The Sources of
Russian Foreign Policy
After the Cold War

The John M. Olin Critical Issues Seri

Published in cooperation with
The Harvard University Russian Research Center

The Sources of
Russian Foreign Policy
After the Cold War

EDITED BY

Celeste A. Wallander

Westview Press
A Member of Perseus Books, L.L.C.

The John M. Olin Critical Issues Series

Copyright © 1996 by the Harvard University Russian Research Center

Published in 1998 in the United States of America by Westview Press, Inc., 5500 Central Avenue, Boulder, Colorado 80301-2877, and in the United Kingdom by Westview Press, 12 Hid's Copse Road, Cumnor Hill, Oxford OX2 9JJ

Library of Congress Cataloging-in-Publication Data
The sources of Russian foreign policy after the Cold War / edited by
   Celeste A. Wallander.
      p.   cm. — (John M. Olin critical issues series)
   Includes index.
   ISBN 0-8133-8841-4. — ISBN 0-8133-2833-0 (pbk.)
   1. Russia (Federation)—Foreign relations—1991– 2. Nationalism—
   Russia (Federation) I. Wallander, Celeste A. II. Series.
DK510.764.S68 1996
327.47'009'049—dc20   95-47101
                                                                  CIP

The paper used in this publication meets the requirements of the American National Standard for Permanence of Paper for Printed Library Materials Z39.48-1984.

10   9   8   7   6   5   4   3   2

To Nat and Joey,
who contributed to delays
and make my life wonderful

Contents

Preface

The chapters in this book were originally presented in the 1993–1994 John M. Olin Critical Issues Series at Harvard University's Russian Research Center. In addition, several of the draft chapters were presented as a panel at the 1994 annual meeting of the International Studies Association in Washington, D.C. The seminar series, travel to the ISA convention, and the preparation of this manuscript were supported by a generous grant from the John M. Olin Foundation.

Many members and friends of the Russian Research Center contributed to the successful operation of the seminar series and the production of this volume. I want to thank Tim Colton, director of the Russian Research Center, for supporting the study of Russian foreign policy at the center in general and for endorsing my proposal for this series. Good research requires insightful analysis and critique, and a number of scholars provided that assistance to the authors. Joel Hellman, Douglas Blum, Randall Stone, Robert Darst, Josephine Andrews, and Carol Saivetz served as discussants for the seminar series, and Jeffrey Knopf and Jeffrey Checkel were the discussants for the ISA panel. Lisbeth Bernstein, associate director, and Christine Porto, head administrative officer, were encouraging and helpful at every turn. I would have been incapable of organizing the series without the administrative assistance and constant good cheer of Michele Albanese, Alan Fortescue, and Judy Mehrmann. And finally, the entire project was rescued by the arrival and skill of Anne Wildermuth, who transformed the diverse writings of eight academics into a readable whole.

Celeste A. Wallander

The Sources of
Russian Foreign Policy
After the Cold War

CHAPTER 1

The Sources of Russian Conduct: Theories, Frameworks, and Approaches

Celeste A. Wallander

Faced with the disappearance of the Soviet Union and the task of understanding and explaining Russian foreign policies, scholars can pursue one of two broad options. The first option—and the focus of most discussion and publication since December 1991—is description and documentation of Russian policy. The second option is explicitly and self-consciously theoretical and is less well represented in recent work. It begins with theoretical constructs rather than substantive policy concerns. Although this is not a purely academic exercise, researchers following this approach are less focused upon the policy itself and more intent on the dynamic processes of policy formation, evolution, and change.

The advantage of the first approach lies in its concrete and fine-tuned exploration of the substantive context of Russian policy. Its weakness is twofold: It can become easily dated, and it cannot produce generalizable insights on Russian foreign policy. The weakness of the more theory-based approach is that it is unlikely to be useful as a direct guide to the content of policy. However, if done well, it will provide a more substantial basis for long-term and more general explanation. The contributing authors to this volume adopt a theory-focused approach to Russian foreign policy. They examine seven theoretical models that have been important in the study of Soviet foreign policy. These models focus on the impact of different factors on Russian foreign policy: type of government, ideology, leadership politics, bureaucratic and interest group politics, the European security system, Russia's historic borderlands and "empire," and the international economic system.

Increasing Access, Increasing Dissent: How Theory Guides Interpretation

Unlike researchers during the Soviet period, scholars no longer face the same severe restrictions on access to information about Russian foreign policy. Although Russia's political system is not a democratic one, its combination of greater openness with competing political sources has expanded our access to information enormously. So in Russian foreign policy studies, we *know* quite a lot. But as yet, it is not clear just how much we *understand*. To understand as well as to know, we need good theoretical frameworks that can make sense of events and information.[1]

Most current disagreement about Russian foreign policy among U.S. scholars and policymakers arises not from varying access to information, which is generally available to any researcher, but on interpretation of events and explanation of the sources of behavior. For example, the influential journal *Foreign Affairs* has published many articles since 1991 in which authors disagree substantially on what Russia is up to in its foreign relations and on whether the United States should adopt a cooperative, competitive, or even hostile position toward the country.[2] For the most part, however, the authors agree on the basic facts: that the Yeltsin government is beset by economic and political problems of enormous dimensions and complexity and that Russian foreign policy has become more assertive and confrontational. Different policy prescriptions arise not from attention to different facts but from implicit explanatory models that try to make sense of what the available information means. These questions can be answered only by an understanding of how the Russian government operates, what are its bases of support, the relationship of society and interest groups to Russian political authority, and the relationship of Russian domestic politics to its foreign policy.

Rather than relying on implicit models of Russian foreign policy, it makes sense to think more systematically about alternative explanations and the factors that constitute them. The question is where to begin, especially in the study of a new country and a renewed subject of inquiry. An obvious place is with approaches and theoretical traditions in the study of Soviet foreign policy. These provide a good base for exploring alternative explanations for foreign policy, and they provide a good standard for assessing change and continuity from Soviet to Russian foreign policy. To the extent that models of Soviet foreign policy and behavior were based on distinctively Soviet factors, such as the political structure of the Soviet state or the imperatives of Soviet ideology, Russian foreign policy ought to look quite different.

International relations studies offer two basic approaches to understanding the foreign policies of states: (1) the constraints and opportunities of the international system and (2) the economic, social, and political characteristics of states.[3] In practice, explanations of national foreign policies combine both approaches. Adam Ulam's classic history of Soviet foreign policy, *Expansion and Coexistence,* explains the outcome of the first major event in Soviet foreign policy—the Brest-Litovsk Treaty of 1918—in terms of both the constraints of a hostile international environment and the revolutionary ideals and objectives of the Bolshevik leadership.[4] In the following section, I offer one framework for organizing explanations for Soviet (and Russian) foreign policy that draws upon both traditions and which is the basis for the seven chapters that follow. The framework includes theories of regime type, the role of ideology in foreign policy, leadership politics, bureaucratic and interest group politics, the external security environment, and the constraints and opportunities of the international economy.

Explanations for Soviet Foreign Policy

Regime Types and Political Institutions

In one of the most influential articles written in the field of Soviet foreign policy studies, George Kennan sought to explain Soviet foreign policy in terms of the totalitarian structure of the Soviet political system and its revolutionary Leninist heritage.[5] He argued that the Soviet regime lacked internal sources of legitimacy yet made severe political and economic demands upon its citizens that could not be sustained solely by repression. This led Soviet leaders to focus on the revolutionary Leninist ideology that would justify Soviet hardship and legitimate the Communist regime. Therefore, he argued, the repressive and illegitimate political institutions of the Soviet state produced a foreign policy focused upon the external revolutionary socialist mission and the presence of a hostile capitalist international system. This focus in turn produced expansionist Soviet foreign policies. The type of political regime has systematic effects on the content of foreign policy, according to this type of explanation, because the institutions and processes of the political order preclude certain policies and tend to produce others.

Lenin also explained the Soviet Union's hostile relations with the West in terms of regime types. He argued that the falling profits and insufficient domestic demand endemic to capitalist economic systems would not lead to internal collapse, as Marx had concluded, but to imperialism. Access to new sources of raw materials and to new markets in the colonial world could save capitalist interests in the short run, so those interests would use their control of states to seek colonies abroad. Thus, "imperialism" was intrinsic to capitalism, not an aberration. Since capitalist domestic political economic orders must expand on the international scene to survive, they could not tolerate the existence of different political economic orders—particularly socialist orders. From the economic nature of capitalism and its political guise in the form of nation-states, Lenin claimed to explain war, expansionism of the European great powers, and the West's hostility toward socialist countries.[6]

An important problem for a regime-type theory of Soviet foreign policy is that it implies a degree of continuity in Soviet foreign policy from 1917 to 1991 that is not borne out by the historical record. Although some authors have argued that the continuities in Soviet foreign policy and politics are more important than marginal and tactical shifts,[7] most have focused on the importance of changes over time and have tried to explain them.

Some authors explained change in Soviet foreign policy while retaining a regime-type explanation by arguing that the Soviet domestic political order changed with Stalin's death. The end of political terror, in this view, fundamentally altered the rules of the Soviet political game and changed the system from Kennan's Stalinist totalitarianism to something less repressive and transformative.[8] Foreign policy would be different because of the departure from Stalinist practices. In particular, the end of political terror meant that the Soviet political elite was more secure, which promoted the development of a competitive political process. Competition meant change in Soviet political processes, with attendant effects on foreign policy.[9]

Other authors argued that the post-Stalinist political order produced a foreign policy of caution and risk aversion. Dennis Ross characterized this post-Stalinist political regime as an oligarchy in which the Soviet elite most valued personal and bureaucratic security. The processes of the post-Stalinist Soviet state favored consensus decisionmaking and placed a premium on elite political coalition maintenance. The result was a foreign policy of caution and risk aversion.[10] So Ross argued that in contrast to the Stalinist system, which required an expansionist foreign policy for regime legitimacy, the requirements of leadership consensus in the partial authoritarian regime produced a policy of cautious opportunism.

Still others agreed that the post-Stalinist political system required consensus within the leadership. But instead of producing caution and risk aversion, the combination of old political institutions and new political processes produced an even more expansionist and predatory foreign policy than had been the case under Stalin. The persistence of Stalinist political institutions in a political environment where coalition politics mattered and new political groups made demands on the leadership produced "offensive détente" and "overcommitted, contradictory policies."[11]

The change in domestic political constraints played a role in explanations of Khrushchev's intervention in Hungary in 1956, near-intervention in Poland in 1956, and the decision to deploy nuclear missiles to Cuba in 1962.[12] Similarly, according to this explanation, the incentives for an expansionist foreign policy grew in the Brezhnev period as he built his political coalition, exhibiting its effects first in growing Soviet interventionism in the Middle East by the late 1960s and in the Soviet invasion of Czechoslovakia in 1968 and culminating in the growth of Soviet Third World interventionism in the 1970s.

Explanations for Gorbachev's new thinking in foreign policy often focused on the domestic political and institutional changes he implemented beginning in 1987. These studies had a somewhat different focus: Instead of domestic political institutions and processes producing a certain type of Soviet foreign policy, the desire to develop a new Soviet foreign (and domestic) policy led Gorbachev to reform the Soviet domestic political system. The Soviet withdrawal from Afghanistan and acceptance of change in Eastern Europe, it was argued, were accomplished only because Gorbachev had succeeded in altering the political and institutional constraints on reformist directions in Soviet foreign policy.[13] Moving farther from the post-Stalinist Soviet political system, according to this foreign policy model, permitted dramatic change in Soviet policies and behavior.

Ideology

An alternative tradition in Soviet foreign policy studies begins not with the Stalinist state as baseline but with Leninist ideas as the source of Soviet foreign policy behavior. The role of ideology as a belief system, or of more specific and particular ideas within that system, permeated the study of Soviet foreign policy, but some authors accorded it great weight in their explanations.[14] The core premise of Leninist ideology was a belief in the fundamental conflict of interest between capitalist states and the new socialist states of the twentieth century. Lenin's thesis in *Imperialism, the Highest Stage of Capitalism* was not a dispassionate theory of foreign relations but became the ideological basis for Soviet foreign policy. Insofar as it posited inescapable hostility and threat, scholars argued that it would produce an unchangeable expansionist and aggressive Soviet foreign policy.[15]

One problem for explanations of Soviet foreign policy based on ideology was that there was a great deal of change and variation in Soviet policy. Soviet leaders pursued at different times over a seventy-four-year period expansionist, opportunistic, accommodating, and even reticent foreign policies. Alexander Dallin wrote: "Over the course of Soviet history the same formal ideology has permitted . . . such a wide range of different, conflicting, and at times mutually incompatible courses of action that it cannot be properly seen as a 'guide to action.'"[16] To cope with this anomaly, authors focused on two ways that ideology could be a guide to action in varying Soviet foreign policy.

One focus was the concept of an "operational code." Although particular policies might change in response to different circumstances, the basic prisms and principles of Leninist ideology remained intact and could serve to explain underlying consistencies in Soviet policy and behavior.[17] Nathan Leites emphasized that Bolshevik ideology, through its view of the nature of politics and the world, prescribed rules of thumb for the conduct of domestic and foreign policy. These beliefs about politics, in Leites's view, provided a systematic guide to patterns in Soviet behavior. Ideology prescribes that the Communist Party "must never risk already conquered major positions for the sake of uncertain gains," that "in attempting to obtain concessions, anything less than the exertion of maximum pressure is ineffective," and that "mastery in the skill of retreating is as necessary as mastery in the skill of advancing."[18] In one of the more systematic evaluations of the role of ideology in Soviet behavior, Hannes Adomeit studied the 1948 and 1961 Berlin crises using an "operational code" framework.[19] He argued that despite apparent revisions in the particular policies from Stalin to Khrushchev, both Stalin and Khrushchev followed the same precepts derived from Leninist precepts: calculation and careful preparation, pushing to the limit with timely retreat in the face of superior power, and constructing a fallback position.[20]

Three problems are apparent with this explanation for foreign policy: It is far removed from the specific content of Leninist ideology in the usual sense of the concept (values and understandings of the social world), the precepts are not much different from a maxim derived from the rationality assumption—"pursue your interests intelligently at acceptable costs and risks"—and the framework fails to explain important Soviet crisis policies such as those in the Cuban crisis of 1962 and the 1979 intervention in Afghanistan.

Other authors focused on the potential for change in Leninist ideology. Although maintaining the fundamental thesis of international relations as a clash between hostile social systems, Soviet political figures and academics often disagreed about the broader range of subsidiary propositions. William Zimmerman showed that change began soon after 1953 and that the basic Leninist conception of international relations and Soviet interests was compatible with a broad range of views on issues such as the importance of states versus classes as international actors and the possibilities for and importance of "peaceful coexistence" in Soviet-American relations.[21] More recently, an extension of Zimmerman's approach found further evolution from the original Bolshevik framework in ideas about the problematic relation between politics and economics and the indeterminacy of historical evolution in international relations.[22] The argument that ideology mattered but changed was especially important in studies of Soviet Third World policy.[23]

More recently, ideology approaches in Soviet foreign policy studies focused on "learning," especially in response to the appearance and importance of "new thinking" in Gorbachev's foreign policy. Although researchers did not cast their efforts in this light,[24] their work continued the tradition of assessing the weight and role of ideas in Soviet foreign policy. Learning entails a change in ideology insofar as it "involves a transformation in mode of thinking—a reassessment of fundamental beliefs and values that draws on the consensual knowledge of an epistemic community."[25]

Despite its rich empirical insight into changing Soviet foreign policy, the learning literature remained weak in linking the causal effect of ideas and changes in ideas to foreign policy and behavior. Although it is clear that some Soviet leaders changed their beliefs during their careers, and that the mix of beliefs within the Soviet leadership changed over time, the learning literature has not demonstrated that this change and variation had a causal effect independent of Soviet domestic political processes.[26] Did Soviet leaders change foreign policies because they learned or did they learn because they had to change policies? These are the same problems that confront studies of the role of ideology in Soviet (and now Russian) foreign policy. Without a model of domestic politics that deals with the competition among leaders and groups within a set of political institutions, learning explanations can demonstrate a correlation of idea change with policy change but do not demonstrate a central causal role for ideas.[27]

Leadership Politics

A third traditional approach to the explanation of Soviet foreign policy focused on leadership politics. Although not entirely contradictory to the regime-type explanation, explanations that focus on leadership politics presume greater variability in Soviet foreign policy over time—between and within leaderships. Leadership explanations can also include a role for ideas in foreign policy because they focus on the policy prescriptions of dominant, ascending, and unsuccessful leaders or coalitions.

However, in leadership explanations, the causal link to foreign policy and behavior is quite different. In leadership politics explanations, foreign policy is the result of competition for power by a small set of Soviet leaders—primarily the Politburo. In a system without constitutional provisions for governance and succession, leadership depended on the constellation of supporters in the Party. Leaders mobilized clients and sought support from allies and doled out political and economic benefits to supporters when they prevailed.[28]

Thus, explanations for foreign policy in terms of leadership politics constituted classic "Kremlinology." Given the "curious enclave of democracy"[29]—the Politburo—in which no single leader could impose his will but had to maneuver constantly to attract support and defeat opponents, policy in the Soviet system was produced by a "competitive oligarchy" and intense political conflict.[30] Although policies and "ideas" were central to the explanation—and to the method of Kremlinology—they had little independent effect on outcomes, which were a result of political power and the skill of Politburo figures in forging winning coalitions among themselves.

In traditional leadership models, foreign policy is a result of the personal and political linkages within the elite and the forms of political power its members and coalitions bring to bear. One would expect to see changes in Soviet foreign policy among leaderships as well as within them. But foreign policy would be a product of political conflict. The actual ideas and policies did not drive Soviet foreign policy and were secondary to the struggle for power. Soviet leaders might have had different interests and views, but compared to the problem of improving or maintaining position in the leadership, advancing ideas or interests was less important.[31]

In contrast, a more recent set of leadership politics studies integrated the causal dynamics of political conflict and competition with the policies that leaders advocated and adopted. In early leadership politics studies, it was not clear why competing Soviet elites would adopt different policies at all if they were irrelevant to the outcomes and if power was the objective. For the leadership politics model to work as an explanation for foreign (or domestic) policy, the policies advocated within the competitive political elite would have to play some role. Rather than purely personalistic or opportunistic alliances, leadership coalitions might be built around like-minded Politburo members who sought to implement their policies as well as retain political power for its own sake. If this were the case, then the policies certain leaders advocated—as well as the perks of power and privilege—could become a basis for competing coalitions, and successful leaders would build authority as well as power.[32]

Furthermore, if authority plays a role in political power, and if policies and ideas play a role in authority, success and failure of policies would have an effect on maintaining power within a collective leadership. Stalin reportedly hid from view for nearly two weeks following the German attack on the Soviet Union in June 1941, and Ulam suggests that he might have feared overthrow for the political and military policies that resulted in the disastrous defeat.[33] At least one cause of Khrushchev's fall in 1964 (though this seems to have been an event caused by multiple factors) was his failed gamble to deploy Soviet nuclear missiles to Cuba in 1962 and the clear humiliation of the Soviet retreat.

As developed since earliest Kremlinological versions, a leadership politics explanation of Soviet foreign policy therefore encompasses not only power and competition in a collective leadership as sources of foreign policy but makes policy choice and policy effects endogenous to the explanation. Although foreign policy remained the result of the power of individual leaders, their successful coalitions, and intense competition within the Politburo, the choice of foreign policies was not random: It reflected leaders' calculations about which positions would gain support and which foreign policies would succeed. Both the directions and changes in Soviet foreign policy under the Khrushchev and Brezhnev leaderships may be explained by the dynamics of competitive coalition building in post-Stalinist leadership conditions, and the particular policy positions taken conform to an authority-building explanation, largely because of the linkages between domestic policy agendas and foreign policy and because of responsiveness in the content of policy advocacy to foreign successes and failures.[34]

Despite its improvements in analytical power over simple ideology models, a simple leadership politics model of Soviet foreign policy fails to explain precisely its central concept—where political power comes from and what role it plays in the political processes and outcomes at issue. To argue that leaders seek power and that the configuration of power within the leadership determines foreign policy begs the question if we identify "powerful" leaders and coalitions by their successful outcomes. Although it is some improvement to argue that policy success is itself a source of power in the form of authority, that still does not tell us how successful groupings within the Politburo might have been put together in the first place.

Interest Groups and Bureaucratic Politics

Interest group and bureaucratic politics models provide clues to this problem. While recognizing that the notion of interest group influence in Soviet foreign policy does not have quite the same meaning as in the study of U.S. foreign policy, some researchers began to focus on evidence of conflict among political, economic, and social groups and institutions in Soviet politics as a key to understanding policy outcomes.[35] In interest group and bureaucratic politics models, the members of Soviet political institutions and groupings such as the military, the KGB, industrial managers, party organs, and intellectuals had distinct interests. Through their structured participation in policy formation and implementation, groups sought to affect policy they cared about or were benefited by. Groups could affect Soviet politics by influencing and serving as power resources for the top political figures competing for political power.[36]

This model shifts the causal focus to the material interests, values, leadership access, and resources of groups in the Soviet system. The Politburo made decisions and took action, but policy ideas and institutional resources affected the making of foreign policy. Studies identified varying institutional interests, both by deduction (the military must favor greater military spending) and by analysis of speeches, newspaper reports, and professional articles. Most studies relied upon implicit theories of which groups held significant power in the Soviet system and expected that foreign policy would tend to favor important and powerful groups.

For example, Harry Gelman explained the rise and decline of Soviet détente policy in terms of Brezhnev's domestic political coalition. The rise of détente was due to the clear interests of military and industrial institutions in limiting competition with the West and gaining access to Western technology. The Party institution with the strongest and most direct influence in foreign policy was the International Department, which advocated détente as a way to limit Western intervention against the growing tide of revolutionary change in the Third World. The views and interests of these groups prevailed in policy decisions, according to Gelman, because Brezhnev relied on them in his dual position as head of the Communist Party and of the Defense Council. Détente failed, he argued, because the fundamentally conservative interests of the groups constituting Brezhnev's coalition were inconsistent with any fundamental transformation of Soviet politics.[37]

Interest group and bureaucratic politics models were especially important in studies of Soviet intervention. In contrast to explanations for Soviet interventionism that saw an overall strategic plan,[38] analyses of domestic debate and the influence of political institutions in policy advocacy and bargaining accorded greater independent causal significance to domestic priorities and political power. Studies of Soviet interventions in Eastern Europe and the Third World demonstrated that members of state and party institutions often disagreed quite substantially on whether and how to intervene in foreign conflicts. Most of these studies attribute eventual intervention decisions to the relative power and advantage of hard-line groups in Soviet politics.[39]

Variation in Soviet foreign policy is therefore easily explained by interest group models as a result of changes in domestic political coalitions, representing different interests and different priorities. For example, Michael Sodaro accounts for variation in Soviet policy toward Germany in terms of the degree of reliance on coalition politics in the Soviet leadership, the extent of agreement on basic policies, and the views of ascendant groups within the secondary and intellectual elites such as regional party secretaries and scholars of academic institutes.[40]

However, an interest group politics model can too easily explain too much variation in Soviet foreign policy. If ideas, interests, coalitions, and institutional power vary as considerably as interest group and bureaucratic politics models suggest, the models would serve little predictive or explanatory value. Some models, such as Gelman's, provide better predictive value because they specify which groups and institutions were likely to wield political influence in the Soviet system. But models such as Gelman's cannot explain change in foreign policy. They specify which groups possessed political resources and influence in the Soviet system, but if their interests, power, and influence were stable, Soviet foreign policy could not have changed as substantially as it did from the Khrushchev era, to the Brezhnev era, to the revolutionary changes of the Gorbachev era.

Two important modifications of interest group models can provide both the predictive power and the explanation for significant change necessary for constructing a theory of Soviet, and Russian, foreign policy. First, a model of Soviet domestic politics that incorporates the economic system and priorities as well as more traditional political institutions can explain the periodic attempts to reform the economy to bolster light industry, production of consumer goods, agriculture, and technological innovation. Change in domestic economic priorities in turn entails change in domestic political power and coalitions. When economic reform became a priority for at least a portion of the Soviet leadership, the configuration of domestic political interests and ideas changed, and so did Soviet foreign policy.[41]

Second, a powerful and dynamic model of Soviet foreign policy must link domestic political economic priorities and competing interests to variation in successful and failed foreign policy. A model of foreign policy based solely on internal political and economic factors implies that the international political and economic system is irrelevant to articulation of interests, to marshaling of resources for political competition, and as a source of constraint and opportunity—against all good sense and evidence. A powerful model of foreign policy must show why and how international relations—the external security and international economic environment—affect competition over policy.

External Effects on Soviet Politics and Foreign Policy

Usually without developing explicit models along these lines, many researchers explained Soviet domestic politics and foreign policy in these terms. In his history of the early years of Soviet foreign policy, Kennan argues that the Allied intervention in the Russian Civil War from 1917 to 1920 was an ill-conceived yet halfhearted and ineffective attempt to aid anti-Bolshevik forces in an effort to prevent the Bolsheviks from pulling Russia out of World War I. The intervention failed, but in the process it also compromised opponents of the Bolsheviks. So important was this intervention to strengthening the Communists internally, writes Kennan, that "I think it may well be questioned whether Bolshevism would ever have prevailed throughout Russia had the Western Governments not aided its progress by this ill-conceived interference."[42]

Others have argued that Stalinist development through collectivization of agriculture and rapid, centralized industrialization was partly the result of perception of Soviet backwardness in the late 1920s and the 1930s and of Soviet vulnerability.[43] The achievement of Soviet power after World War II alleviated this sense of threat and vulnerability. But Soviet nuclear inferiority remained a source of domestic political vulnerability for Khrushchev, who had promised to reduce defense spending while achieving security by developing a superior strategic nuclear capability. When he failed to achieve either military parity or significant foreign policy victories, Khrushchev was driven by his domestic political vulnerabilities to attempt a cheap and easy victory in equalizing the strategic nuclear balance by deploying Soviet intermediate-range missiles in Cuba.[44]

The most carefully articulated studies of international effects on domestic politics are those on the sources of Gorbachev's "new thinking."[45] In these models, domestic political and economic groups do not merely have different interests and different domestic power resources; in addition, the international system and events affect interests and coalition formation. For example, Gorbachev sought to portray choice of security policy as one between the status quo, which was leaving the Soviet Union a crippled superpower, versus reform and new thinking in security, which would allow the Soviet system to sustain advanced technology and a modern military with a modern military doctrine.[46] Pointing to the Strategic Defense Initiative (SDI), Afghanistan, and North Atlantic Treaty Organization's (NATO) advances in conventional forces, Gorbachev sought to find a base of support within the Soviet military for his domestic reforms.

Studies of the effects of the external security environment on Soviet politics and foreign policy tend to posit a somewhat indirect relationship: The security environment affects coalition building by affecting the plausibility of alternative policy prescriptions. Studies of the effects of the international economic environment on Soviet domestic politics and foreign policy tend to posit a much more direct linkage. In these models, certain domestic and political actors have material interests in the nature of the relationship between the international and domestic economies. This affects both their incentives to support different foreign policies and their resources.

For most of its history, the Soviet domestic economy was closed to the outside world and its limited foreign trade was centrally controlled. As a resource-rich country, there was little the Soviet Union needed to import to survive, and the Stalinist model of development prescribed that the country forgo the advantages of trade to avoid the economic and political dependence trade risked. This began to change in the 1960s, when the Soviet Union imported substantial amounts of food to make up for the failures of its agricultural sector and imported technology to correct for the effects of an economy that could not generate innovation. Soviet interest in détente was a response to the need to limit the arms race and to seek a political ratification of the postwar division of Europe, but it was also a response to Soviet economic weakness.[47] The Brezhnev leadership sought to improve conditions without fundamentally altering the political and economic system and pursued a strategy meant to remedy domestic economic failures by participating in the international economy. Export of Soviet resources—primarily oil and natural gas—was increased to pay for the imports, and the policy of détente was launched to create an environment to sustain the limited cooperative foreign policy.

This limited opening to the international economy in the late 1960s and throughout the 1970s ultimately had very significant effects on the Soviet domestic political economy and foreign policy. Inflation in the Soviet domestic economy was transmitted through rising import prices paid for through government subsidies, paid for in turn by the printing of rubles. At the same time, falling prices for Soviet exports required the government to borrow abroad to cover the difference between Soviet export earnings and import payments. Increased openness to the international economy also created new coalitions of intellectuals and officials in certain industries who obtained direct benefits from participation in the world economy and from the advanced technological environment. These groups were to become part of Gorbachev's political support coalition.[48] Domestic economic reform and the need for the resources and discipline that participation in the international economy would bring were the fundamental reasons for Gorbachev's new thinking policy abroad and perestroika at home. In this regard, it is not too much of an exaggeration to conclude that the effects of the international economic environment—as well as the security constraints of competition with the United States and Soviet overextension in the Third World—were a major contribution to the end of the Cold War.[49]

To summarize, models of the external effects on Soviet politics and foreign policy provide constraints for models of the domestic sources of policies. They suggest why some policies may fail or succeed. They provide a dynamic element to domestic theories that indicate how domestic power and interests may shift and therefore why and how policy can change. In short, they provide us with an explanation and prediction of why foreign policy should be an issue at all in domestic politics and why domestic politics should be systematically related to foreign policy.

Explaining Russian Foreign Policy

The organization of our inquiry into the sources of Russian conduct after the Cold War follows the framework I outlined in the previous section. In some respects, fundamental changes underlie Russian politics and policies while important aspects of continuity remain. It is easy to become overwhelmed by the complexity of change and continuity in trying to explain Russian foreign policy. To avoid this, each of the authors has used one of the approaches to Soviet foreign policy I have discussed as a starting point for developing and evaluating explanations for Russian foreign policy since 1991.

In Chapter 2, Jack Snyder looks at the importance of regime type and questions the commonly held presumption that post-Communist regimes will produce more pacific foreign policies. He argues that although many of the post-Soviet states, including Russia, have abandoned authoritarian political institutions and centralized command economies and replaced them with free elections and democratic institutions, these states are at best merely partial democracies. They lack the established and stable democratic and liberal political orders that can produce the "democratic peace," and the process of incomplete democratization may produce even more aggressive and unstable foreign policies than did the authoritarian political regimes of the late Soviet era. In particular, he argues, the institutions of partial democracy and the dynamics of democratization enhance the power and role of ethnonationalist movements, which tend to produce belligerent and expansionist foreign policies.

We are more likely to see, in contrast to the ideological monopoly of the Soviet system, a plurality and competition of ideas and policies than a new monopoly. But one ideological tradition has achieved predominance in Russian politics and is especially important for Russian foreign policy: Russian nationalism as successor to Marxism-Leninism. Astrid Tuminez focuses upon this in Chapter 3. As political ideology, nationalism defines criteria for membership in the nation, national self-image and other-image, and a statement of national mission. In this regard, she argues, there are several contemporary variants of Russian nationalism ranging from malignant national patriotism to inward-looking nativism. Statist and national patriotic versions have achieved the upper hand, but given the substantial variation in Russian nationalist foreign policy prescriptions, no one variant can be understood as dominant, and political institutions and the international environment play an important role in competition over foreign policy and the role of nationalist ideology.

State institutions and Russian nationalism provide context and content of foreign policy, but they do not explain the political process. Extending his previous work on Soviet leadership politics, James Richter argues in Chapter 4 that Russian political leaders compete for power in part by adopting foreign policies that legitimate their domestic policies and claims. He shows how the "politics of identity" is an instrumental battle for control of the resources and authority of the state. Unlike in the Soviet political environment in which competition was restricted to elites, in Russian politics potential leaders play to a wider audience and need to substantiate claims that their policies will serve the common good. In this regard, symbols and national identities are instruments of political competition. With the collapse of old political institutions and instability of new ones in Russia, Richter argues, Russia's identity as an international player and the international environment is likely to be more important in the competition for political leadership.

In the chaos of post-Soviet Russia, it is difficult to identify the sources of political and economic power, and therefore it is difficult to identify which groups are influential in formulating Russian foreign policy. Kimberly Marten Zisk examines one group that we know to have been influential in Soviet foreign policy—defense industrialists. In Chapter 5, she argues that the managers of Russian defense industries will be key players in Russian domestic politics and foreign policy because of the size and importance of those industries in Russia's economy and society. Unlike Soviet defense managers—who had a clear and rather straightforward interest in substantial military spending and little interest in moderate foreign policies—Russian defense industrialists operate in a different environment. Conversion, privatization, and the opening of the Russian economy to the international market create the potential for the defense industry's interests in integration, Westernization, and cooperative Russian security policies. However, she argues, in the Russian context individual defense firms do not have common interests and policy preferences in foreign trade and therefore have limited influence in foreign policy to date.

Although in Chapters 2, 3, 4, and 5 the authors focus on Russian domestic politics and the formulation of Russian foreign policy, the external international environment plays some role in each of their studies. In Chapter 6, Bruce Porter assesses explicitly the effect of the European security environment on Russian politics and foreign policy. He argues that the absence of an objective foreign threat has contributed to domestic stress and disunity, unlike in previous Russian history when an atmosphere of threat or foreign competition generated unity and effective development and mobilization. Ironically, disunity engendered by the absence of external threat could result in a benign and cooperative Russian foreign policy, he argues, if bolstered by an external environment that offers support for Russian security and development.

A peculiar feature of Russia's post-Soviet external security environment is the "near abroad"—newly independent countries that were part of the Soviet Union until 1991. These countries are without exception less powerful than Russia, yet they are an important and troublesome security environment for Russia nonetheless. Military and economic integration in the Soviet era left these countries very interdependent, and Russians left in the "near abroad" with the breakup of the Soviet Union became a significant issue in Russia's foreign policy. In Chapter 7, Ted Hopf argues that Russian intervention to protect its minorities in now-foreign countries depends in large part on how Russians define their identities. He points out that ethnic conflict is not inevitable but depends in part on state and social practices that can include, ignore, or harm certain groups. He compares this process in Estonia, which adopted an exclusionary definition of ethnic identity, and Uzbekistan, which adopted inclusion. He concludes that as a consequence of its exclusionary ethnic policies, Estonia contributed to the increasing salience of the intervention issue and to threats and pressure from Moscow. Uzbekistan's quite different approach provoked no Russian pressure or threat.

One would expect that with the end of the Cold War and the disappearance of the Communist economic system, the most significant new influence on Russian politics and foreign policy would be the international economy. The political constraints of the Stalinist system, which severely limited foreign trade and repressed domestic political economic demands, have been lifted, so participation in the international economy should create new domestic interests in favor of trade and success should increase political resources for those groups. Matthew Evangelista writes in Chapter 8 that given Russian energy resources, we should see dramatic changes in the Russian energy sector and strong interest in that sector for participation in the international economy. However, he argues, such an expectation ignores the effect of preexisting institutions on domestic interests and political strategies. He shows that Soviet—and now Russian—coal miners have not lobbied to be free of state restrictions to participate freely in the international market. They have reacted to reforms for the most part by seeking to preserve state subsidies and social justice because they understand market competition in terms of the socialist "labor theory of value." Although the international economy has created new economic opportunities, the lack of market institutions at the domestic level has proven more significant for continuity in domestic interests and their relation to foreign economic policy.

Finally, in Chapter 9 I discuss the important connections in the arguments and evidence presented in this volume. I conclude that the key to understanding future Russian foreign policy is to understand two sets of linkages: those between ideas, institutions, and interests and those between domestic political power and the international environment.

Notes

I would like to thank Jeffrey Anderson and Lisbeth Bernstein for their helpful comments.

1. Stephen M. Meyer, "Soviet National Security Decision Making: What Do We Know and What Do We Understand?" in *Soviet Decision Making for National Security,* ed. Jiri Valenta and William Potter (Boston: George Allen and Unwin, 1984), pp. 255–297.

2. These articles include Zbigniew Brzezinski, "The Premature Partnership," *Foreign Affairs* 73 (March-April 1994): 67–83; Dmitri Simes, "The Return of Russian History," *Foreign Affairs* 73 (January-February 1994): 67–82; Stephen Sestanovich, "Russia Turns the Corner," *Foreign Affairs* 73 (January-February 1994): 83–98.

3. These are familiar in international relations as the "third image" and "second image" respectively. Kenneth Waltz, *Man, the State, and War* (New York: Columbia University Press, 1954).

4. Adam Ulam, *Expansion and Coexistence: Soviet Foreign Policy, 1917–1973* (Fort Worth, Tex.: Holt, Rinehart, and Winston, 1974).

5. George Kennan [X, pseud.], "The Sources of Soviet Conduct," *Foreign Affairs* (July 1947), reprinted in *Foreign Affairs* 65 (Spring 1987): 852–868.

6. V. I. Lenin, *Imperialism, the Highest Stage of Capitalism* (New York: International Publishers, 1939).

7. Charles Gati, "The Stalinist Legacy in Soviet Foreign Policy," in *Soviet Foreign Policy in a Changing World,* ed. Robbin F. Laird and Erik P. Hoffmann (New York: Aldine Publishing Company, 1986), pp. 16–28.

8. Whether the post-Stalinist system was "merely" authoritarian or some intermediate form that retained some of the features of totalitarianism has been a contested issue in Soviet studies. On the original statement of the issue see Carl J. Friedrich and Zbigniew K. Brzezinski, *Totalitarian Dictatorship and Autocracy* (Cambridge: Harvard University Press, 1956). For challenges and critiques, see Joseph LaPalombara, "Monoliths or Plural Systems: Through Conceptual Lenses Darkly," *Studies in Comparative Communism* 8 (Autumn 1975): 305–332; and Jerry F. Hough, "The Soviet System: Petrification or Pluralism?" in *The Soviet Union and Social Science Theory,* by Jerry F. Hough (Cambridge: Harvard University Press, 1977).

9. For an early analysis of the importance of this change for Soviet foreign policy, see Alexander Dallin, "The Domestic Sources of Soviet Foreign Policy," in *The Domestic Context of Soviet Foreign Policy,* ed. Seweryn Bialer (Boulder: Westview Press, 1981), esp. pp. 348–353.

10. Dennis Ross, "Risk Aversion in Soviet Decision Making," in *Soviet Decision Making,* ed. Valenta and Potter, p. 242.

11. Jack Snyder, "The Gorbachev Revolution: A Waning of Soviet Expansionism?" *International Security* 12 (Winter 1987/88): 93–131; at pp. 94, 104.

12. Zbigniew K. Brzezinski, *The Soviet Bloc: Unity and Discord,* revised and enlarged edition (Cambridge: Harvard University Press, 1967); Arnold L. Horelick and Myron Rush, *Strategic Power and Soviet Foreign Policy* (Chicago: University of Chicago Press, 1964).

13. Matthew Evangelista, "Sources of Moderation in Soviet Security Policy," in *Behavior, Society, and Nuclear War,* vol. 2, ed. Philip E. Tetlock et al. (New York: Oxford University Press, 1991); Snyder, "Gorbachev Revolution."

14. In contrast, the role of "ideas" in foreign policy has only recently become much of a focus in international relations. See Judith Goldstein and Robert O. Keohane, eds., *Ideas and Foreign Policy: Beliefs, Institutions, and Political Change* (Ithaca: Cornell University Press, 1993).

15. For example, see the theses in Richard Pipes, "Soviet Global Strategy," *Commentary* 67 (April 1980): 31–39.

16. Dallin, "The Domestic Sources," pp. 357–358.

17. The earliest work was Nathan Leites, *The Operational Code of the Politburo* (New York: McGraw-Hill, 1951); and Nathan Leites, *A Study of Bolshevism* (Glencoe, Ill.: Free Press, 1953).

18. Leites, *The Operational Code,* pp. 68, 75, 82.

19. Hannes Adomeit, *Soviet Risk-Taking and Crisis Behavior* (Boston: George Allen and Unwin, 1982).

20. Ibid., pp. 317–322.

21. William Zimmerman, *Soviet Perspectives on International Relations, 1956–1967* (Princeton: Princeton University Press, 1969).

22. Allen Lynch, *The Soviet Study of International Relations* (New York: Cambridge University Press, 1987).

23. Mark N. Katz, *The Third World in Soviet Military Thought* (Baltimore: Johns Hopkins University Press, 1982); Elizabeth Kridl Valkenier, *The Soviet Union and the Third World: An Economic Bind* (New York: Praeger, 1983); Jerry F. Hough, *The Struggle*

for the Third World: Soviet Debates and American Options (Washington, D.C.: Brookings Institution, 1986).

24. An exception is George W. Breslauer, "Ideology and Learning in Soviet Third World Policy," *World Politics* 39 (April 1987): 429–448. Franklyn Griffiths was an early analyst of the role of ideas in Soviet foreign policy, and he carried this over to an interest in learning under Gorbachev. See Franklyn Griffiths, "The Sources of American Conduct," *International Security* 9 (Fall 1984): 3–46; and Franklyn Griffiths, "Attempted Learning: Soviet Policy Toward the United States in the Brezhnev Era," in *Learning in U.S. and Soviet Foreign Policy,* ed. George W. Breslauer and Philip E. Tetlock (Boulder: Westview Press, 1991), pp. 630–683.

25. Philip E. Tetlock, "Learning in U.S. and Soviet Foreign Policy: In Search of an Elusive Concept," in *Learning in U.S. and Soviet Foreign Policy,* ed. Breslauer and Tetlock, pp. 20–61.

26. For a careful analysis of this issue, see Jack S. Levy, "Learning and Foreign Policy: Sweeping a Conceptual Minefield," *International Organization* 48 (Spring 1994): 279–312, esp. pp. 300–310.

27. For a similar assessment in the context of a single project on learning, see George W. Breslauer, "What Have We Learned About Learning?" in *Learning in U.S. and Soviet Foreign Policy,* ed. Breslauer and Tetlock, at pp. 826–827.

28. See, for example, Robert Conquest, *Power and Policy in the U.S.S.R.* (New York: St. Martin's Press, 1961); and Michel Tatu, *Power in the Kremlin* (New York: Viking Press, 1969).

29. Tatu, *Power in the Kremlin,* p. 529.

30. Dallin, "The Domestic Sources," p. 363.

31. Grey Hodnett, "The Pattern of Leadership Politics," in *The Domestic Context,* ed. Bialer, pp. 87–118.

32. George W. Breslauer, *Khrushchev and Brezhnev as Leaders: Building Authority in Soviet Politics* (Boston: George Allen and Unwin, 1982), chap. 1.

33. Ulam, *Expansion and Coexistence,* pp. 315–318.

34. For studies using this approach, see James G. Richter, *Khrushchev's Double Bind: International Pressures and Domestic Coalition Politics* (Baltimore: Johns Hopkins University Press, 1994); and Richard D. Anderson, Jr., *Public Politics in an Authoritarian State: Making Foreign Policy During the Brezhnev Years* (Ithaca: Cornell University Press, 1993).

35. For the first and best introduction to the interest group approach in Communist studies, see *Interest Groups in Soviet Politics,* ed. H. Gordon Skilling and Franklyn Griffiths (Princeton: Princeton University Press, 1971). For a statement of the bureaucratic politics model of Soviet foreign policy, see Jiri Valenta, *Soviet Intervention in Czechoslovakia, 1968: Anatomy of a Decision* (Baltimore: Johns Hopkins University Press, 1979). In the Soviet context, the difference between bureaucratic politics and interest group politics as influences in foreign policy is not very significant, given that both sets of interests were fundamentally part of and/or organized by the state (on this point, see Dallin, "The Domestic Sources," pp. 398–399 n. 78).

36. See H. Gordon Skilling, "Groups in Soviet Politics: Some Hypotheses," in *Interest Groups in Soviet Politics,* ed. Skilling and Griffiths, pp. 19–45.

37. Harry Gelman, *The Brezhnev Politburo and the Decline of Détente* (Ithaca: Cornell University Press, 1984). Indeed, most studies and explanations of Soviet détente policy accord some causal importance to important domestic political (and economic) groups and

institutions that sought access to greater resources through economic relations with the West or by restraining U.S.-Soviet competition. For a study that focuses on domestic economic interests, see Bruce Parrott, *Politics and Technology in the Soviet Union* (Cambridge: MIT Press, 1985). However, studies of interest group influence in Soviet foreign policy focused in particular on the military or on the Soviet "military-industrial complex." See, for example, Condoleezza Rice, "The Party, the Military, and Decision Authority in the Soviet Union," *World Politics* 40 (October 1987): 55–81; Dale R. Herspring, "Soviet Military Politics," *Problems of Communism* 35 (March-April 1986): 93–97; Roman Kolokowicz, *The Soviet Military and the Communist Party* (Princeton: Princeton University Press, 1967); and Vernon Aspaturian, "The Afghan Gamble: Soviet Quagmire or Springboard?" in Vernon Asparturian, Alexander Dallin, and Jiri Valenta, *The Soviet Invasion of Afghanistan: Three Perspectives,* ACIS Working Paper no. 27 (Los Angeles: University of California, 1980). For a skeptical view of influence of the Soviet defense industry on foreign policy, see Peter Almquist, *Red Forge: Soviet Military Industry Since 1965* (New York: Columbia University Press, 1990).

38. See, for example, Pipes, "Soviet Global Strategy," pp. 31–39.

39. Valenta, *Soviet Intervention in Czechoslovakia;* Jiri Valenta, "Soviet Decision Making on Afghanistan, 1979," in *Soviet Decision Making,* ed. Valenta and Potter; Dina Rome Spechler, "The USSR and Third-World Conflicts: Domestic Debates and Soviet Policy in the Middle East," *World Politics* 38 (April 1986): 435–461; Galia Golan, *Yom Kippur and After: The Soviet Union and the Middle East Crisis* (Cambridge: Cambridge University Press, 1977); Katz, *The Third World.*

40. Michael J. Sodaro, *Moscow, Germany, and the West from Khrushchev to Gorbachev* (Ithaca: Cornell University Press, 1990), esp. chap. 11. On the foreign policy views of regional party secretaries, see Peter Hauslohner, "Prefects as Senators: Soviet Regional Politicians Look to Foreign Policy," *World Politics* 34 (January 1981): 197–233.

41. See Sarah E. Mendelson, "Internal Battles and External Wars: Politics, Learning, and the Soviet Withdrawal from Afghanistan," *World Politics* 45 (April 1993): 327–360; Celeste A. Wallander, "Opportunity, Incrementalism, and Learning in the Extension and Retraction of Soviet Global Commitments," *Security Studies* 1 (Spring 1992): 514–542; and Evangelista, "Sources of Moderation." For an overview of the linkage between the economic system and the politics of economic policy in the Soviet Union, see Timothy J. Colton, *The Dilemma of Reform in the Soviet Union,* revised and expanded edition (New York: Council on Foreign Relations, 1986).

42. George F. Kennan, *Russia and the West Under Lenin and Stalin* (New York: Little, Brown, 1960), p. 114.

43. See Bruce D. Porter, *War and the Rise of the State: The Military Foundations of Modern Politics* (New York: Free Press, 1994), and the sources cited in Porter's chapter for this volume.

44. Richter, *Khrushchev's Double Bind;* Horelick and Rush, *Strategic Power,* part 3; Raymond L. Garthoff, *Reflections on the Cuban Missile Crisis,* revised edition (Washington, D.C.: Brookings Institution, 1989), pp. 11–21.

45. See, for example, Evangelista, "Sources of Moderation," and Mendelson, "Internal Battles and External Wars," for very detailed models of the effects of the external environment on Soviet domestic politics and Gorbachev's security policies. William Wohlforth makes a strong realist argument for the crucial role of the external security environment in Gorbachev's reforms, the collapse of the Soviet Union, and the end of the Cold War. See

William C. Wohlforth, "Realism and the End of the Cold War," *International Security* 19 (Winter 1994/95): 91–129. For exceptions that analyze earlier periods of Soviet foreign policy with well-articulated models, see Richter, *Khrushchev's Double Bind,* and Anderson, *Public Politics.*

46. Stephen M. Meyer, "The Sources and Prospects of Gorbachev's New Political Thinking on Security," *International Security* 13 (Fall 1988): 124–163.

47. Robert Legvold, "The Nature of Soviet Power," *Foreign Affairs* 56 (October 1977): 49–71; Angela Stent, *From Embargo to Ostpolitik: The Political Economy of West German–Soviet Relations* (Cambridge: Cambridge University Press, 1981); Bruce Parrott, *Politics and Technology in the Soviet Union* (Cambridge: MIT Press, 1985), esp. chap. 6.

48. Matthew Evangelista, "Stalin's Revenge: Institutional Barriers to Internationalization in the Soviet Union," in *Internationalization and Domestic Politics,* ed. Robert O. Keohane and Helen Milner (Cambridge: Cambridge University Press, forthcoming), pp. 16–24. For studies that explain these issues in far greater detail and with deeper sophistication than I can suggest here, see Ed A. Hewett (with Clifford G. Gaddy), *Open for Business: Russia's Return to the Global Economy* (Washington, D.C.: Brookings Institution, 1992); and Jerry F. Hough, *Opening Up the Soviet Economy* (Washington, D.C.: Brookings Institution, 1988).

49. Wallander, "Opportunity, Incrementalism, and Learning."

CHAPTER 2

Democratization, War, and Nationalism in the Post-Communist States

Jack Snyder

In the past few years, a virtual army of political scientists has been examining the relationship between democracy and war. In his State of the Union address, Bill Clinton invoked their most notable finding, that no two democracies have ever fought each other in war, to justify a foreign policy dedicated to promoting the spread of democracy. Commentators such as Francis Fukuyama, capturing the heady mood during the collapse of the Soviet empire, speculated that the new wave of democratization would bring with it a history-ending reign of liberal peace.[1]

Alas, the recent evidence on this hypothesis is mixed at best. The protagonists in two of the main post-Communist wars—Croats and Serbs, Armenians and Azeris—have held competitive elections. By some reasonable definitions, most of these states could be called democratizing.[2] In party-list voting, a quarter of the Russian electorate voted for Vladimir Zhirinovsky's militant nationalist party, which routinely threatens intervention in the affairs of Russia's democratic and nondemocratic neighbors. Boris Yeltsin's democratically elected, avowedly liberal government used military aid to promote the overthrow of President Abulfez Elchibey's democratically elected regime in Azerbaijan.[3] Elected parliaments in Estonia and Latvia stubbornly insist on restrictive citizenship laws that risk conflict with Russian nationalists and democrats. Democratic Hungary and democratizing Romania, however, have avoided a conflict over Transylvania that many considered inevitable.

To be fair, this dubious track record would not have been surprising to careful scholars researching the history of democracy and war. Their works have routinely excepted new or partial democracies from the hypothesis that democracies never fight each other. Wars have indeed occurred between elected regimes when, for at least one of the parties, suffrage was highly restricted (the War of 1812), elected representatives lacked direct control over foreign and defense ministries (Germany in 1914), electoral outcomes were choreographed behind the scenes (Spanish-American War), or the elected regime was less than a year or two old or was dominated by a nearly autocratic chief executive (France and the Roman Republic; Ecuador and Colombia in 1863).[4] The British and the Dutch fought repeatedly in the seventeenth century when they were virtually the only major states with meaningful representative institutions.[5]

In short, though mature democracies never fight each other, democratizing states certainly do. In fact, some types of democratizing states seem especially war prone. Many of the great powers went through a period of aggressive, populist, nationalist expansionism during their initial experience with mass political participation—Revolutionary France, Palmerstonian Britain, Wilhelmine Germany, and Japan at the beginning of the 1930s. The Zhirinovsky vote raises the question of whether it will be Russia's turn next.

The war behavior of newly or partially democratizing states is too important to be relegated to the category of cases that are defined out of the sample of peaceful democracies. It should be a major research topic in its own right, in part because of its policy implications. Is it prudent to promote new democracies, or will such states destabilize the international order? Are some pathways to democracy more benign than others, and how can they be promoted?

Two bodies of theory can be tapped for insights on these questions. First, predictions of the war behavior of democratizing states can be deduced from the standard explanations offered for the peace among mature democracies. The consequences of expanded participation, representative institutions, division of powers, and democratic norms may help explain the pacific behavior of full-fledged democracies, but they may also help explain the belligerence of partial democracies. Second, hypotheses about the foreign behavior of democratizing states can be derived from theories of political development, which examine the effects of various paths to modernization on institutional effectiveness, coalition politics, and nationalism.

After defining some terms and deducing some hypotheses from these standard theories, I will illustrate the hypotheses with reference to some historical evidence, particularly from periods when the great powers were democratizing. Finally, I will discuss the value of these hypotheses as explanations for the international relations of several post-Communist states and draw some implications for future cases and for the policy choices of the mature democratic states.

Definitions

The first step in sorting out the puzzle of war-prone democratizing states must be to distinguish clearly between democracy and partial democratization. Studies of the democratic peace define democracy according to a number of criteria. Minimal definitions of democracy advanced by Joseph Schumpeter and most recently Samuel Huntington require periodic elections between candidates who compete fairly for the votes of a substantial portion of the adult population and whose outcome determines who makes state policy, including foreign and military policy.[6]

Some stricter definitions require in addition that a democracy must respect individuals' civil rights or that a government must have surrendered office following an electoral defeat. As further indicators of democracy, though not necessarily part of the core definition, some studies also measure whether the executive branch of government is checked in policymaking by the legislature or the judiciary, whether political parties are well institutionalized, and whether individuals' economic rights are respected.[7]

Some studies point out that states exhibit democratic characteristics in varying degrees. Elections may be sporadic, some people may be barred from voting or running for office, access to the press may be skewed, or election outcomes may not directly determine who governs the country. Some countries may be highly democratic according to certain of these criteria (e.g., Wilhelmine Germany had universal suffrage) but not others (electoral control of executive offices); conversely, other countries might have the opposite mix across these dimensions (e.g., pre-1832 Britain). Quantitative studies have devised schemes for measuring gradations of democracy on several of these dimensions.[8] I will use the term partial democracy to refer to intermediate cases where the prospect of having to compete in elections, no matter how sporadic or unfair, has a substantial effect on the calculations of political elites. I will call a state democratizing if it is a partial democracy that is becoming more democratic on one or more of these dimensions.[9]

A related phenomenon is political participation, which may take such forms as voting and party formation but also mass demands for a voice in politics through political strikes or riots.[10] Also, political participation might increase outside of electoral politics if large numbers of people join mass pressure groups, like the German Navy League before World War I, whose strategy focused more on making direct demands on the government than on organizing for electoral victories. Thus, political participation may increase even though a country is neither democratic nor even democratizing.

Theories of the Democratic Peace

A few scholars argue that the absence of war among democracies is spurious, an artifact of a small number of cases driven by the democracies' geopolitical need to unite to resist aggressor states that happened to be authoritarian.[11] But the vast majority of scholars are convinced that the democratic peace cannot be so easily explained away. They disagree, however, on the reasons for the democratic peace.[12] Their disagreement has implications for thinking about the war behavior of democratizing states. If the variables producing the democratic peace can be isolated, then the condition of those variables in democratizing states might provide clues to their more belligerent behavior. Four explanations merit examination.

Median-Voter Interests

The simplest explanation for the democratic peace was advanced long ago by Immanuel Kant: In a democracy, ultimate power is held by the average citizen, who bears the costs and risks of war.[13] By this logic, democracies will fight only when the costs are low, the benefits high, or the need incontrovertible. Dictators or oligarchies, in contrast, may go to war more lightly, since they can pass the costs on to their long-suffering subjects.

Most scholars have not accepted this explanation, despite its logical simplicity, because they believe that it implies that democracies ought to be more peaceful in general, not just among themselves. In fact, democracies fight as often as other states, and they seem to initiate war about as often. In rebuttal, David Lake has presented quantitative evidence that democratic constraints on the state elite's ability to monopolize profits from empire have indeed made democracies more prudent and cost-conscious in their war fighting.[14] Thus, median-voter interests cannot be disregarded as a possible explanation for the democratic peace.

In partial democracies or democratizing states, there is little reason to expect the median voter to exert a consistent constraint on the war making of the state or other elite groups benefiting from imperialism. Electoral sanctions may be irregular, and officials responsible for foreign and defense policy may face no electoral sanction at all. Antiwar candidates may be prevented from running for election or forced to compete on an uneven playing field. Restricted suffrage may allow the state to pass the costs of war on to groups that do not vote.

Even worse, in partially democratizing states, elites can use their control over resources and the rules of the game to select which mass groups get access to political power. In a strategy of partial democratic opening, elites may divide and rule by co-opting some groups to share in the spoils of war and empire while forcing excluded groups to bear the costs. This strategy has an ancient pedigree. The aristocrats of Athens weathered a political crisis by extending political rights to parts of the lower classes, which included a large number of naval rowers, whose livelihood depended on frequent military expeditions, and to civil servants, whose salaries came from imperial tribute.[15] When this happens, the volatility of mass politics is no longer tempered by the cost-sensitivity of the average voter. Depending on the precise configuration of interests, this might make democratizing states more belligerent than either mature democracies or authoritarian regimes.

Checks and Balances

Some authors try to distinguish the effects of checks on political authorities from voters and checks that stem from the division of power within the government.[16] Thus, it is hypothesized that democracies with intragovernmental separation of powers may be more prudent because of the difficulty in achieving a consensus for war among the branches of government, especially in obtaining legislative approval for military adventures.

This hypothesis has several problems. First, preliminary quantitative research shows only a modest connection between institutionalized intragovernmental checks and war behavior.[17] Second, divided authoritarian governments have often been warlike—for example, the splits between army and navy in imperial Japan or between iron and rye in the Wilhelmine coalition. Without effective checks from voters, elite factions may logroll their separate imperial interests rather than acting as a mutual check.[18] Third, intragovernmental stalemate is a two-edged sword: It might hinder decisions to begin a warlike policy, but it also might prevent the abandonment of an agreed endeavor that has turned out to be risky. Finally, even in cases where democratic checks are fairly strong, a government that is divided between executive and legislative factions, each beholden to different core constituencies, might resemble the imperial logrolling pattern more than the pacific stalemate pattern. The executive-legislative maneuvering that led to the U.S. Cold War consensus in the early 1950s is a possible example.[19]

In newly democratizing states, there is even less reason to expect that checks and balances will have a systematically pacifying effect. One or another branch of government is likely to be dominated by old elite groups with an interest in empire, protectionism, or arms racing left over from the authoritarian period. The role of the military in the Wilhelmine German executive branch and the role of economic interest groups in both the executive and the Reichstag is the quintessential example. In partial democracies, such groups are under loose accountability to the average voter. Moreover, the distribution of powers among the branches is likely to be highly politicized and unstable rather than legally and predictably institutionalized. Checks and balances under those conditions are likely to resemble naked interest group politics more than a constitutionally regulated decisionmaking process. In contemporary Russia, for example, the unstable division of powers among the president, the legislature, and the courts has contributed to nationalist demagogy by parliamentary factions, tenuous political control over the military, and concessions by the executive to demands for an assertive foreign policy.[20]

The Free Marketplace of Ideas

Some scholars argue that democracies are more prudent because they tend to have institutions that guarantee free speech and the diffusion of information needed to evaluate public policies.[21] Critical journalists, congressional fact finders, and independent universities create a climate of informed public debate where truly reckless, unsupportable ideas will usually wither under close scrutiny. Obviously, nobody claims that the free marketplace of ideas always yields optimal results, only that well-institutionalized democracies evaluate policy more effectively than most authoritarian regimes, where elite groups may exploit information monopolies to evade accountability or where underlings may avoid telling bad news to the dictator.

However, there is also the well-established view that democratic public opinion is emotional, fickle, and rooted in profound ignorance, especially concerning foreign affairs. Thus, the incompetence of consumers in the free marketplace of ideas may cancel out the benefits of public accountability. But recent, rigorous research contends that the U.S. public has been fairly rational in responding to information about foreign affairs when elites have provided them with sensible interpretations of events in the mass media.[22]

Democratizing states may have the worst of both worlds as regards public debate on foreign affairs. Mass publics are engaged in politics, so the incentive for demagogy is strong, but the marketplace of ideas is likely to be highly imperfect. Elite interest groups or the state may enjoy monopolies of crucial information. Institutions providing intellectual accountability—the journalistic media, universities, parliamentary oversight bodies—may be weak, dependent on the state or interested parties, and lacking in professionalism. Under such conditions, the free market of ideas may be flooded with shoddy goods, subject to no systematic quality control. Moreover, publics unaccustomed to weighing evidence in public debate may be closer to the traditional, volatile stereotype than is the rational public portrayed by recent studies of the United States.

Democratic Norms

Some scholars argue that the crucial difference between democracies and other regime types lies in their norms for settling political disagreements and recognizing political legitimacy.[23] Successful democracies, it is argued, operate domestically according to norms of cooperative bargaining and dispute settlement, which carry over into patterns of bargaining and adjudication in their foreign relations. Thus, Anne-Marie Slaughter shows that a democracy is more likely to treat disputes involving foreign states as legal questions, rather than power-political issues, if the other state shares its democratic norms.[24] Democracies generally expect each other to be cooperative, rule-following, and nonthreatening, and so a self-fulfilling prophecy is created. In contrast, it is argued, democracies see authoritarian regimes as illegitimate and expect them to be threatening.[25]

This line of argument enjoys great popularity at present, but it suffers from some significant logical and empirical shortcomings. Logically, it is peculiar that proponents of the normative explanation define democracy primarily in terms of its institutions—for example, fair elections determining the government—yet they deny that the direct consequences of those institutions—for example, checks on policy by the median voter or separation of powers—have a decisive effect on the war behavior of the state. Moreover, they have not adequately explored the connection between the norms, such as the civil rights of individuals, and the institutions that enforce them, such as courts, legislatures, and police. Logically, it seems odd to set norms apart as a competing explanation to institutions when the casual interconnections between norms and institutions are inextricable.

Finally, the most extensive tests of the normative argument have so far been based on dubious, surrogate measures of the strength of democratic norms, such as the number of years a democracy has endured and the extent of domestic violence perpetrated by the state. These measures might be capturing not only normative differences across cases but also differences of coalitions, strategies, and interests.[26] Moreover, present normative arguments beg the question of where the norms come from and how they are causally related to democratic institutional arrangements.

Despite these conceptual and empirical problems, it is still worthwhile to ask how norms might affect the behavior of democratizing states. In principle, a number of quite different arguments seem possible. One might expect democratic norms to be weak in a newly democratizing state, on the grounds that ideas and habits from the old regime are likely to persist in public life. For example, Gabriel Almond and Sidney Verba's *The Civic Culture* and the follow-up studies to it found that Germans' commitment to democratic norms was purely pragmatic among the first generation of the Federal Republic's citizens but that it subsequently deepened and became internalized.[27] Conversely, one might expect the commitment to democratic ideology to be particularly strong among the first generation of committed activists who mobilized popular support to overthrow the old regime. For example, Donald Kagan says that Pericles and other young democrats were "intoxicated with a bright new ideology" and that "like the young ideologues of the French and Russian revolutions," they thought that "noble ideas would sweep all before them."[28] Or both of these might be true: Democratic norms may be weak in states that democratize as a result of a partial, tactical elite opening to participation by some popular groups whereas populist—though not necessarily democratic—norms may be strong in states that democratize as the result of a successful mass movement. In the latter case, the principle of popular sovereignty may be intensely felt, but procedural norms of democracy and civil rights may be weak. Ethnonationalist states are likely to fall into this category.

Neither of these patterns bodes well for a pacific foreign policy. In the case of the partial elite opening, the merely tactical commitment to democracy would seem to provide little scope for a flowering of norm-driven cooperation with other democracies. In the case of the ethnopopulist state, the violation of the civil rights of ethnic minorities, which is legitimated by the norms of the new state, risks conflict with neighboring states and the broader community of democratic states.

However, there is another side to this coin. Although some democratizing states do become belligerent, others do not. In some cases, this may be because democratizing elites may face strong international incentives to adhere to the normative expectations of powerful, mature democratic states. Elites governing a new democracy must be concerned about the risk that their state will slip back into its old authoritarian pattern, destroying the democratic regime on which they have staked their political fortunes. Thus, they have powerful reasons to cooperate with their natural allies abroad, well-established democracies that have an interest in promoting the consolidation of the democratic regime. For that reason, the democratizing elite may submerge any geopolitical interests that conflict with its foreign

backers in order to gain outside support against the more threatening domestic opposition.[29] Moreover, the democratic elite has a strong incentive to solidify its external alliance by touting its thoroughgoing acceptance of democratic norms and
implementing whatever civic reforms the outsiders deem necessary.

Theories of Modernization, Expanding Participation, and War

Another body of theory bearing on the link between democratization and war examines the political consequences of social modernization. A number of the best-
known classical theorists of large-scale social change—Alexander Gerschenkron, Karl Polanyi, Barrington Moore, and their intellectual descendants—have
argued that social, economic, and political stresses at the transition to modernity
are likely to give rise to nationalism and war. Increased political participation and
partial democratization are typically part of this syndrome of disruptive social
change. Thus, our most basic theories of comparative politics and macrosociol-
ogy lead us to expect a link between democratization and war.

Such theories should not be considered alternatives to hypotheses derived from
the literature on the democratic peace. Rather, they can be thought of as a deeper
level of causation, identifying some of the underlying processes that shape the
variables that are of interest to theorists of the democratic peace: namely, the
power and interests of social groups, institutional checks and balances, social
norms, and the structure of the marketplace of ideas.

What explains the apparent connection between democratization and war, in
the views of the theorists of political modernization? Long-run social changes—
such as the development of capitalist economic relations, industrialization, urbanization, increases in education and political awareness, and resulting changes
in the social power of classes and groups—typically lead to demands for increased political participation by formerly excluded groups. This may lead to nationalism and war by a number of paths.

Institutional Lag and State Building

As modernization accelerates, social change typically races ahead of existing social institutions. The development of institutions to channel participation and to
reconcile contending interests lags behind the increased demand for democratization.[30] Not only are state administrative bureaucracies, legislatures, parties, and legality poorly institutionalized, but state boundaries and citizenship rules may be
up for grabs. In this context, both old and new elite groups are likely to promote an
intense nationalism in an attempt to mobilize people to build an effective state to
fill the gap between participation and institutions.[31] Or, as John Matthews puts it in
his dissertation in progress, nationalism is an ideological substitute that fills the legitimacy gap when institutions are weak but participation levels are high.[32]
Scholars of nationalism, most recently Liah Greenfeld, have noted the strong connection between expanded political participation and the rise of nationalism.[33]

Several theorists offer variations on this theme. Alexander Gerschenkron, for example, argued that the role of nationalism as a mass ideology for state building is especially strong in late-developing countries. Nationalism serves as the ideological substitute for liberalism in those cases where an activist state or monopolistic cartels promote a national development strategy to catch up with early-industrializing, laissez-faire states. As Gerschenkron contended in *Bread and Democracy*, war and protectionism can be the by-products of this process.[34]

Charles Tilly finds yet another connection among state building, war, and nationalism. In his view, military competition spurs the development of military and other state bureaucracies, which co-opt social groups into a nationalist consensus in order to expand their resources for waging war.[35] Former Azerbaijani president Abulfez Elchibey made exactly this appeal, arguing that only a popular ethnonationalist regime could mobilize taxes and soldiers for the war with Armenia. But he fell from power when he could not deliver on this pledge.[36] In yet another variation on this theme, Barry Posen and Eugen Weber show how military bureaucracies in the era of mass warfare inculcate nationalism in order to increase the fighting power of their troops.[37] Finally, the mass ethnonationalist approach to state building almost necessarily leads to war in regions where ethnic groups live intermingled or where state boundaries are mismatched with ethnic or linguistic residence patterns.

Political Competition: Elites, Masses, and Coalitions

A second path linking war, nationalism, and expanded political participation goes through coalition politics and through the political strategies of elite groups vis-à-vis mass groups and vis-à-vis other elites. Modernization and pressures for expanded participation threaten the rule of old elites, create opportunities for rising elites, and mobilize a pool of potential mass supporters for both. Several theorists and historians have explored the consequences of these dynamics for nationalism and war.

Arno Mayer, for example, shows how elites of the ancien régime used international crises to gain nationalist legitimacy as a prop to their eroding right to rule, a tactic that has been echoed by Serbian president Slobodan Milosevic's campaign of ethnic cleansing and by Ukrainian president Leonid Kravchuk's symbolic diplomacy over the Black Sea Fleet.[38] Similarly, Hans-Ulrich Wehler shows how the ideology of mass militant nationalism was used in an attempt to maintain the power of Wilhelmine Germany's old elites in the face of an expansion of political participation. And Geoff Eley has shown how the rising German middle class became a "sorcerer's apprentice" in this game.[39] More generally, Liah Greenfeld shows that nationalism in Britain and France originally meant popular self-rule and was aimed at traditional elites.

Another factor that may affect the propensity of democratizing states to drift toward war and nationalism is the nature of the social structure from which they are making a transition. In Germany and Japan, old elites having an interest in protectionism, empire, and military instruments played a central role in shaping political institutions, coalitions, and ideas in the era of increasing participation. Barrington Moore, for example, saw the rise of militant dictatorships as the result of the weakness of the bourgeoisie in the coalition politics of late-developing states.[40] However, contemporary democratizing states may not have analogous elites. Stephen Van Evera argues that more egalitarian post-Communist states democratizing from a different baseline should have a more benign outcome.[41] Nevertheless, it may still turn out that post-Communist militaries, industrialists, and neo-Communists could be partial analogues to the Schlieffens, the Krupps, and the Junkers of yore.

Economic Change

A third link among democratization, war, and nationalism comes through economic change. Many scholars of nationalism, notwithstanding their theoretical diversity, argue that mass nationalism is the result of the process of economic development that had its roots in eighteenth- and nineteenth-century Europe. Ernest Gellner argues that nationalism arose from the functional necessity to create a homogeneous national mass culture to make the modern industrial economy work efficiently. Nationalism is at its most intense and militant during the shakedown period during which this homogenization is taking place.[42] Amending Gellner to take into account the nationalism that slightly preceded industrialization, Michael Mann argues that nationalism reflected the rise of preindustrial commercial capitalism, which strengthened the economic and social power of the popular forces of the nation.[43] Karl Polanyi, making an argument that has direct contemporary relevance to the Zhirinovsky phenomenon, contends that fascist nationalism was one possible result of the contradiction between mass democracy and the painful economic adjustments required by the system of laissez-faire economics and the gold standard.[44] This outcome was especially likely in relatively large states like Germany and Japan, where a strategy of autarky in an expanded empire looked like a feasible means to avoid dependence on the world market.

Thus, through all three of these mechanisms—institutional lag, political competition, and economic dislocation—incipient democratization resulting from the modernization process may give rise to war and nationalism. However, this does not always happen. There are numerous cases where a gap between participation and institutions in a modernizing society does not produce militant nationalism. Huntington's study of praetorian societies, for example, included many peaceful Latin American states, where elites successfully repressed mass groups and so did not have to compete to mobilize them via a popular nationalist ideology. It was primarily his "mass praetorian" regimes, such as Weimar Germany and perhaps interwar Japan, that developed mass-energized nationalist regimes that went on the warpath.[45] The temptations that accompany great-power military capabilities also played a role in these two cases.

In short, there are strong reasons to expect a connection among democratization, nationalism, and war in countries that are undergoing dramatic social and economic change, struggling to build a new state, or experiencing a gap between high political participation and weak governing institutions. This connection is not universal, and there is no well-developed theory specifying the conditions under which it will and will not occur. However, great-power status, mass politics, ethnic intermingling, and the presence of atavistic elites with an interest in or tradition of imperial expansion seem to be some of the risk factors.

Historical Evidence: The Great Powers

Despite the large quantitative literature on democracy and war, there are few if any systematic, quantitative studies that trace the connections between democratization and war. Edward Mansfield and I are beginning a project along these lines. In the interim, a qualitative discussion of a few cases may at least provide some illustrations.[46]

One particularly striking sample of cases is the great powers. Almost all of them have fought wars during the early stages of the expansion of political participation. The fact of the wars is not in itself so important, because the great powers were almost always fighting wars, but the exceptionally aggressive and strategically excessive character of several of these wars makes them noteworthy.

These cases provide some anecdotal support to a number of the hypotheses linking war, nationalism, and democratization outlined above. The most consistent and striking theme, however, is the central role of elite competition for mass political support under conditions of expanding political participation in fostering belligerent foreign behavior in all of the cases. Under conditions of rapid social change, old and new elites used nationalism to vie for mass backing in an institutional context of imperfect democratic competition. Elite groups, often having traditional interests in imperial or military activities, exploited the imperfect accountability, unequal franchise, and propaganda asymmetries typical of partial democracies to channel political participation in the direction of nationalism and external expansion. Thus, the hypotheses of modernization theory and of the democratic peace help to explain this outcome.

Britain

Britain's expansion of mass political participation after the Reform Act of 1832 provided an impetus contributing to the Crimean War. In that era, suffrage was sufficiently widened to meet Michael Doyle's definition of democracy, yet oligarchical factions retained their dominance as a result of unequal representation and the absence of a secret ballot. Public opinion in this partial democracy started off relatively pacific, but over time elite propaganda and coalition strategies won over the middle classes to more warlike strategies.

During the 1840s, mass opinion on foreign affairs was dominated by Richard Cobden's pacifist, free-trading Anti–Corn Law League, which lobbied against protectionist and militarist policies that it claimed served the interests of only the military-feudal elite. But middle-class pacifism evaporated when agricultural protection was abandoned and when the threat of a revolutionary working class arose with the Chartist movement of 1848. The middle class then realigned with moderately conservative oligarchs, such as Lord Palmerston, who offered an aggressive, pseudoliberal foreign policy to open markets abroad while blocking further liberal reforms at home. This strategy of liberal imperialism had been well prepared over two decades of demonizing autocratic Russia through Palmerston's systematic manipulation of the popular press. In this new political context, middle-class elites enthusiastically backed the Crimean War, which they thought would advance their commercial and ideological interests as well as provide a chance to press for a greater middle-class role in the effort to rationalize government in order to prosecute the war more efficiently. The moderate majority of the ruling oligarchy were lukewarm about the war but felt hemmed in by Palmerston's social imperialism.[47]

Germany

The story of German social imperialism in an era of expanded political participation is more familiar and even more clear-cut. Bismarck had opened the democratic floodgates of universal suffrage, through which he hoped to use conservative rural votes to neutralize urban liberals, but the rise of the working class and the increasing political awareness of other popular classes turned this ploy against subsequent German elites. As I have already outlined above, the Wilhelmine elite tried to use nationalist themes, international crises, the control of levers of propaganda and information, and executive branch insulation from the electoral process to shape access to political coalitions on terms that would maintain the old elite's power. Rising middle-class elites turned these weapons against the old governing elite, arguing that if international rivalry was really as the government portrayed it, then the old elite was criminally negligent for its laxity in prosecuting the conflict. Like a much more extreme version of the Palmerstonian case, a situation of partial democracy and manipulated public debate created an opportunity for social imperialism, which escaped the old elite's control.[48]

Japan

Increased political participation also served as the backdrop for Japan's turn toward imperialism in the 1930s. By the late 1920s, Japan was moving toward a two-party system with periodic, competitive elections whose outcome was the main determinant of who held government office. One of the parties, the Minseito, tended to favor further expansion of the franchise, free trade with the West, and a gradual approach to gaining influence in China consistent with the open-door concept. At least on one occasion, the Minseito gained power in part because its opponents failed to rein in the excesses of the military in Manchuria.

Thus, as with Cobden's Anti–Corn Law League, increased political participation seemed to promote a moderate, peace-oriented foreign policy in the Japan of the late Taisho period.

The Japanese military and other radical nationalists, however, harbored a different vision of Japanese democracy, where voting and parliaments would have diminishing weight. They envisioned a populist, corporatist state where the military and sympathetic bureaucrats would take power from the corrupt, old aristocratic and economic elite and carve out a self-sufficient, industrialized, militarized Asian empire that would protect the people from the vagaries of the world market. This would also protect the military from naval arms control and constraints on military operations imposed by the Taisho politicians and backed by Taisho voters. The Great Depression gave the military their chance to begin to implement this strategy through faits accomplis in a climate of mass public support. This support was not automatic, however. It was built only through a campaign of mass public propaganda, physical intimidation of political opponents, and the creation of pork barrel incentives, as in the opportunity to colonize agricultural land in Manchuria.[49] Japanese imperial policy became increasingly extreme as a younger generation of true-believing populist officers gained influence over the traditional officers who were necessary to set the imperial strategy in motion.[50]

France

Growing mass political participation was a central factor in several of France's most dubious wars. In revolutionary France, the democratic Brissotin faction consciously provoked a war with monarchist Austria as a means of polarizing French politics and undercutting King Louis's strategy of appeasing the French democrats.[51] Arguably, Napoleon I's use of military force to spread the Enlightenment was a way of tapping popular ideals and energies that served as a substitute for democracy at home. Even more obviously, Napoleon III came to power through elections but used the legitimacy acquired through wars for popular causes to escape democratic constraints.[52]

Russia

The stresses of democratization did not play as central a role in Russia's wars, but some similar themes are recognizable. Before World War I, pan-Slav expansionism and sympathy for the Serbs were typical among the politically attentive intelligentsia. Rising middle-class groups in the Duma, including the industrial elite, were inclined to favor a reformed political system, resting on a broader social base, as a way of strengthening Russia's power vis-à-vis its geopolitical competitors. In response, the old elite sought to demonstrate that it remained able to fight effectively for Russian interests abroad. And of course after 1917, increased political participation played a role in the conflict involving Russia's revolutionary regime, its neighbors, and the intervening great powers.[53] For the most part, however, the interplay of democratization and foreign policy remains a matter for Russia's future, not its past.

In summary, most of the great powers fought a popular war during their initial surge of democratization. Many of these conflicts were geopolitically dubious. In tracing the domestic political processes that contributed to war, several theoretical hypotheses receive some support. Partially democratic institutions skewed outcomes toward warlike or nationalist coalitions when voter preferences were filtered through a process that was managed by elites, which expressed an interest either in imperial policies per se or in the legitimation bonus of nationalist politics. Likewise, the free marketplace of ideas favored nationalist or imperialist ideas when such elites enjoyed informational or propaganda advantages. However, in democratizing states, overly warlike policy was often an unintended consequence that occurred when elites lost control of the popular forces that they attempted to shape.

In newly democratizing states, populist norms of radical action on behalf of the people tended to be strong, but democratic-procedural norms tended to be weak. Thus, it was easy for dictators to claim to be liberal democrats on the grounds that they had loose, plebiscitary backing to prosecute a popular war. War, democratization, and state building were repeatedly connected by the attempt of rising elites to use the occasion of war to insist on a greater political and administrative role in the interests of energizing and rationalizing the war effort. Nationalist exploitation of mass economic distress played a role in some of these cases, but so did nationalist claims of economic opportunity through expansion.

In short, most of the theoretical hypotheses linking democratization, nationalism, and war can be illustrated by two or more of the great-power cases. This is not surprising, since many of these theories emerged from the study of the European great powers. Whether these hypotheses would fare as well against a larger sample of cases, and whether they can be applied fruitfully to contemporary cases, remain to be seen.

Democratization and War in the Post-Communist States

The experience of the post-Communist states confirms the proposition that democratizing states are at risk for militant nationalism and war, even among each other. Two states engaged in military conflict, Serbia and Croatia, are arguably democracies by minimal Schumpeterian criteria. They do not, however, meet the peaceful change of government test. Armenia, also a Schumpeterian democracy, has informally supported the Karabakh Armenians in their war with Azerbaijan, which chose the ethnonationalist Abulfez Elchibey as its president in free and fair elections until he was overthrown following military defeats.[54] In addition, incipient post-Communist cold wars between Russia and its Ukrainian, Estonian, and Latvian neighbors involve nationalistic democratizing states on both sides. The other post-Communist wars in Tadzhikistan, Georgia, and Moldova should perhaps be set aside, since they are complex civil-international struggles that have only a little to do with nationalism and even less to do with democracy; wars are not caused *only* by democratization!

The greater theoretical problem is that the democratization hypothesis seems to overpredict war among the post-Communist states. One notable example is the much-anticipated war between Hungary and Romania over the Hungarian minority in Transylvania. Indeed, the forbearance of the Hungarians in the face of multiple provocation—Romanian farmers attacking Hungarians with scythes, Serbs driving Hungarians from their homes in parts of Voivodina, and Slovaks trying to gerrymander Hungarian districts—is almost a miracle. Former Communists are making a comeback in the face of economic difficulties, but nationalist demagogue Istvan Czurka has made few converts. Arguably, the relatively strong, pluralistic Hungarian civil society jumped in a single leap from its Communist past into fully institutionalized democracy, avoiding the predicted evils of partial democratization.

Perhaps more revealing than gross correlations between degrees of democratization and belligerence are the more specific hypotheses about how democratization leads to international conflict. The hypotheses derived from the literature on the democratic peace get mixed results. The argument that legislative checks keep democracies peaceful fares quite poorly. In Russia, Ukraine, Armenia, and Azerbaijan under Elchibey's predecessor, Ayaz Mutalibov, parliament was consistently more belligerent than the chief executive.[55] The argument about the free marketplace of ideas fares better: The press in the Balkans and Caucasus is notoriously myth-ridden and skewed by nationalist content. And even in the less egregious post-Soviet cases, the professionalism of foreign affairs writing outside Moscow is so underdeveloped that informed public assessments of nationalist arguments are nearly impossible.

The argument about norms of dispute resolution is harder to assess. It is true that almost all of the post-Soviet states have faced difficulties in resolving political disputes both at home and abroad. But little insight is to be gained by attributing Yeltsin's high-handedness toward the parliament and toward the near abroad to a weakness of Russia's democratic norms. Yeltsin's foreign minister, Andrei Kozyrev, spent 1992 and 1993 touting the value of democratic norms in domestic and international affairs, yet by the beginning of 1994 he was forced to jump aboard the nationalist, pro-Serb, neo-imperial bandwagon like virtually everyone else in Russian politics.[56] More concrete causal explanations can be found by studying the political tides and coalitions that lie behind the norms.

Also elusive is the question of whether the institutional imperfections of partial democracies foil or distort the realization of the median voter's true preferences. There is little reason to doubt that the median voter in Serbia, Croatia, Armenia, and Estonia approves the assertive nationalist policy of its government. Given a choice, voters in these countries have consistently chosen ethnonationalist candidates, though not necessarily the most extreme ones. In the Serbian case, it has been argued that the average voter's preferences have been cleverly manipulated. Milosevic used various undemocratic stratagems—intraparty maneuvers to oust the liberal faction and faits accomplis by the military and the Croatian Serbs—to create a nationalist climate of opinion that might otherwise not have existed. Nonetheless, Milosevic's main electoral opposition, both in the Yugoslav period and more recently, has come from politicians even more militantly nationalist than he.

In Russia, the election of a substantial number of nationalist politicians was in part the unintended consequence of a protest vote based primarily on the poor economic performance of the Yeltsin regime. Surveys suggest that on most policy dimensions the general public is less nationalist and less oriented toward the use of force abroad than are Russian elites. According to a well-designed study by William Zimmerman, 56 percent of a sample of Russia's foreign policy elite were inclined to "send military aid if asked to aid a country of the former Soviet Union" whereas only 34 percent of the general public held that opinion. According to 77 percent of the elite sample, the "national interests of Russia extend beyond its current territory," but only 57 percent of the general public agree. The public was more nationalist than the elite (81 percent to 69 percent) only on the use of unspecified means to "defend the interest of Russians abroad."[57] Other polls, however, show that the mass public has a low level of interest in foreign policy and is often unwilling to express any opinion on foreign issues. In contrast, the elite expresses elaborate views on foreign affairs.[58]

The rise of nationalism in Russian politics has more to do with the forging and legitimation of elite coalitions than with a groundswell of mass sentiment.[59] Nationalism is a useful component of a counterliberal ideology binding together an emerging coalition of neo-Communist elites, industrialists, and the military. Nationalism substitutes for communism as an ideology stressing the role of the strong state in defending the Russian national interest against economic and security threats, real or imagined, domestic and foreign. In Wilhelmine Germany, most middle-class voters cared little about the fleet per se; it just came as part of a coherent, plausible political and ideological package. In general, recent Russian developments highlight the relevance of several theories rooted in the German experience, notably Polanyi's arguments linking nationalism to the backlash against laissez-faire and Gerschenkron's view of nationalism as the ideology of late, state-centered development.

The case of Azerbaijan sheds light on the limits of the Tilly-Posen dynamic connecting military mobilization and popular nationalism. Elchibey's political program looked like a textbook case of the expansion of mass political participation to mobilize economic and human resources for a nationalist war. It turned out, however, that administrative corruption and incompetence undercut the goal of national collective action. Both national sentiment and military mobilization fizzled, and Elchibey was overthrown by a Russian-backed clientelistic regime headed by former Communist boss Geidar Aliev. The Tilly-Posen thesis may be correct, but it evidently depends on certain preconditions that were lacking in the Azerbaijani case.[60]

In short, several of the theories linking democratization, nationalism, and war help illuminate a number of the post-Communist cases. For the most part, these cases neither prove nor refute the theories. More often, they show the need for qualifying the theories before applying them in this new context, and they demonstrate the broad range of variation in war behavior and nationalism across cases of democratization.

Implications for Policy

The relationship among democratization, nationalism, and war is complex and contingent. A great deal more research is needed to prescribe policies knowledgeably. At this stage, only a few broad conclusions can be drawn.

Although mature democracies have never fought each other, the road from a society's authoritarian past toward a stable, democratic future is likely to be bloody. Promoting democratization in large, nuclear-armed states like Russia and China is at best like spinning a roulette wheel. Often, however, history will set this wheel to spinning whether the West gives it a nudge or not. When that is the case, there are strong reasons to take a hand in the process, trying to minimize the carnage that sometimes accompanies a democratic transition.

The theories of democratization, nationalism, and war examined in this chapter point to a few guidelines for policy. Most of them conform to conventional wisdom, but some are underappreciated. To ease the international security consequences of democratic transitions, the West should seek to strengthen institutions of democratic accountability, remove imperfections from the free marketplace of ideas, aggressively use its influence to promote civic-territorial rather than ethnic forms of national identity, invest in social safety nets to buffer the victims of economic change, buy off or dismantle elite groups with imperial interests, and focus its efforts on the great powers, where the temptations of aggressive nationalism may be greatest and where the resulting wreckage would be most serious.[61]

If social scientists begin to study democratization and war with as much care as they have democracy and war, perhaps future presidential speeches will temper their calls for the promotion of democracy with reminders of the dangers of a halfhearted policy that gets countries only halfway to that goal.

Notes

I am grateful to Rachel Bronson, Otilia Giron, Ted Hopf, Robert Keohane, David Lake, John Matthews, Edward Mansfield, Bruce Russett, Randall Stone, and Celeste Wallander and other participants at a seminar at Harvard's Russian Research Center for providing useful comments.

1. "Transcript of Clinton's Address," *New York Times,* 26 January 1994, p. A17; Francis Fukuyama, "The End of History?" *National Interest,* no. 16 (Summer 1989): 3–18.

2. Commission on Security and Cooperation in Europe, *Human Rights and Democratization in the Newly Independent States of the Former Soviet Union* (Washington, D.C.: GPO, January 1993); idem, *Human Rights and Democratization in Croatia* (Washington, D.C.: GPO, September 1993); Timothy Colton, "Politics," in *After the Soviet Union,* ed. Timothy Colton and Robert Legvold (New York: Norton, 1992), pp. 17–48.

3. Thomas Goltz, "Letter from Eurasia: The Hidden Hand," *Foreign Policy* 92 (Fall 1993): 92–116; Fiona Hill and Pamela Jewett, "'Back in the USSR': Russia's Intervention in the Internal Affairs of the Former Soviet Republics and the Implications for United States Policy Toward Russia," report of the Ethnic Conflict Project of the Strengthening Democratic Institutions Project, John F. Kennedy School of Government, Harvard University (January 1994).

4. Bruce Russett, *Grasping the Democratic Peace* (Princeton: Princeton University Press, 1993), pp. 16–18.

5. Lisa Martin, "Legislative Delegation and International Engagement," in *Liberalization and Foreign Policy,* ed. Miles Kahler (forthcoming).

6. Joseph Schumpeter, *Capitalism, Socialism, and Democracy,* 2d ed. (New York: Harper, 1947); Samuel P. Huntington, *The Third Wave: Democratization in the Late Twentieth Century* (Norman: University of Oklahoma Press, 1991), pp. 5–13, esp. p. 6; see also Russett, *Grasping,* pp. 14–16.

7. Russett, *Grasping,* pp. 14–16; Michael Doyle, "Liberalism and World Politics," *American Political Science Review* 80 (December 1986): 1151–1169, esp. p. 1164.

8. Ted Robert Gurr, Keith Jaggers, and Will Moore, *Polity II Handbook* (Boulder: University of Colorado, 1989).

9. The categories of partial democracy and democratizing state are defined here in a multidimensional way. These concepts might be broken down further into one-dimensional indicators for the purposes of identifying domestic correlates of war. For example, the behavior of partial democracies might be evaluated separately for each of Gurr's dimensions. Moreover, partial democracy might be distinguished from unstable democracy; that is, it is a retrogression from or oscillation between democratic and authoritarian forms. For the most part, I hope to take up such distinctions in future studies, not here.

10. Samuel P. Huntington, *Political Order in Changing Societies* (New Haven: Yale University Press, 1968).

11. John Mearsheimer, "Back to the Future: Instability in Europe After the Cold War," *International Security* 15 (Summer 1990): 5–57.

12. Russett, *Grasping,* chaps. 1–2.

13. Doyle, "Liberalism," p. 1160, quoting Immanuel Kant, *Perpetual Peace* (Cambridge: Cambridge University Press, 1970), p. 100.

14. David Lake, "Powerful Pacificists," *American Political Science Review* 86 (March 1992): 24–37. Moreover, democracies are much less likely to engage in preventive war, and democratic great powers are better at learning to avoid or correct imperial overextension. Randall Schweller, "Domestic Structure and Preventive War: Are Democracies More Pacific?" *World Politics* 44 (January 1992): 235–269; Jack Snyder, *Myths of Empire* (Ithaca: Cornell University Press, 1991).

15. Donald Kagan, *The Outbreak of the Peloponnesian War* (Ithaca: Cornell University Press, 1969), pp. 140–141, also pp. 65, 70; Josiah Ober, *Mass and Elite in Democratic Athens: Rhetoric, Ideology, and the Power of the People* (Princeton: Princeton University Press, 1989), p. 84.

16. Russell, *Grasping*, pp. 38–40.

17. Ibid., pp. 86–93.

18. Snyder, *Myths of Empire*, pp. 43–49.

19. Ibid., chap. 7.

20. For a good overview, see Alexei Arbatov, "Russia's Foreign Policy Alternatives," *International Security* 18 (Fall 1993): 5–43.

21. Stephen Van Evera, "Primed for Peace: Europe After the Cold War," in *The Cold War and After,* 2d ed., ed. Sean Lynn-Jones (Princeton: Princeton University Press, 1993) (first published in *International Security* 15 (Winter 1990/91): 7–58), at p. 213.

22. Benjamin Page and Robert Shapiro, *The Rational Public* (Chicago: University of Chicago Press, 1991); Miroslav Nincic, "The United States, the Soviet Union, and the Politics of Opposites," *World Politics* 40 (July 1988): 452–475.

23. Russell, *Grasping*, pp. 30–38; Doyle, "Liberalism."

24. Anne-Marie Slaughter Burley, "Law Among Liberal States: The Act of State Doctrine," *Columbia Law Review* 92 (1992): 1907–1996.

25. Doyle, "Liberalism," pp. 1156–1157, 1162–1163.

26. Russell, *Grasping,* 86–93; William J. Dixon, "Democracy and the Peaceful Settlement of International Conflict," *American Political Science Review* 88 (March 1994): 14–32.

27. Gabriel Almond and Sidney Verba, *The Civic Culture* (Princeton: Princeton University Press, 1963).

28. Kagan, *Outbreak,* 83.

29. This would be a form of what Stephen David calls omnibalancing. See David, "Explaining Third World Alignment," *World Politics* 43 (January 1991): 233–256.

30. Huntington, *Political Order.*

31. Jack Snyder, "Nationalism and the Crisis of the Post-Soviet State," *Survival* 35 (Spring 1993): 5–26.

32. John Matthews, Ph.D. diss. in progress, Department of Political Science, Columbia University, 1994.

33. Liah Greenfeld, *Nationalism: Five Roads to Modernity* (Cambridge: Harvard University Press, 1992), chaps. 1, 2.

34. Alexander Gerschenkron, *Economic Backwardness in Historical Perspective* (Cambridge: Belknap, 1962), p. 25; idem, *Bread and Democracy in Germany* (Ithaca: Cornell University Press, 1989; orig. ed. 1943).

35. Charles Tilly, *Coercion, Capital, and European States* (Cambridge: Blackwell, 1990), chap. 4.

36. Elizabeth Fuller, "Azerbaijan's June Revolution," *RFE/RL Research Report* 2 (13 August 1993): 24–29.

37. Barry Posen, "Nationalism, the Mass Army, and Military Power," *International Security* 47 (Fall 1993): 80–125; Eugen Weber, *Peasants into Frenchmen* (Stanford: Stanford University Press, 1976).

38. Arno Mayer, *The Persistence of the Old Regime* (New York: Pantheon, 1981); on Milosevic, see V. P. Gagnon, Jr., "Ethnic Nationalism and International Conflict: The Case of Serbia," *International Security* 19 (Winter 1994/95): 130–166.

39. Hans-Ulrich Wehler, *The German Empire* (Leamington Spa: Berg, 1985); Geoff Eley, *Reshaping the German Right* (New Haven: Yale University Press, 1980).

40. Barrington Moore, Jr., *Social Origins of Dictatorship and Democracy* (Boston: Beacon, 1966).

41. Van Evera, "Primed for Peace," pp. 214–215.

42. Ernest Gellner, *Nations and Nationalism* (Ithaca: Cornell University Press, 1983).

43. Michael Mann, "The Emergence of Modern European Nationalism," in *Transition to Modernity,* ed. John A. Hall and Ian Jarvie (Cambridge: Cambridge University Press, 1992), pp. 137–166.

44. Karl Polanyi, *The Great Transformation* (Boston: Beacon, 1957; orig. ed. 1944), esp. chap. 19.

45. Huntington, *Political Order,* 198.

46. Edward Mansfield and Jack Snyder, "Democratization and War," *Foreign Affairs* 74 (May-June 1995): 79–97; and idem, "Democratization and the Danger of War," *International Security* 20, no. 1 (Summer 1995), pp. 5–38. For additional literature, see Russett, *Grasping,* esp. pp. 16–20; also Zeev Maoz, "Joining the Club of Nations: Political Development and International Conflict, 1816–1976," *International Studies Quarterly* 33 (1989): 199–231.

47. Snyder, *Myths of Empire,* chap. 5.

48. Ibid., chap. 3.

49. Ibid., chap. 4; Louise Young, "Mobilizing for Empire: Japan and Manchukuo, 1931–1945" (Ph.D. diss., Columbia University, 1992).

50. On the radicalization over time of Japan's strategic culture during this period, see Charles Kupchan, *The Vulnerability of Empire* (Ithaca: Cornell University Press, 1994).

51. T.C.W. Blanning, *The Origins of the French Revolutionary Wars* (London: Longman, 1986), chap. 3.

52. Lynn Case, *French Opinion on War and Diplomacy During the Second Empire* (Philadelphia: University of Pennsylvania Press, 1954).

53. Stephen Walt, "Revolution and War," *World Politics* 44 (April 1992): 321–368.

54. On Armenia, see Commission on Security and Cooperation in Europe, *Human Rights,* pp. 98–108; Nora Dudwick, "Armenia: The Nation Awakens," in *Nations and Politics in the Soviet Union,* ed. Ian Bremmer and Ray Taras (Cambridge: Cambridge University Press, 1993), pp. 261–287. On Azerbaijan, see Fuller, "Azerbaijan's June Revolution."

55. Andrei Kozyrev, *New Times,* no. 4 (1994).

56. V. P. Gagnon, "Serbia's Road to War," *Journal of Democracy* 5 (April 1994): 117–131; Branka Magas, *The Destruction of Yugoslavia: Tracking the Break-Up, 1980–1992* (London: Verso, 1993), pp. 194–198 and passim.

57. William Zimmerman, "Markets, Democracy and Russian Foreign Policy," *Post-Soviet Affairs* 10 (April-June 1994): 103–126, at p. 115.

58. Suzanne Crow, "Why Has Russian Foreign Policy Changed?" *RFE/RL Research Report* 3 (6 May 1994): 1–6, at pp. 3–4.

59. On the nationalist foreign policy consensus among the Russian elites, see Suzanne Crow, "Russia Asserts Its Strategic Agenda," *RFE/RL Research Report* 2 (17 December 1993): 1–8. Crow argues that "it is the ideas of the elite that are driving the country's foreign policy today, not a 'spontaneous explosion of civil feelings' of patriotism." See Crow, "Why Has Russian Foreign Policy Changed?" p. 4.

60. Fuller, "Azerbaijan's June Revolution."

61. For discussions of how to exert such influence, see Ted Hopf, "Managing Soviet Disintegration: A Demand for Behavioral Regimes," *International Security* 17 (Summer 1992): 44–75; Stephen Van Evera, "Managing the Eastern Crisis," *Security Studies* 1 (Spring 1992): 361–382.

CHAPTER 3

Russian Nationalism and the National Interest in Russian Foreign Policy

Astrid S. Tuminez

Promising a new era of nearly unbridled Russian imperial expansionism, Vladimir Zhirinovsky and his Liberal Democratic Party captured approximately one-quarter of party votes to the Russian Duma, or lower legislative chamber, in the December 1993 elections. This victory heralded a new and triumphant phase in the rise of nationalism as a driving force in post-Soviet Russian politics. It also lent credence to what observers had earlier underlined as a looming danger in Russia: the rise of malevolent nationalist ideology and the attendant renewal of authoritarianism at home and aggression abroad.[1]

Zhirinovsky's victory and the ensuing attempt of Russian politicians of all colors to grab the nationalist/patriotic mantle raise several questions: What exactly is the content of Russian nationalism, and is such nationalism universally malevolent? Who are the key proponents of nationalist ideology, and what are their goals? Under what conditions is Russian nationalism likely to be empowered and, therefore, have an impact on the definition of Russia's national interest and, implicitly, on Russian foreign policy?

Many scholars who write on Russian nationalism, both before and after Zhirinovsky's debut on Russia's political stage, argue that nationalism is intrinsically dangerous. It embodies exclusivist and chauvinist ideas and, therefore, promotes a discriminatory and aggressive definition of the state's national interest.[2] However, although nationalism may often be negative, it need not be exclusively harmful. In fact, nationalism can aid consolidation of reform, economic development, and the pursuit of collective welfare. As one author argues, nationalism is "an inevitable concomitant of social life and of many generous human impulses."[3] In this chapter, I highlight the variable quality of Russian nationalism: It varies in content, degree of empowerment, and impact on the national interest in Russian foreign policy. I describe below four strands of Russian nationalism that range from the most benign to the most malevolent. These are liberal nativism, Westernizing democracy, statist nationalism, and national patriotism.

41

Statist nationalism, with overlapping strands of national patriotism, is currently dominant in post-Soviet Russia. It has malevolent implications, but it is not the most chauvinistic or aggressive version of Russian nationalism. Its effects on policy are unclear and will depend largely on whether elite proponents emphasize the more extreme aspects of their ideology. Further, it remains to be seen if the public will identify with statist nationalism in a sustained fashion. I examine three sets of variables to explain the empowerment of statist nationalism from the late 1980s to 1994: (1) elite political and material interests, which are served well by the purveyance of statist nationalism; (2) permissive elements in the domestic environment; and (3) threats in the international system and the weakness of international norms and structures to help Russia resolve these threats.

The rest of this chapter is divided into two sections: The first part defines key concepts and outlines a framework of inquiry for studying nationalism, its empowerment, and impact; it explains in detail the variables I mention in the preceding paragraph. The second part applies the framework of the first part to analyze post-Soviet Russian nationalism. I end with some tentative conclusions on the impact of nationalist ideas on Russia's national interest.

Defining the Framework of Inquiry

Nationalism and Nations

Nationalism is a concept that scholars have yet to define consensually.[4] I define nationalism as an elite-generated political ideology that includes (1) criteria for membership in the nation; (2) a definition of self-image and other-image; and (3) a statement of the national mission. I focus on nationalism as a *political ideology* because I am interested primarily in its use as a political instrument. Nationalist ideology is most relevant in the realm of social action when its proponents are mobilized and use nationalism to gain, increase, and/or exercise state power. Nationalism and the state are inextricably linked because nationalists either seek their own state or strive to make their state conform to the substantive content of their ideology.[5]

Nationalism is malleable and changes over time and under different circumstances; however, it always highlights the nation as the locus of individual and collective loyalty. I define the nation as a community of people who share a high culture—that is, a system of ideas, signs, and associations and ways of behaving and communicating—and who share common perceptions of duties and benefits within their community.[6]

The Content of Nationalism

Nationalism, as a political ideology, varies on a spectrum that is benign on one end and malevolent on the other. I describe below some criteria for determining the character of nationalist ideas.

Membership in the Nation.   Nationalism is likely to have malevolent implications if ethnic, rather than civic, criteria determine membership in the nation. Ethnic nationalism depends on a common language, culture, or ancestry and includes pan-ideologies such as pan-Slavism. Civic nationalism, in contrast, includes in its membership all citizens within a designated territory, regardless of cultural or linguistic background.[7] Ethnic nationalism can push states toward the goal of unification—that is, an ethnic group scattered territorially will seek to rescue the irredenta or unify all its members in one national state.[8] Ethnic nationalism also implies the threat of disenfranchisement, persecution, or forced assimilation of minorities or outsider groups who reside within the state.

National Self-Image and Other-Image.   The greater the degree of chauvinism in a nation's self-image, the more dangerous nationalism is likely to be. The self-image can be proud, yet relatively honest and self-critical, or chauvinistic and exaggerated in its sense of uniqueness. Chauvinism thrives on mythmaking that glorifies the nation while denigrating other groups. Such mythmaking has dangerous implications, particularly if internalized by elites and their mass constituencies.

Chauvinistic myths and attitudes can create distorted perceptions of the historical balance of rights and wrongs between groups and can lead to an exaggeration of the malevolence of others along with a minimization of one's wrongdoings. Such perceptions can encourage aggression against nonmembers of the nation who are perceived as dangerous enemies of the past and present. Chauvinism can also lead to a repetition of past aggression that has not been recognized as a wrongdoing. Finally, it can justify malicious behavior against outsiders on the grounds that the national group is "unique" or "special" and possesses greater rights and privileges than others.

Another important component of the national self-image is its view of war and the military. The more exaggerated the military component of the self-image is, the more likely that nationalism will be of a malevolent nature. Who are the military heroes and how prominent are they in the national culture? Do people believe that the nation's greatness lies chiefly in its military strength and prowess? Is there a belief that war and conquest strengthen the national character, and is there a vigilant effort to inculcate military values in members of the nation?

National Purpose.   Nationalism is dangerous if the national mission is defined primarily in hegemonic and messianic terms. The national mission can be benign: It can be defensive toward outsiders and focused on improving collective welfare, maintaining the territorial status quo, and strengthening internal cohesion and unity. Or it can be hegemonic, imperialistic, and messianic, leading the nation to pursue expansive and aggressive policies. Objective realities including the existence of disputed territories and the dispersal of ethnic groups can mitigate or aggravate any messianic or imperialistic tendencies.

Nationalism and the National Interest in Foreign Policy

I use the term "national interest" to refer to a set of primary goals that a state determines as central to its well-being and long-term survival. Several factors contribute to the definition of the national interest, including geography, natural resources, character of the ruling elite, and ideology; this chapter focuses on ideology as a determinant of the national interest. The ideology of nationalism can fulfill various functions related to foreign policy making. Maximally, it can provide a rigid prescription of what the national interest ought to be. In the former Yugoslavia, for example, Serbian nationalism has defined assistance to the Serb irredenta in Bosnia-Herzegovina as a nonnegotiable priority of Serbian foreign policy. Another function of nationalism is to provide the conceptual lens through which policymakers view the world and weigh options; this need not lead to rigidity, but certainly to a demarcation of the limits of acceptable and viable goals that leaders can articulate and pursue.[9] In fact, in almost all cases, nationalism tends to narrow the range of definition of the national interest because its proponents can label unpatriotic or traitorous those who stray from the nationalist fold. Finally, nationalism can legitimize a regime in power and justify aggressive goals that such a regime might pursue in the name of the nation.[10]

Hypotheses on the Empowerment of Nationalism

Nationalism can have an impact on the national interest when it is empowered. Empowerment comes when nationalist ideas are propagated in legitimate and effective fora; when they are attached to powerful symbols; and when key institutions such as the military, foreign ministry, executive and legislative organs, mass media, and others rally support for these ideas. Ultimately, empowerment means that channels are opened for nationalist ideas to influence state priorities and actions.

The empowerment of nationalism requires, at the outset, the existence of adequately motivated *agents* to purvey the ideology. In addition, the appropriate *environmental context* for success is necessary. I propose below three sets of factors—all of which are related to agents of nationalism and the environment in which they operate—to explain the empowerment of nationalist ideology: (1) the nature and extent of elite interests; (2) the domestic political context; and (3) the international system. The hypotheses I articulate apply to the empowerment of both benign and malevolent nationalism, but with greater emphasis on the latter. Further, these hypotheses are only plausible and not necessarily proven; their application to the post-Soviet case is only one attempt to test their explanatory power.

Agents: The Nature and Extent of Elite Interests

The larger the gains that elites can make from nationalistic propaganda, the more likely they are to focus their energies and organizational skills on such an undertaking. And even though nationalist ideas may have dangerous or malevolent implications, these may be of little or no concern to self-interested elites.[11] Two types of elite interests are notable: (1) tangible political and economic gains and (2) more abstract interests such as legitimacy, psychological satisfaction, and prestige. When elites face serious crises of legitimacy—for example, after a humiliating military or diplomatic defeat or during severe economic crisis—they may use malevolent nationalism to regain public trust and consolidate domestic support.

Certain elite institutions also benefit from malevolent nationalist ideas and thus have strong incentives to propagate them. One is the military, whose mission of war preparation and war fighting is served well by chauvinistic and hegemonic nationalism. Military elites may propagate these ideas to cultivate public support and loyalty and facilitate the state's extraction of resources for military needs.[12]

The Environment: The Domestic Political Context

The Existence and Competence of Independent Evaluative Units.   Evaluative units refer to individuals, groups, and institutions that assess the validity of nationalist ideas and debate their implications.[13] These include scholars, universities, civilian associations, and a free press. Evaluative units function best when society observes the norm of free speech; when thinkers and opinion makers are committed to a norm of combating myths and ideas that encourage chauvinism, aggression, or imperialism; and when consumers of information are relatively sophisticated.[14] When evaluative units are few and/or incompetent, nationalist elites can propagandize malevolent ideas with relative ease.

State Policy Vis-à-Vis Nationalists.   The empowerment of any kind of nationalism depends to a large extent on the state's policy vis-à-vis nationalist ideas and their proponents. The state can pursue opposition, tolerance, or collusion, thereby granting nationalists varying levels of access to state power and resources. Serious and competent state opposition is likely to obstruct the rise of nationalist ideology or cause its ultimate demise, depending on what instruments the state applies. The state generally has a preponderance of resources compared to other sectors of society and can operate with a comparative advantage against nationalist proponents. Resources are not enough, however. Competent and reliable state structures and policies are also critical. If state institutions are weak and leaders blunder seriously, they may well add to the legitimacy of nationalists, including those who propagate extremist ideas.

Tolerance by the state can help nationalists gain moderate or great success, even to the point of assuming state power. Finally, collusion almost always guarantees that nationalism will be empowered in the variant that state leaders prefer, however benign or malevolent. Exceptions may occur in cases where state power is weak or divided or if the state regime is overthrown by opposing forces.

The Degree of Delegitimation of Ideas and Institutions.   The more severe the delegitimation of ideas and institutions and the more a society feels insecure as a result, the easier it is for malevolent nationalism to spread and gain adherents. Delegitimation entails the breakdown of society's basic organizing principles—

for example, monarchy, parliamentarism, socialism, or capitalism—and its key institutions. Nationalism is an ideology of cohesion and legitimacy, and elites can easily use it to bolster their position and, specifically, to blame outsiders for the ills of the nation.[15] In the nineteenth and early twentieth centuries nationalism proved an effective ideology for promoting or restoring cohesion, order, and legitimacy to the state and became the ideology of choice for many elites seeking legitimacy and power in transitional contexts. Finally, when popular participation or mass politics accompanies delegitimation, nationalist elites may try to outdo each other's rhetoric as they vie for public support.[16] This helps explain why extreme variants of nationalism may co-opt more moderate ones.

The Environment: The International System

If nationalists can effectively portray, first, that threats in the international system are high and, second, that the state can competently repulse these dangers only by adopting aggressive nationalism, then such nationalism will likely be empowered. External threats can be military or economic, and geography, demography, history, and relative economic and military power all play a role in the state's calculation of such threats. Although nationalists can certainly conjure outside perils to benefit their ideology, objective factors can increase or decrease the credibility of their propaganda. However, the international system can hinder malevolent nationalism if it offers resources other than self-help to allow a state to defend against security threats.[17] If interdependence, international norms, and cooperative regional or international action are preferable to self-help, extreme nationalism and its proponents are less likely to predominate.

Finally, the greater material, financial, and political support the international system proffers to proponents of malevolent nationalism, the more likely its ideas will be empowered.[18] The availability of such support can legitimize nationalism at home and abroad and help its proponents purvey their ideas and pursue relevant political and/or military action. Conversely, if the international community withholds support and/or threatens sanctions against proponents of malignant nationalism, it will be more difficult, though not impossible, for such an ideology to become dominant.

The Reemergence of Russian Nationalism Under Gorbachev

Russian nationalism traversed a rough and uneven path in the first six decades of Communist rule, from Lenin to Brezhnev.[19] It reached its apex under Stalin and never quite enjoyed again the same status despite alleged support in high places in the late 1960s and early 1970s. Gorbachev's policies of glasnost and perestroika, begun in the mid-1980s, created a new window for Russian nationalists to propagate their ideas and participate in the country's political life. Some of the most active nationalists in the first years of glasnost were those concerned about

Russia's historical and cultural monuments, the environment (e.g., the fate of Russia's northern rivers), social problems (e.g., alcoholism and high mortality rates), and the truth about the Stalinist past. On the negative side, nationalists united by their antisemitic convictions also mobilized and coalesced in Pamyat', an organization that attracted a lot of Western attention.

Four developments stand out in the Gorbachev period. First, glasnost stimulated a revival of nationalist ideas, past and present. Previously unavailable works of nineteenth-century conservative nationalist thinkers and historians were widely read.[20] Russian intellectuals and publicists also wrote a barrage of nationalist articles in both the popular media and Russian scholarly journals. The revival of nationalism certainly was not tantamount to a consolidation of nationalist ideas or their proponents. Ideological differences among nationalists persisted, but they were able to insert some of their ideas into prominent policy debates in Moscow.

Second, concessions by the state under Gorbachev legitimized Russian nationalist demands and aspirations. For example, contravening previous Communist policy, Gorbachev allowed thousands of Orthodox churches to reopen and granted demands for Russia to have its own republican institutions within the Soviet Union. This policy reflected a pattern of state accommodation of, and indecision toward, centrifugal nationalism and revived national identity in Russia and other Soviet republics.

A third development was the creation of political institutions and processes that were open to full participation by nationalists. The Soviet elections of 1989, Russian Supreme Soviet elections in 1990, and Russian presidential elections in 1991 were particularly important. Although most members of the national-patriotic bloc lost in these elections, they nonetheless gained political experience and public exposure necessary for future political battles. Those few nationalists who did win seats in the Soviet and Russian parliaments joined forces with Communists to form an active and outspoken opposition to the democratic camp.

Finally, groups that one might characterize as conservative, authoritarian, chauvinist, and imperialist to one extent or another hijacked nationalist themes. These groups actively promoted ideas and slogans on a strong, hegemonic Russian state, on discipline and order, and on defense of Russia's national interests. They identified themselves as true defenders of Russia, in contrast to "democrats" who had surrendered Russia's interests to the West; emphasized deceptive "all-human values" over Russian uniqueness; and created chaos in Russia's social and economic life. Russian liberals in the USSR Supreme Soviet attempted in early 1990 to discredit the authority of nationalists to speak "in the name of the Russian people and Russia," but this effort soon fizzled. In fact, the disintegration of the Soviet Union in December 1991 seemed only to prove what nationalists had warned all along about the destructive impact of the liberal-democratic program for Russia.

After the Soviet Union: Russian Nationalism

The propagation of Russian nationalism has intensified since the Soviet Union's collapse. Discussions in the media and academic journals, as well as demonstrations on Moscow's streets, reveal a serious preoccupation with what Russia is, what its relations are with new neighbors, and what role the country should play in a postimperial context. Below, I describe my typology of current Russian nationalist ideas, which strives to capture the benign or malevolent elements of nationalist tenets on membership in the nation, self- and other-image, and the national mission. This categorization does not correspond with strictly delineated ideological lines separating one group of nationalists from others. Indeed, nationalists often have overlapping ideas, and those with seemingly contradictory convictions have been known to join in political coalitions. Further, given Russia's politically fluid context, nationalists tend to make tactical changes in their rhetoric as required by political exigencies. This categorization, however, does reflect the "menu" of nationalist ideas in Russia today.

The Content of Nationalism

Liberal Nativism.   The most prominent representatives of this strand are the historian and humanist Dmitrii Likhachev and the writer Aleksandr Solzhenitsyn. Nativists[21] generally define the nation as an ethnic entity encompassing Great Russians, Little Russians (Ukrainians), and White Russians (Belorussians). However, they do not believe in the nation's unification by violent means; hence, they are willing to limit Russia to the current boundaries of the Russian Federation.[22]

Nativism promotes a Russian self-image rooted in the morality and Christianity of the Orthodox faith. Its proponents reject Marxism-Leninism as an alien ideology imposed on Russia and condemn Soviet tyranny as a product of that ideology rather than an expression of the "Russian character." They see a return to native peasant values and Russian Orthodoxy as the key to Russian renewal. Some nativists promote monarchy as the system of government best suited for Russia, but this idea is considerably weak. Others emphasize Russia's democratic roots and see democracy as a viable option for the nation. At the same time, people like Solzhenitsyn emphasize that democracy has its weaknesses and pitfalls, which Russia must avoid.

The self-image of nativists is generally inclusive of other peoples and cultures. Likhachev and Solzhenitsyn, for example, advocate the flourishing of languages and cultures of all national groups in the Russian Federation. This inclusiveness, however, precludes wholesale acceptance or imitation of Western ideas and styles. Nativists often juxtapose Russia with the West and claim that the former is potentially superior to the latter. Although the West is doing better than Russia by some indicators, Russia will eventually flourish and surpass the latter in terms of moral and spiritual development.[23]

Russia's mission is primarily defensive and inward-looking: to restore and defend the physical and spiritual well-being of the land and people. This means, inter alia, arresting the degradation of the environment, improving the state of Russian demography, giving land to the peasants, reeducating the youth in moral and spiritual values, stemming the tide of crime in Russia, preserving Russia's cultural and historical legacies, rebuilding a strong state (without imperial coercion), protecting the human rights of Russians in the former Soviet Union, and fending off Western economic, political, or cultural exploitation.[24] Nativists see the revival of Russian national consciousness as a healthy phenomenon and a prerequisite to Russia's fulfillment of its mission.

Westernizing Democracy.   Boris Yeltsin, Andrei Kozyrev, and Yegor Gaidar probably represent best the "Westernizing democrats." They define the nation primarily in civic terms—that is, Russia includes all citizens within Russia's territorial boundaries (hence Yeltsin's frequent use of the multiethnic *rossiian* as opposed to the ethnic term, *russkii*). At the same time, the civic definition of the nation does not preclude recognition of ethnic Russians and Russian speakers outside Russia. Russians abroad are also rightful affiliates of the nation, and the nation must look out for their interests. This should be done largely through negotiations and the use of international legal norms and institutions.[25] However, leaders should not preclude forceful intervention in extreme cases where Russians abroad may be killed for advocating union with Russia.[26]

Like their nativist counterparts, Westernizing democrats reject Marxism-Leninism and the Soviet system, which they identify as the cause of many of Russia's problems. Their self-image of Russia is that of a great power whose immense potential can be realized through democracy, market reform, and integration and participation in the international community. They reject categorical assertions of Russian uniqueness and veer away from blatant claims to restore the Russian or Soviet empire. Westernizing democrats see Russia as the rightful leader in the former Soviet Union (FSU) region and would prefer close integration among FSU states and perhaps reunification of the Slavic states of Russia, Ukraine, and Belarus.[27] As for the West, they see it as a model and partner but as one whose national interests may not always coincide with Russia's.[28]

The national mission from the viewpoint of Westernizing democrats includes preserving the Russian Federation's territorial integrity, protecting Russian citizens within and outside Russia, modernizing the economy, achieving a special role as peacekeeper in the former Soviet Union, and attaining full partnership with the international community.[29]

Statist Nationalism.   Statist nationalism defines as members of the Russian nation both ethnic Russians and Russian speakers; territorially, proponents argue that Russia is not only the Russian Federation but also the "historical" borders of the old empire. Some of the early articulators of statist nationalism include former Russian vice-president Aleksandr Rutskoi;[30] Yeltsin adviser Sergei Stankevich; Minister of Defense Pavel Grachev; former chair of the Supreme Soviet Committee on International Affairs Evgenii Ambartsumov; chair of the Democratic Party of Russia Nikolai Travkin; and Vladimir Lukin, former ambassador to the United States.[31]

Centrist statists portray a Russian self-image infused with great-power history and ideas. They see Russia as a temporarily demoralized entity that will inevitably regain its natural position as a world power. They reject communism but deplore the disintegration of the former Soviet Union. In fact, many statists left the Democratic Russia movement (an alliance whose early format included nativists and Westernizing democrats) because they disagreed with the movement's support for Soviet disintegration. They argue that a Russian great-power renaissance cannot happen within the chaotic context of democratization; thus, they favor authoritarian rule, albeit temporary, for Russia.[32]

Eurasianism figures prominently in the self- and other-image of statist nationalists. They claim that Russia is a unique entity positioned between East and West and is a "nation of nations" that can potentially gather again its former units in a closely integrated structure.[33] Statists see their nation as a rightful hegemon among its neighbors. They argue that Russia should be the guarantor of political and military stability in the former Soviet Union, including the Baltics, and that it should continue to have a military presence in the newly independent states. Unless Russia takes charge, the North Atlantic Treaty Organization (NATO) or other international bodies like the Organization on Security and Cooperation in Europe (OSCE) will likely interfere in the region and in Russia's internal affairs.[34] Statists admit limited partnership with the West but emphasize that Russia must go its own way in spheres where it has unique, historical interests.[35] In other cases, they label the West a great enemy of Russia.[36]

Russia's mission, according to statists, includes defending Russians and Russian speakers in the FSU (using both legal norms and force, when necessary); maintaining territorial integrity while seeking a larger, leading role in the FSU; restoring the borders of the former Soviet Union via referendum or other expressions of the people's will; creating a new, unifying idea that would consolidate support for the state and revive discipline, authority, and order in the economy, the army, and society in general; and discarding the Yeltsin/Kozyrev Western-oriented foreign policy in favor of one that distinctly defends Russian national interests.[37]

National Patriotism. National patriotism is the ideology of the Red-Brown[38] coalition, which includes some of Russia's most vocal and notorious nationalists. Key representatives of this group are Aleksandr Prokhanov, editor of the newspaper *Den'*; Dmitrii Vasiliev, head of Pamyat' National Patriotic Front; General Aleksandr Sterligov, former KGB official and now leader of the Russian National Assembly; Gennadii Zyuganov, chair of the Russian Communist Party; Viktor Anpilov, leader of the Russian Communist Workers Party; and the fascists Aleksandr Barkashov and Vladimir Zhirinovsky. National patriots define the nation primarily in ethnic terms, though some will not openly admit this.[39] They also insist that Russia is the territorial equivalent of the former Soviet Union, and some claim that only one ethnic group should lead the country—Russians. They support the use of force to restore the former Russian/Soviet empire and to defend the interests of ethnic Russians outside the Russian Federation.[40]

Some national patriots reject Marxism-Leninism and the Soviet legacy, whereas others adopt the "single stream" view of history—that is, the Soviet Union was legitimate because it was a continuation of the great Russian state.[41] Despite these differences, national patriots unite in their self-image of Russia as a great, imperial power. Many of the ideas that infuse the self-image of national patriots come from Eurasianism, which characterizes Russia as a unique, organic, and self-sufficient geographic and cultural entity; its imperial borders are "natural."[42] National patriots believe that Russia flourishes when the state is strong, centralized, and authoritarian and that Russians must accord the highest priority to state requirements. Thus, they largely reject the democratic model for their state.[43] They consider a strong military the key to Russian greatness in the past and future. The armed forces are the "savior of the Fatherland" in its critical moments, and, as Aleksandr Prokhanov declares, the Soviet army "connected the past and the present, the old and the young, and guaranteed [Russia's] stability and sovereignty."[44]

National patriots emphasize that Russia is a victim of the Soviet system, which allowed other republics to prosper at Russia's expense. They blame a "Zionist conspiracy" or "Jews hiding behind Russian surnames" for the destruction of the Russian state and the environment.[45] They see the West as a threat to Russian culture and statehood, an exploiter of Russia's natural resources, and a spiritually hollow and inegalitarian society. In some instances, they depict the West as a country of "civilized barbarism" and the relentless antagonist of a blameless Russia.[46]

Finally, national patriots argue that the national mission is to restore the previous empire under strong Russian leadership; protect Russian citizens abroad; overthrow the Yeltsin Western-oriented government; block arms control agreements; restore military power and prestige; correct negative social trends in the family and society; and establish law and order. Occasionally, Russia's mission has a Stalinist and fascist flavor. For example, Mikhail Antonov, leader of the Union for the Spiritual Revival of the Fatherland, has called for a full-fledged attack on the "rootless and cosmopolitan" intelligentsia (i.e., Jews). Others have called for purging cities like St. Petersburg of all non-Russians or dismissing leaders who are not Russian by nationality.[47]

The Empowerment of Nationalism

An examination of the Russian debate from 1989 to 1994 over national identity and Russia's national interest reveals that elements of two strands of nationalism, statism and national patriotism, have come to the fore in Russian political discourse. Because the most extreme elements of national patriotism—for example, noxious antisemitism and fascism—remain on the periphery of Russian discourse, I will label this dominant nationalist ideology simply *statist nationalism.* Besides rhetorical evidence on the empowerment of statist nationalism, mass action such as demonstrations and support for nationalist media also indicate the salience of these ideas. Further evidence of empowerment is that some state leaders and institutions have begun to adopt statist nationalist rhetoric.[48] Proponents of these ideas (statists and moderate national patriots) have been able to propagate their ideology in legitimate and effective fora; attach them to powerful symbols; and obtain support from state actors and institutions. As a result, their ideas have had a palpable impact on the definition of Russia's national interest.

From 1989 to 1994, patriots and statists have been able to increase the fora for propagating their ideas and have moved their agenda from the periphery of former Soviet politics to the mainstream of public debate. They have preached openly their ideas in print, TV, and other media and in institutions like the former Supreme Soviet and the current Duma. Indeed, proponents of statist nationalism have effectively consolidated the legitimacy of their ideas as an alternative to the Yeltsin/Kozyrev Westernizing democratic line that was dominant soon after the Soviet Union's disintegration. The increasing number of people that patriots and statists have been able to mobilize for street demonstrations also bolster the legitimacy of their ideas. Such demonstrations drew no more than a few hundred people in 1991, but in 1992–1993, tens of thousands of people participated in them.

Besides propagating their ideas in diverse and effective fora, statists and their co-thinkers among the national patriots have also linked their ideas to powerful symbols. Symbols legitimize ideas and intensify their mobilizational effect. In Russia, such symbols as motherland (*rodina*), the Great Fatherland War (*velikaia otechestvennaia voina*), Russians abroad, Eurasia, and "great power/state" (*velikaia derzhava*) have been largely appropriated by statists and patriots.[49] These symbols are rooted in Russian history and resonate tremendously among a populace demoralized by loss of empire, loss of international prestige, and economic hardship. Other potentially powerful symbols are the monarchy and the church. Nativists use these symbols, but their mobilizational power is weak in a society modernized and secularized by seventy years of Soviet rule.[50]

Finally, state actors and institutions, including leaders of the former Supreme Soviet and the new Duma, the military, and the defense industry, have increasingly shown support for statist nationalism. In contrast, nativists have been largely unable to garner such support and seem to have the weakest institutional base of all the nationalists. Many Westernizing democrats have been (and are) officially in power and have used their institutional base to promote their ideas. This was true especially of the Foreign Ministry and the executive branch during 1991–1992. Official and institutional support for Westernizing democracy, however, has been diluted, and Kozyrev and Yeltsin and the institutions they represent have increasingly adopted positions closer to statist nationalism on such issues as Russians abroad, Russia's great-power status, and Russia's territorial claims on its neighbors. Many initially nativist and Westernizing democratic nationalists have also drifted increasingly toward statist ideas.[51]

What explains the empowerment of statist nationalism? I explore below the salience of material, political, and other interests that drive the elite proponents of this ideology. I then explain permissive factors in the domestic and international environments that have facilitated these elites' propagation of statist nationalism.

Elite Interests. For a particular strand of nationalism to become dominant, its adherents must propagate it through sustained effort. Such effort, in turn, depends on strong economic, political, or other inducements. One clear interest driving elite proponents of statist nationalism in Russia is political power through the state. State power is attractive because the state, despite initial market reform, continues to control a large amount of resources for physical comfort, security, and status. Under the Soviet regime, Communist elites enjoyed many perquisites of power. However, these privileges ended with the demise of the Soviet Union. Former Communist elites want to regain their privileges, and one potentially effective way to do so is to harness nationalism as a platform from which to catapult themselves back to power. This explains why former Communists and others who have fallen out of the official sphere of power are some of the most active proponents of statist nationalism. Others who already occupy official positions purvey statist nationalism to legitimate themselves and their claims to various prerogatives. This is true of the democratic reformers who have been on the defensive since the December 1993 electoral victory of Communists and nationalists. This is also true of regional leaders who have tried to wrest control from the center over economic resources in the periphery.

Another group of leading statists comes from the military/security establishment or the military-industrial sector.[52] This group also represents a segment of society that enjoyed great privileges but who, all of a sudden, found themselves denied of former wealth, power, status, and respect. This includes Rutskoi; Sterligov, an ex-KGB officer; Stanislav Terekhov, from the Officers' Union; General Albert Makashov; and Minister of Defense Grachev. Officials like Grachev may not be seeking to regain lost personal privileges but rather are using nationalism to generate support for the demoralized Russian military and to justify Russian military presence and demands in the post-Soviet states. It is well known that the Russian military lost numerous assets due to the breakup of the Soviet Union and is suffering numerous other vicissitudes as well.[53]

Finally, statist nationalism serves the intangible psychological interests of the intelligentsia and other elites who are highly demoralized by Russia's loss of great-power status, the dark revelations about the Stalinist past, and the social and demographic problems plaguing the Russian nation. Indeed, the rise of Russian national consciousness in the late and post-Soviet period may be termed "sacrificial" rather than triumphalist; it is a nationalism born out of shame for the

Stalinist legacy, the nation's moral degradation, and the country's material poverty.[54] Under these circumstances, elites understandably want to reassert an ideology of national greatness, uniqueness, and power.

Domestic Politics. Gorbachev's policies of glasnost and democratization infused new life into society's near-moribund "evaluative units," including the media, academic journals, television, and civil organizations. The public responded enthusiastically to the first burst of uncensored information and pluralistic opinion. The array of nationalist ideas in Russia is impressive, but criticism of these ideas—particularly ahistorical, illogical, and extremist notions—has not been rigorous. Public fatigue, distrust, and cynicism have also grown: fatigue with glasnost and pluralism; distrust of official media attempts to combat extremist nationalism;[55] and cynicism regarding the ideas of Westernizing democrats, which many associate with the destruction of the state (i.e., the breakup of the Soviet Union) and economic hardship. The weakness and incompetence of evaluative units in Russia are unlikely to change soon. Such incompetence stems from years of ideologized social science, historiography, and journalism. Many observers, including scholars, swing to one extreme ideology or other and accept or reject ideas wholesale without a full examination of their accuracy and merit. Genuine dialogue is rare among proponents of different versions of Russian nationalism; these people "rarely interact, . . . resent each other . . . , and have no respect for each other."[56]

In post-Soviet Russia, state policy has included opposition, accommodation, and co-optation. In particular, the Yeltsin government has opposed the most extreme elements of national patriotism—as evidenced in the October 1993 crisis—but has increasingly embraced statist nationalism. The Yeltsin government accommodated statist nationalism, first, because the challenges of a fluid political system required tactical partnership with statist nationalists, as in Yeltsin's cooperation with Rutskoi in 1991–1992. Yeltsin chose Rutskoi, a military man with solid credentials, to bolster his candidacy in the 1991 presidential elections. Subsequently, Yeltsin found it difficult to get rid of an elected vice-president whose nationalism was not entirely consistent with the official line.

Second, the loosening of political controls and decentralization of power (e.g., among executive, legislative, and judicial institutions) induced the executive power to tolerate not only statist nationalism but even extreme national patriotism. For example, Yeltsin banned the National Salvation Front after its establishment in 1992, but the Constitutional Court canceled the ban. In another case, the Russian Press Ministry filed suits to close down the nationalist publications *Sovetskaia Rossiia* and *Den',* but the courts rejected these suits. Further, when the Ministry of Defense fired an officer for virulent nationalism, the courts ordered his reinstatement.[57] Other state institutions, like the former Supreme Soviet and Congress of People's Deputies, also provided a haven and pulpit for patriots and statists. Deputies such as Ambartsumov, Sergei Baburin, and Oleg Rumiantsev used the legislative forum often to disseminate statist ideas and influence foreign policy. Ex-parliament speaker Ruslan Khasbulatov, a late "convert" to nationalism, also supported patriots and statists in an attempt to gain allies against Yeltsin.[58]

Third and perhaps most important, the Yeltsin government has been besieged on many fronts and censured for its economic policies, deference to the West, and failure to protect Russians in the near abroad. Given its enormous challenges and the existence of a genuine social base in support of statism, it is no surprise that the government has moved from accommodation to adoption of statist nationalism.[59] This ideology promises order, discipline, the restoration of state power, and hegemony in the former Soviet sphere and is a satisfactory rhetorical riposte to Russia's ills. As such, it is attractive to public opinion and to official elites anxious to reinforce their political base.

Delegitimation has occurred in the ideological, political, economic, and social spheres. Ideologically, both Marxism-Leninism and democratic Westernism have been highly discredited. The former can be safely pronounced dead, and the latter is barely alive. Reformers and Westernizers in the late Soviet and early post-Soviet period created many myths that reality debunked: the desirability of democracy, the prosperity of a market economy, and the advent of a good life once Communist power was eliminated. Instead, most people saw the demise of Communist power result in severe poverty, crime, and ethnic and other conflicts. Westernizing democrats have destroyed the old order but appear incapable of replacing it with a better alternative.[60] Thus many elites, from ex-Communists to ex-democrats, have seized statist nationalism as a new ideology because it is untarnished relative to other ideologies.

In politics, intense disagreement and power rivalry among different actors have paralyzed new institutions and obstructed consensus and effective governance. The movement that catapulted Yeltsin to power, Democratic Russia, has splintered; Yeltsin's political compromise with the more centrist Civic Union has also dissipated; and Yeltsin's own team has divided into rival blocs in the wake of the October 1993 crisis.[61] It is clear as well that the so-called victory of the Yeltsin government against parliamentary and nationalist rivals in October 1993 created neither political stability nor efficiency. The scene of tanks shooting at the Russian White House, with the blessing of Western leaders, only reinforced the image in many minds of an incompetent, weak, and even illegitimate government guilty of shedding Russian blood and eliminating by force a body of elected representatives. In fact, some interpret the electoral victory of statists and national patriots in December 1993 as a popular backlash against the government's actions in the October crisis.[62]

The economic and social aspects of delegitimation are well known. Russian society has been stratified into small sectors of nouveaux riches (who are conspicuous consumers) and large masses who live on or below the poverty line. Official unemployment rose from 367,500 in October 1992 to 1 million in August

1993. This may not seem high for a country with 150 million people, but most unemployment in Russia is unregistered, so the figure may be actually in the tens of millions.[63] Moscow is also home to an estimated 2 million refugees, Russian and non-Russian, who have fled from other former Soviet republics because of discrimination, ethnic conflict, and economic travails. Further, the crime rate in Russia has nearly doubled from 1985 to 1992.[64] Public opinion surveys reflect frustration with these developments; dissatisfied citizens blame democrats and the ex-Soviet leadership over anyone else for current problems and declare that a more desirable government should provide security first over freedom.[65]

The International System. The international system at large has not been a significant source of material and other support for proponents of statist nationalism.[66] At the same time, actions of the international community, particularly Western democracies, may dampen any official tendencies toward extreme national patriotism in Russia. Officials like Yeltsin and Kozyrev may speak increasingly in statist terms, but they are unlikely to propagate fascist and other extreme nationalist ideas because it would rouse the opprobrium of their Western colleagues and audience.[67]

The international factor most relevant to the empowerment of statist nationalism is Russia's near abroad, or *blizhnee zarubezh'e,* which refers to new states of the former Soviet Union. Genuine threats have arisen in the near abroad that validate the arguments of statists and help them cultivate popular support. One is the status and treatment of Russians and Russian speakers outside Russia. Although it is true that statists and their co-thinkers in the national patriotic camp exaggerate the problems of Russian irredenta, there are also solid reasons why Russians abroad feel threatened and discriminated. As their conditions worsen, Russians abroad will likely flee in greater numbers to Russia and tax a system that already is unable to handle current refugee needs. Another problem is the outbreak of ethnic and other conflicts in the near abroad. Some of these conflicts have killed thousands, including an indeterminate number of Russians. The escalation of these conflicts and any possible use of chemical or nuclear weapons further heighten security threats to Russia.[68]

A third threat from the near abroad is the rise of new military, possibly nuclear, powers on Russia's borders. Relations with Ukraine, in particular, have been contentious, and disputes over ownership of the Black Sea Fleet and control of the Crimea are unlikely to be resolved soon. To date, the international community, particularly Western democracies, has not been a reliable partner for untangling any of the paramount issues on Russia's security agenda. United Nations (UN) and OSCE mediation in places like Nagorno-Karabakh, Moldova, and Abkhazia have been inadequate and ineffective. Further, some Western leaders' categorical opposition to Russian membership in NATO, along with acceptance of such membership for East European countries, creates the impression that the West wants to build a new anti-Russian bloc. This situation bolsters the validity of statist nationalism because it highlights threats to Russia and advocates a "can-do" attitude: Russia is a great state that can overcome its challenges through self-help and need not rely on an unpredictable, even inimical, West.

The Impact on the National Interest

What is the impact of Russian statist nationalism on the definition of Russia's national interest? A detailed process-tracing of changes in Russian foreign policy rhetoric or behavior is beyond the scope of this chapter; however, I want to show at least a correlation between statist nationalist ideas and major contours of Russian foreign policy. Russian statist nationalism has had an impact on the national interest in shifting the parameters of the state's foreign policy priorities. In a sense, the empowerment of statist nationalist ideas has changed what is "politically correct" in Russian foreign policy.

In Russia's first year as a post-Soviet state (1991–1992), Yeltsin and Kozyrev's foreign policy mainly followed the line that Gorbachev and Shevardnadze had started. They defined Russia's national interest in terms of increased partnership with Western developed countries; active participation in international organizations such as the United Nations and OSCE; and acute streamlining of formerly extensive Soviet ties with Third World countries. Although Kozyrev did pay lip service to the primacy of Russian relations with CIS states, it was obvious that foreign policy energies were spent at first mostly on Western countries and international institutions. In 1992–1993, statist and patriotic forces, many of whom also opposed Gorbachev's foreign policy, sustained an effort to discredit Yeltsin and Kozyrev's approach. A quick examination of three central national-interest issues illustrates how, since 1991, Russian foreign policy has evolved farther from the "Westernizing democratic" line and closer to statist nationalist preferences.

Territorial Boundaries and Irredenta.   Claims involving territorial borders and Russians abroad followed almost immediately the breakup of the Soviet Union. These issues inevitably rose to the top of national interest debates because territorial integrity and citizenship are two items that any new state must clarify and defend. In the former Soviet Union, many borders between republics were set arbitrarily by Stalin and had shifted many times in the course of Soviet history.[69] Moreover, the relatively free movement of peoples of various nationalities had created a multiethnic mosaic in the country. Russians, in particular, settled in many areas outside Russia, forming near-majorities in republics that were nominally non-Russian such as Kazakhstan and Latvia; in fact, Russians abroad are estimated at about 25 million people.

Several issues are paramount on Russian territory and irredenta. First is the issue of territories that used to belong to Russia or have large Russian populations, such as Crimea and Sevastopol in Ukraine and the Trans-Dniestr region in Moldova. The Russian population of Trans-Dniestr have been the most vigilant and violent in asserting their claim of independence from Moldova and in seeking association with Russia. A second key issue is the treatment of Russians abroad; problems range from citizenship rights for Russians in Estonia and Latvia to violence against Russian border guards in Tadzhikistan and elsewhere.[70]

Kozyrev and Yeltsin have traditionally taken a moderate stance on the issue of Russians abroad. Kozyrev has asserted that the best way to protect Russian irredenta is to foster friendly relations with its host states. He has also warned that extremist elements are exploiting the Russians abroad issue in order to implement strong-arm tactics against Russia's neighbors.[71] In contrast, statists and patriots have consistently supported more forceful means for protecting the "rights" of Russians in neighboring states. Newspapers such as *Den'* and TV programs such as Nevzorov's "600 Seconds" have sensationalized the plight of Russians, and leaders like Rutskoi, Grachev, Stankevich, and others have explicitly supported secessionism that will unite former parts of the empire with Russia.[72]

The impact of statist nationalism is twofold. First, official Russian rhetoric on territorial and irredenta problems has become more aggressive. Both Russia's foreign policy and military doctrine enshrine the protection of Russian minority rights. More recently, Kozyrev stated that it is Russia's national interest to take a "forceful role" in the conflict in Tadzhikistan.[73] The ex–Supreme Soviet also passed a resolution claiming that Sevastopol, home of the Black Sea Fleet in Ukraine, was and is part of Russian Federation territory.[74] A second, more important, impact deals with the Russian government's actions in conflicts in the near abroad. Russian officials, at most, may be giving orders to Russian military personnel abroad to engage in activities that heighten the risk of disintegration of new FSU states unless they return to Moscow's orbit. At the very least, Moscow is aware of these activities but is unwilling to do anything to stop renegade military personnel in the near abroad.[75]

The conflict in Trans-Dniestr in Moldova is an unequivocal example of Moscow's destabilizing activities in the near abroad. The Russian Fourteenth Army, under the leadership of Major-General Aleksandr Lebed, has used force on behalf of secessionist Russians in the Trans-Dniestr without explicit authorization by civilian authorities. Lebed often employs explosive and chauvinistic rhetoric yet has never been reprimanded or held otherwise responsible for his words or actions by Moscow.[76] Trans-Dniestr sets a precedent that diverges from moderate, legal-institutional options for the Russian irredenta problem; it may well be a harbinger for other Moscow-supported confrontational tactics on behalf of Russians abroad.

Russian Hegemony in the FSU.   Statist nationalism has influenced Russia's national interest in favor of a hegemonic role in the FSU region. As noted, statist nationalism emphasizes the "benevolence" of the Russian empire, Russia's "unique" role as a "bridge" among diverse nations, and Russia's greatness as an imperial state. It is an ideology incompatible with the reality of a much-shrunken Russian state. In contrast, other nationalist ideologies such as nativism underline the costs of empire and Russia's dire need to focus on its long-neglected material, moral, and social problems at home. The rhetoric and actions of Russian officials indicate that the former approach is prevailing over the latter.

Russian leaders have recently articulated priorities that favor Russian regional hegemony. Foreign policy statements focus less on integration with the developed West and the international community (though that option has not been abandoned) than on the formalization of Russia's leading or "special" role vis-à-vis its neighbors. In February and March 1993, Yeltsin and the Russian ambassador to the UN referred to Russia's "special responsibility" in the FSU and asked the UN to grant Russia special powers for peacekeeping in the region. A few months later, Yeltsin told a group of military officers that Russia must maintain and formalize its military presence in Moldova, Georgia, Armenia, and Central Asia and that Russia should offer to lease Black Sea Fleet bases in Sevastopol in Ukraine.[77] Kozyrev has also repeated these ideas, emphasizing that the FSU region is a "zone of special responsibility and special interest"; that a complete Russian pullout from these regions would be an "unwarranted loss" because Russia had won influence in these areas over centuries; and that Russian "peacekeeping" would protect Russian national interests and stem conflict more effectively than mediation by the international community.[78]

It is only natural that Russia should seek to protect its interests in the cauldron of instability and conflict in the FSU, but what is notable is the diminished emphasis on the role of international actors and the increased manifestation of Russian hegemony and assertiveness. Only a little over a year ago, for example, Yeltsin asked that NATO troops be deployed in the war-torn enclave of Nagorno-Karabakh. But members of his government have since condemned the notion of using NATO because it will lead to interference in Russia's internal affairs and will weaken Russian statehood and sovereignty.[79]

War in Yugoslavia. Statist nationalism has influenced Russian priorities in favor of a moderate and sometimes supportive position toward Serbia. Statists and patriots consistently deplore "one-sided" international sanctions against Serbia. More extreme elements depict Serbia as a victim of international "intervention" that targets not only Serbs but also Slavs and Orthodox believers in general. They argue that in the future, Russians in Ukraine and Belarus may well find themselves in a position similar to that of their embattled Serbian kin, who have been held hostage by Westernizing Croats and Slovenians. When that happens, the international community will intervene to prevent Russia from aiding its irredenta.[80]

Statists and patriots have actively maligned Yeltsin and Kozyrev's foreign policy, which has largely supported Western sanctions against rump Yugoslavia throughout and sent sympathetic visits to Belgrade. In one incident, the national-ist paper *Den'* published a classified memo written by the Russian ambassador to the UN, Yurii Vorontsov, which, in reference to further sanctions against Yugoslavia, argued: "It is very important not to oppose . . . the western countries and the U.S., where public opinion is strong against [Serb leader] Milosevic."[81] This leak ignited an explosion among nationalists in the former Supreme Soviet, who questioned the legality of Russian actions in the UN. Pressure from patriots and statists eventually caused Foreign Minister Kozyrev to weaken his rhetoric on Russian solidarity with Western policy on Yugoslavia and, in April 1993, Russia abstained from a UN vote on additional sanctions against rump Yugoslavia.[82] Russian officials expressed disapproval of a U.S.-led initiative to lift the arms embargo against Bosnia's Muslim government in response to the Serbs' umpteenth rejection of a multilateral peace settlement.[83]

Conclusion

As with most analyses of post-Soviet politics, one's conclusions on Russian na-tionalism can be only tentative at best. The political landscape in Russia is still shifting, and the fate of statist nationalism and its proponents is far from deter-mined. Having issued this caveat, I propose the following conclusions. First, Russian nationalism is not a homogeneous concept. The ideas of nativists and Westernizing democrats definitely have fewer malevolent implications than those of national patriots or statists. Second, proponents of milder forms of national-ism, including nativists and Westernizing democrats, have been less effective than their extremist colleagues in sustaining nationalist propaganda for the pur-pose of Russian renewal or rebirth. This has narrowed the range of policy ideas and options for defining and pursuing Russia's "national interest." The "narrow-ing" process is closing off options for more moderate, nonchauvinistic, and non-imperialistic articulations of Russia's national interest.

Third, the current empowerment of statist nationalism does not denote the un-mitigated triumph of aggression, chauvinism, and/or imperialism in Russian for-eign policy. Although these ideological elements are present in state officials' rhetoric, domestic political division and an army in disarray will likely impede the pursuit of intensely aggressive behavior. Moscow is likely to engage in more saber-rattling than truly alarming behavior.[84] It will continue to exploit opportu-nities for hegemony in the near abroad while seeking the fig leaf of international community approval. Further, the most extreme elements of the nationalist spec-trum are still deeply divided and unable to maintain effective coalitions or organi-zations; hence, their influence in the near future will remain limited.

Finally, the choices and policies of the state will matter greatly. Nationalism can be a force for good or ill, and the state has at its disposal many instruments for strengthening one or the other version. The Yeltsin government has adopted ideas of statist nationalism to cultivate popular support and legitimacy and to anchor itself in ideas that have historical resonance in Russia. The central question remains: Will this government succeed in using nationalism to consolidate the Russian state without also giving in to the malevolence of chauvinism and imperialism?

Notes

The author would like to acknowledge support for this research project from the U.S. Institute of Peace and the Social Science Research Council.

1. On the dangers of Russian nationalism, see Galina Starovoitova on Radio Ekho Moskvy, 14 October 1992; Hélène Carrere d'Encausse, *Decline of an Empire* (New York: Harper and Row, 1979); Robert Conquest, ed., *The Last Empire: Nationality and the Soviet Future* (Stanford: Hoover Institution Press, 1986); Roman Szporluk, "Dilemmas of Russian Nationalism," *Problems of Communism* 38 (July-August 1989): 15–35; and Walter Laqueur, "Russian Nationalism," *Foreign Affairs* 71 (Winter 1992/93): 102–116.

2. Alexander Yanov's well-known book on Russian nationalism, for example, presents all variants of nationalist thought as part of a "new right" movement that sooner or later degenerates into tyranny and fascism. See Alexander Yanov, *The Russian New Right* (Berkeley: UC Institute of International Studies, 1978).

3. Leonard W. Doob, *Patriotism and Nationalism: Their Psychological Foundations* (New Haven: Yale University Press, 1964), p. 263. See also John Breuilly, *Nationalism and the State* (Chicago: Chicago University Press, 1985), pp. 234–245; Hugh Seton-Watson, *Nations and States* (Boulder: Westview Press, 1977).

4. For example, Ernest Gellner and Eric Hobsbawm define nationalism as a "political principle which holds that the political and national unit should be congruent," whereas Hans Kohn defines it as a "state of mind" in which individuals' supreme loyalty is to their own nation-state. See Ernest Gellner, *Nations and Nationalism* (Ithaca: Cornell University Press, 1983); Eric J. Hobsbawm, *Nations and Nationalism Since 1780* (Cambridge: Cambridge University Press, 1990); and Hans Kohn, *The Idea of Nationalism* (New York: Collier Books, 1944). Alexander Motyl summarizes meanings of nationalism in "The Modernity of Nationalism," *Journal of International Affairs* 45 (Winter 1992): 308–312.

5. An ideology is a set of assertions, beliefs, and aims that constitutes or strives to constitute a sociopolitical program. My definition draws from Breuilly and Paul Brass, both of whom emphasize the political aspect of nationalism. See Breuilly, *Nationalism and the State*, p. 3; and Paul R. Brass, *Ethnicity and Nationalism: Theory and Comparison* (New Delhi: Sage Publications, 1991), chaps. 1–3.

6. My definition draws on Gellner, *Nations and Nationalism,* p. 7; and Samuel E. Finer, "State and Nation-Building in Europe: The Role of the Military," in *The Formation of National States in Western Europe,* ed. Charles Tilly (Princeton: Princeton University Press, 1978), p. 144.

7. Liah Greenfield, *Nationalism: Five Roads to Modernity* (Cambridge: Harvard University Press, 1992), pp. 1–12.

8. Myron Weiner discusses the potential for conflict over irredenta in "The Macedonian Syndrome," *World Politics* 23 (July 1971): 665–683. Serbian aggression and ethnic cleansing in the former Yugoslavia exemplify the dangers inherent in ethnic nationalism.

9. Scholars disagree on the impact of ideology on foreign policy making. For a skepti-

cal view, see Hans Morgenthau, *Politics Among Nations* (New York: Knopf, 1967), chap. 7; for the affirmative argument, see Adam Ulam, "Russian Nationalism," pp. 3–18 in *The Domestic Context of Soviet Foreign Policy,* ed. Seweryn Bialer (Boulder: Westview Press, 1981); Jack Snyder, "The Gorbachev Revolution: A Waning of Soviet Expansionism?" *International Security* 12 (Winter 1987/88): 93–131; and Jeff Checkel, "Ideas, Institutions, and the Gorbachev Foreign Policy Revolution," *World Politics* 45 (January 1993): 271–301.

10. The impact of nationalism on the national interest in foreign policy recalls the debate among former Sovietologists on the role that Marxist-Leninist ideology played in Soviet foreign policy. For contrasting views, see Seweryn Bialer, "Soviet Foreign Policy: Sources, Perceptions, Trends," in *The Domestic Context,* ed. Bialer, pp. 409–441; Ulam, "Russian Nationalism," pp. 3–18; George Breslauer, "Ideology and Learning in Soviet Third World Policy," *World Politics* 39 (April 1987): 429–448; and Hannes Adomeit, "Capitalist Contradictions and Soviet Policy," *Problems of Communism* 33 (May-June 1984): 1–18.

11. This is a key theme in Jack Snyder, *Myths of Empire* (Ithaca: Cornell University Press, 1991).

12. C.J.H. Hayes, *Essays on Nationalism* (New York: Macmillan Company, 1926), pp. 156–195; and Finer, "State and Nation-Building," pp. 154–163. This does not imply, however, that military institutions are always proponents of malevolent nationalism.

13. Stephen Van Evera, "Hypotheses on Nationalism," *International Security* 18 (Spring 1994): 5–39, at pp. 32–33.

14. On the last point, see Jack Snyder's chapter in this volume.

15. On the issue of national identity and political legitimacy, see James Richter's chapter in this volume.

16. Jack Snyder argues this in "Nationalism and the Crisis of the Post-Soviet State" in *Survival* (Spring 1993): 5–26; in his *Myths of Empire,* pp. 66–111; and in his chapter in this volume.

17. See chapters by Kenneth Waltz in *Neorealism and Its Critics,* ed. Robert Keohane (New York: Columbia University Press, 1986); and Robert Keohane and Joseph Nye, *Power and Interdependence* (Glencoe, Ill.: Scott, Foresman and Company, 1989).

18. See Weiner, "The Macedonian Syndrome."

19. On the evolution of nationalism during the Soviet period see Astrid S. Tuminez, "Russian Nationalism and the National Interest in Russian Foreign Policy," paper presented at the Annual Meeting of the American Political Science Association, Washington, D.C., 2–5 September 1993; John B. Dunlop, *The Contemporary Faces of Russian Nationalism* (Princeton: Princeton University Press, 1983).

20. On the ideas of these thinkers, see Andrzej Walicki, *A History of Russian Thought* (Stanford: Stanford University Press, 1979), pp. 52–59, 291–309; Richard Pipes, *Karamzin's Memoir on Ancient and Modern Russia: A Translation and Analysis* (New York: Atheneum, 1974); and Walter Laqueur, *Black Hundred: The Rise of the Extreme Right in Russia* (New York: HarperCollins, 1993), pp. 8–13; 298–302.

21. I borrow the term "nativist" from Dimitry Pospielovsky.

22. See, for example, Eduard Volodin, *Literaturnaia Rossiia,* 26 January 1990, pp. 3–4.

23. This image of Russia and the West echoes the ideas of nineteenth-century Slavophiles. See Walicki, *A History of Russian Thought,* pp. 92–114. Some nativists have expressed antisemitic, anti-Western, and imperialist sentiments.

24. Dmitrii Likhachev, "The National Nature of Russian History" (Second Annual W. Averell Harriman Lecture, Columbia University, 13 November 1990), pp. 11–18; "Ot pokaianiia k deistviiu," *Literaturnaia gazeta,* no. 37, 1987; "A chto ostanetsia Rossii?" *Den'* 3, no. 83 (1993): 8; and "O Russkoi intelligentsii," *Novyi mir,* no. 2 (1993): 3–9. See also Aleksandr Solzhenitsyn, *Kak nam obustroit' Rossiiu* (Paris: YMCA Press, 1990), and idem, *Pis'mo vozhdiam Sovetskogo Soiuza* (Paris: YMCA Press, 1974); Szporluk, "Dilemmas of Russian Nationalism"; Hélène Carrere d'Encausse, *Decline of an Empire,* chap. 9; Dimitry Pospielovsky, "Russian Nationalism: An Update," *RFE/RL Report on the USSR,* 9 February 1990, pp. 8–17; Dunlop, *The Contemporary Faces of Russian Nationalism,* pp. 144–200; Roman Solchanyk, "Ukraine, Russia, and the National Question: An Interview with Aleksandr Tsipko," *RFE/RL Report on the USSR,* 17 August 1990, pp. 19–24; and "Esli natsiia ne ponimaet tsennosti gosudarstva, ona opasno bol'na," *Komosomol'skaia pravda,* 14 January 1992, p. 3.

25. See Kozyrev's interview in *Kuranty,* 16 April 1993, p. 6; and Boris Yeltsin, "Russia Is Strong in Intellect, Resources, and Culture," *Rossiiskie vesti,* 21 April 1993, pp. 1–2.

26. My interview with Boris Fedorov, former Russian finance minister, Berlin, 25 August 1994.

27. Ibid.

28. Andrei Kozyrev, "Russia: A Chance for Survival," *Foreign Affairs* 71 (Spring 1992): 1–16; and "Rossiia obrechena byt' velikoi derzhavoi," *Novoe vremia,* no. 3 (1992): 20–24.

29. On the ideas of Westernizing democrats, see "Kozyrev Presents Overview of Foreign Policy Tasks," *Rossiiskie vesti,* 3 December 1992, p. 2; "Foreign Ministry Document Outlines Foreign Policy," *Interfax* (Moscow), 1 December 1992; "Russian Diplomacy Reborn," *International Affairs* (Moscow), no. 3 (March 1991): 120–134; Arkadii Lapshin, "From the Russian Point of View," *International Affairs* (Moscow), no. 10 (October 1991): 79–81; Aleksei Kiva, "A Superpower Which Ruined Itself," *International Affairs* (Moscow), no. 2 (February 1992): 13–22; Vadim Zagladin, "Russia at World Crossroads," *Novoe vremia,* no. 48 (1992): 23–26; and "Russia Calls for CIS Integration," *RFE/RL News Briefs,* 15–19 March 1993, p. 5.

30. Rutskoi began as a centrist statist, but his nationalist rhetoric became more extreme in the summer and fall of 1993 as the political battle between him and Yeltsin intensified. He is easily the most extreme of the statists and, in some cases, may fit better with the national patriots (the fourth and most aggressive group of nationalists in my typology). I include him among the statists because his persona and rhetoric form a bridge between statists and less extreme national patriots such as Gennadii Zyuganov and others.

31. See Rutskoi's comments in *Nezavisimaia gazeta,* 13 February 1992. Arkady Volskiy has also stated that all former "Soviet people" are genetically the same; therefore they naturally belong in an imperial union. See *RFE/RL Post-Soviet/East European Report,* 6 October 1992, p. 5. Lukin once declared himself an "enlightened patriot" but then told me in an interview that he did not want to be called a "nationalist" or "patriot." Despite his protestation, his rhetoric often includes statist nationalist ideas. My interview with Vladimir Lukin, Moscow, 3 June 1994.

32. In Stankevich's words, "at all times, in all countries, intensive reform efforts . . . were implemented only by leaders who were somewhat authoritarian. . . . Never and nowhere has a transition of society to a qualitatively new state been accomplished during . . . a flourishing parliamentary democracy." *Washington Post,* 7 October 1991; see also

Stanislav Govorukhin, *Velikaia kriminal'naia revoliutsiia* (Moscow: Andreevskii flag, 1993); my interview with Aleksandr Rutskoi, Moscow, 8 June 1994; and the platform of Rutskoi's new movement, "Vozzvanie sotsial-patrioticheskogo dvizheniia 'Derzhava'," manuscript.

33. Igor Malashenko, "Russia: The Earth's Heartland," *International Affairs* (Moscow), no. 7 (July 1990): 46–54.

34. Valentin Larionov, "Geostrategiia nas obiazyvaet," *Krasnaia zvezda,* 4 December 1992, pp. 2–3.

35. This is true, for example, of Russian "long-standing interests" in Serbia or its ties with Third World countries such as India, fostered over many years of Soviet rule. See Vsevolod Rybakov, "Great Russia—A Myth or a Reality?" *Novoe vremia,* no. 30 (1992), pp. 4–7.

36. Rutskoi, for example, blames Russia's problems on Western interference in support of "a great democrat, Boris Nikolaevich Yeltsin." See Aleksandr Rutskoi, "V zashchite Rossii," *Pravda,* 30 January 1992; "Rutskoi Calls for Government to Be Disbanded," *RFE/RL News Briefs,* 1–4 June 1993, p. 2; and my interview with Rutskoi, 8 June 1994.

37. My interview with Rutskoi, 8 June 1994; "Committee Chairman on Russian National Interests," *RFE/RL News Briefs,* 8–12 February 1993, p. 5; and "Civic Union Discusses Foreign Policy Concept," *RFE/RL News Briefs,* 18–22 January 1993, p. 3.

38. The "red-brown" appellation refers to the mixed membership of this group: neo-Communists and nationalists. Their predecessors include the National Bolsheviks, who mixed nationalism with support for Soviet communism. See Dunlop, *The Contemporary Faces of Russian Nationalism,* pp. 254–265.

39. In October 1993 I interviewed Sterligov, Zhirinovsky, Stanislav Kuniaev (chief editor of *Molodaia gvardiia*), and General Viktor Filatov (former editor of *Voenno-istoricheskii zhurnal*) in Moscow. Except for Filatov, all initially claimed that the Russian nation was not defined ethnically. In the course of the interviews, however, it became evident that they used ethnicity and language as key criteria for membership and, particularly, *leadership* in the nation.

40. In the words of Sergei Baburin, "Russia is the former Soviet Union. . . . It is politicians, not the people, who want national states. As for the will of the people and the 'referendums' on independence—[those] are the biggest lie of all." See *Nezavisimaia gazeta,* 9 January 1992; and Marina Shakina, "The Discreet Charm of a Russian Nationalist," *Novoe vremia,* no. 47 (1992): 10–13.

41. National patriots gloss over the history of the Stalin era. They are less interested in a full exposure of the past than in blaming recent and current leaders such as Gorbachev and Yeltsin for destroying the great Russian state. See Wendy Slater, "Russian Communists Seek Salvation in Nationalist Alliance," *RFE/RL Research Report,* 2 (26 March 1993): 8–13.

42. One national patriot remarked to me that the years of Stalinist rule, 1937 to 1953, were golden years, when Russians were truly able to live by Russian rules. My interview with Filatov, 15 October 1993.

43. The original Eurasianists included the linguist N. S. Trubetskoi; the geographer P. N. Savitsky; the legal scholars V. N. Il'in and N. N. Alekseev; the historians M. M. Shakhmatov and G. V. Vernadsky; and the philosophers G. V. Florovsky and L. P. Karsavin. Their ideas are elaborated in Petr Nikolaevich Savitskii, *Exodus to the East (Iskhod K Vostoky)* (Sofia: Rossisko-Bulgarsko Knigoizdatel'stvo, 1921). The more recent

Eurasianists began to publicize their ideas in 1989, first through the newspaper *Poslednii polius,* which closed after two issues. Since then, the newspaper *Den'* has taken up the Eurasianist idea; a biweekly journal dedicated to Eurasianism, *Elementy,* also appeared in 1992. See V. Solovei, "Sovremennyi russkii natsionalizm: Ideino-politicheskaia klassifikatsiia," *Obshchestvennye nauki,* no. 2 (1992): 125.

44. See interviews with Prokhanov and Colonel Viktor Alksnis by Michael Shuster, National Public Radio, October 1992; "Afganistan: ispytanie ognem," *Literaturnaia gazeta,* 29 April 1987, p. 6; Sergei Khovanskii, "Afghanistan: The Bleeding Wound," *Détente,* no. 6 (Spring 1986): 2–4; and Vera Tolz and Elizabeth Teague, "Prokhanov Warns of Collapse of Soviet Empire," *RFE/RL Report on the USSR,* 9 February 1990, pp. 1–3.

45. Nikolai Lysenko in "Nasha tsel'—sozdaniie velikoi imperii," *Nash sovremennik,* no. 9 (1992): 122–130; and my interview with Filatov, 15 October 1993.

46. When asked about the nuclear arms race, Prokhanov once declared, "My people are not guilty. Guilty are the black imperialist forces [led by the United States]." See my interview with Kuniaev, 14 October 1993; and Stephen Shenfield, "Making Sense of Prokhanov," *Détente,* no. 5 (1987): 28–89, at p. 51.

47. Douglas Smith, "Formation of New Russian Nationalist Group Announced," *RFE/RL Report on the USSR,* 7 July 1989, pp. 5–8; "Anpilov Wants Khasbulatov Replaced by a Russian," in *RFE/RL News Briefs,* 3–7 May 1993, p. 2; Adi Ignatius, "Mayor of Moscow? Spider the Metalhead Is Ready to Serve," *Wall Street Journal,* 18 February 1993, pp. A1, A13; and Celestine Bohlen, "Irate Russians Demonize Traders from Caucasus," *New York Times,* 20 October 1992, p. 3.

48. See David Filipov, "Nationalism Moves into Mainstream," *Moscow Times,* 29 July 1994, pp. 1–2; and Gennadii Zyuganov, *Derzhava* (Moscow: Informpechat', 1994).

49. Rutskoi's new political movement established in May 1994 is called "Derzhava" and the title of Zyuganov's latest propaganda monograph is also *Derzhava.*

50. A 1991 survey by Vox Populi in Moscow found only 51 percent of females and 27 percent of males to be believers, but not necessarily of the Orthodox faith. See Oksana Antic, "Patriarch Aleksii II: A Political Portrait," *RFE/RL Report on the USSR,* 8 November 1991, pp. 16–18; and Laqueur, "Russian Nationalism," p. 111. Aleksandr Solzhenitsyn's return to Russia in May 1994 has thus far not catalyzed institutional support for nativism, either.

51. This includes Viktor Aksyuchits, Mikhail Astafev, Nikolai Travkin, Sergei Stankevich, Oleg Rumiantsev, Evgenii Ambartsumov, and Anatoly Sobchak. The movement toward statist nationalism continues. A leader of Gaidar's Russia's Choice party informed me that his party's greatest mistake in the December 1993 elections was failing to present itself as a patriotic/nationalist group that was concerned about Russia's great-power status. They intend to correct this mistake in the future. My interview with Sergei Blagovolin (Chair of Russia's Choice, Moscow branch), Moscow, 6 June 1994. Boris Fedorov also enthusiastically declared to me, "I am a nationalist!" He and other democrats would have hesitated to use this label in the past. My interview with Fedorov, 25 August 1994.

52. See Pavel Felgengauer, "Zakrytye goroda Rossii," *Nezavisimaia gazeta,* 30 June 1992, p. 5; Vitalii Goldanskii, "Russia's Red-Brown Hawks," *Bulletin of the Atomic Scientists* 49 (June 1993): 24–27; and John B. Dunlop, "Zhirinovsky's World," *Journal of Democracy* 5 (April 1994): 30. Military supporters of the breakaway Trans-Dniestr

Republic in Moldova also have clear, material interests that are served by statist nationalist ideas. See Stephen Foye, "Russian Troops Abroad: Vestiges of Empire," *RFE/RL Research Report,* no. 1 (28 August 1992): 15–17.

53. Boris Tarasov, "Voennaia strategiia Rossii: Evraziiskii aspekt," *Nash Sovremennik,* no. 12 (1992): 112–117; "Zakony 'voennogo paketa' dolzhny deistvovat' v polnom ob'eme," *Krasnaia zvezda,* 12 October 1993, p. 1; "Russia's Military: A Shriveled and Volatile Legacy," *New York Times,* 28 November 1993, pp. 1, 18–19; and Stephen Foye, "Armed Forces Confront Legacy of Soviet Past," *RFE/RL Research Report,* no. 1 (21 February 1992): 9–13.

54. My interview with Alla Latynina, Moscow, 31 May 1994; Solzhenitsyn, *Kak nam obustroit',* pp. 3–5; and Carrere d'Encausse, *Decline of an Empire,* pp. 171–195.

55. Popular distrust of state-supported media, particularly television, has grown in the wake of government censorship and manipulation of mass media during and after the October 3–4, 1993, crisis. See Vera Tolz and Julia Wishnevsky, "The Russian Media and the Political Crisis in Moscow," *RFE/RL Research Report* 2 (8 October 1993): 12–15.

56. Vera Tolz, "Russian Westernizers Continue to Challenge National Patriots," *RFE/RL Research Report* 1 (11 December 1992): 1. On general problems of historiography in the Soviet period, see Nancy Whittier-Heer, *Politics and History in the Soviet Union* (Cambridge: MIT Press, 1971). Many of my interviews with nationalist leaders also reveal a lack of critical thinking. As Rutskoi framed it, "I hate gray. I like black and white." My interview with Rutskoi, 8 June 1994.

57. Julia Wishnevsky, "Media Still Far from Free," *RFE/RL Research Report* 2, no. 20 (14 May 1993), pp. 86–91; "Courts Stand for Press Freedom," *RFE/RL News Briefs,* 14–21 May 1993, p. 3; and *Nezavisimaia gazeta,* 3 April 1993, p. 2.

58. On 20 March 1993, for example, Khasbulatov allowed the unofficial, statist nationalist, anti-Yeltsin All-Army Officers Assembly to use the facilities of the "White House" parliamentary center for a meeting to discuss, among other things, Yeltsin's declaration of emergency rule in Russia. See Stephen Foye, "The Defense Ministry and the New Military 'Opposition,'" *RFE/RL Research Report* 2 (14 May 1993): 68–73.

59. Dmitrii Orlov, "Vosstanie protiv razuma," *Segodnya,* 26 October 1993, p. 9; and Filipov, "Nationalism Moves into Mainstream," pp. 1–2.

60. Aleksandr Tsipko, "'Demokraticheskaia Rossiia' kak bol'shevistskaia i odnovremenno pochvennicheskaia partiia," *Nezavisimaia gazeta,* 9 April 1993, p. 5.

61. "Komanda reformatorov raskololas' pered vyborami potomu, chto nikogda ne byla monolitnoi," *Izvestiia,* 26 October 1993, p. 2.

62. Street interviews with Russians in Moscow, 3–4 October 1993; my interview with Latynina, 31 May 1994; and my interview with Fedorov, 25 August 1994.

63. See John Lloyd, "Growing Numbers Join Russia's 'Working Poor,'" *Financial Times,* 1 August 1994, p. 14; Celestine Bohlen, "Underworld in Moscow: Gangsters Kill in the Streets and Twist the Economy," *International Herald Tribune,* 17 August 1993, pp. 1, 6; Sheila Marnie, "How Prepared Is Russia for Unemployment?" *RFE/RL Research Report* 1 (4 December 1992): 44–50; and "Russia Opens Up Market but Few Have the Money," *New York Times,* 18 November 1993, p. A3.

64. "Russia's Growing Refugee Problem," *RFE/RL News Briefs,* 28 June–2 July 1993, p. 4; and "Rising Crime Becomes a Political Issue," *RFE/RL Research Bulletin,* 1 June 1993, p. 3.

65. "Sociological Survey: Who's to Blame?" *Novoe vremia,* no. 9 (1993): 8; "Roundup: Life in Russia," *RFE/RL Research Report* 1 (8 May 1992): 57–58; "Survey Finds Low

Confidence in Leaders and Growing Support for Strong Government," *RFE/RL Research Bulletin,* 19 January 1993, pp. 3–4; and Mark Rhodes, "Political Attitudes in Russia," *RFE/RL Research Report* 2 (15 January 1993): 42–44.

66. However, there has been some support for national patriots from members of the European new right and even Saddam Hussein, but this support has been minuscule and has had no real impact in empowering national patriotism wholesale. See "Predal Rossiiu-predal Evraziiu!" (Roundtable of the newspaper *Den'*), *Den',* no. 22 (50): 3; and "Predaval li Saddam Khusein Sergeia Baburina?" *Izvestiia,* 26 October 1993, p. 1.

67. Institutions like the Organization on Security and Cooperation in Europe (OSCE) and countries like the United States have declared their preference for democratic norms and market reform and their disapproval of chauvinistic and imperialistic ideas and behavior. See William Korey, *Human Rights, the Helsinki Process and American Foreign Policy* (New York: Institute for East-West Studies, 1993).

68. Richard J. Krickus, "Latvia's 'Russian Question,'" *RFE/RL Research Report* 2 (30 April 1993): 29–34; Steven Erlanger, "In the Baltics, There May Be No Home for Russians," *New York Times,* 22 November 1992, pp. A1, A12; John Lloyd, "Painful Legacy of an Empire," *Financial Times,* 9 July 1992; "Russia to Spy on Ex-Republics," *Boston Globe,* 29 October 1992, p. 6; and Steven Erlanger, "Moscow Fears for Troops in Tajikistan," *New York Times,* 30 September 1992, p. A12.

69. See Gabriel Schoenfeld, "Outer Limits," *Post-Soviet Prospects* (Center for Strategic and International Studies), no. 17 (January 1993).

70. Daniel Shorr, *The Citizenship and Alien Law Controversies in Estonia and Latvia* (a report published by the Harvard Project on Strengthening Democratic Institutions), April 1994. The civil war between Muslim guerrillas (aided by Afghan mujahideen) and the former Communist government in Tadzhikistan has killed at least 20,000 people and created half a million internal refugees. Some of the casualties have been Russian troops, border guards, and their families, who are still stationed in the area. In 1992, Russian border guards in Azerbaijan were also the victims of Russophobic sentiment. See Schoenfeld, "Outer Limits," pp. 2–3.

71. *Kuranty,* 16 April 1993, p. 6.

72. See Eduard Kondratev, "Vizit Rutskogo v Pridenstrov'e," *Izvestiia,* 6 April 1992; and ITAR-TASS, 8 April 1992; Igor Shafarevich, "U Rossii est' budushchee," *Den',* no. 1 (81) (1993): 7.

73. Kozyrev noted as well that UN and OSCE participation would be welcome, but the tone of his statement connotes a new Russian assertiveness on issues in the "near abroad." See *RFE/RL Daily Report,* 4 August 1993; "Andrei Kozyrev: partnerstvo i soiuz ne oznachaiut sliianiia," *Moskovskie novosti,* 24 October 1993, p. 15; and *Izvestiia,* 18 November 1993, for most of the text of Russia's new military doctrine.

74. *Rossiiskaia gazeta,* 13 July 1993, p. 1.

75. Thomas Goltz, "Letter from Eurasia: The Hidden Russian Hand," *Foreign Policy,* no. 92 (Fall 1993): 92–116.

76. See these articles by Vladimir Socor in *RFE/RL Research Report:* "Russian Forces in Moldova," 1 (28 August 1992): 38–43; "Russia's Fourteenth Army and the Insurgency in Eastern Moldova," 1 (11 September 1992): 41–48; and "Russia's Army in Moldova: There to Stay?" 2 (18 June 1993): 42–49. Kozyrev has also desisted from acknowledging the extremism of Russian nationalists in Trans-Dniestr, even after the fact that some nationalist fighters from the region fought on the side of parliament during Moscow's October 1993 crisis. See *Izvestiia,* 8 October 1993; and Interfax, 16 October 1993.

77. ITAR-TASS, 1 March 1993; "Yeltsin on Special Status for Russia," *RFE/RL News Briefs,* 1–5 March 1993, p. 1; and "Yeltsin Calls for Retention of Military Bases Abroad," *RFE/RL News Briefs,* 7–11 June 1993, pp. 5–6.

78. Kozyrev, "Partnerstvo i soiuz," p. 15; his comments on Moscow Russian Television Network, 1948 GMT, 27 April 1993; and an interview in *Nezavisimaia gazeta,* 24 November 1993. These statements are more strident than earlier ones, which emphasized respect for the sovereignty and legislation of neighboring states and noninterference in their internal affairs. See *Krasnaia zvezda,* 13 April 1993, pp. 1, 3.

79. "'Atlanticists' Versus 'Eurasians' in Russian Foreign Policy," *RFE/RL Research Report* 1 (29 May 1992): 19; Tarasov, "Voennaia strategiia Rossii," pp. 112–117; and "Russia Criticizes New Ukrainian Security Concept," *RFE/RL News Briefs,* 24–28 May 1993, p. 2.

80. See "Brat'ia-Slaviane," *Den'* 3, no. 83 (1993): 5; the analysis of the Eurasianist Center for Metastrategic Research in "Geopolitika Iugoslavskogo konflikta," *Elementy,* no. 2 (1992): 2–5; and "Mnenie obozrevatelia," *Pravda,* 2 June 1992, p. 3.

81. Interfax, 3 June 1992.

82. Kozyrev said he felt "sick at heart" for this decision. See "Kozyrev Regrets Abstaining on UN Vote," *RFE/RL News Briefs,* 26–30 April 1993, p. 3.

83. "Russia Warns Clinton Not to Allow Bosnia Arms," *New York Times,* 4 September 1994, p. 4.

84. After months of threatening language, for example, Russian troops nonetheless completed their pullout from Estonia and Latvia on the agreed deadline. See "Last Russian Troops Leave Latvian and Estonian Bases," *New York Times,* 1 September 1994, p. A3.

CHAPTER 4

Russian Foreign Policy
and the Politics
of National Identity

James Richter

In March 1992, Sergei Stankevich, then an adviser to Russian president Boris Yeltsin, wrote that "foreign policy with us does not proceed from the directions and priorities of a developed statehood. On the contrary, the practice of our foreign policy . . . will help Russia become Russia."[1] This remark raises two central issues in the study of comparative foreign policy. First, Stankevich suggests that Russia's interests are not fixed by its geopolitical position but instead emerge as decisionmakers evaluate that position in relation to a "developed statehood," which I interpret to mean a set of stable state institutions and the myths of identity that sustain them. Second, his statement that "the practice of our foreign policy . . . will help Russia become Russia" raises the agent-structure problem as defined by constructivist approaches to international relations. According to the constructivists, the state and the international system should not be treated as analytically distinct but as mutually constitutive.[2] Russian leaders define "the directions and priorities" of Russia's foreign policy in light of expectations based on Russia's previous interactions with the international environment, expectations that are institutionalized in decisionmaking procedures as part of Russia's "developed statehood."

The Russian foreign policy debate since Stankevich wrote these words provides an excellent opportunity to examine both these issues in an empirical case study. In March 1992, the Russian state had no established identity. Many of the institutions of the old order had disintegrated or had been left stranded by the collapse of communism. As a new state with new borders and new neighbors, Russia had no authoritative history of foreign relations upon which to define its international role. These conditions enabled politicians and intellectuals to articulate enormously varied prescriptions for the "directions and priorities" of Russia's foreign policy, ranging from calls to integrate Russia into an international community of Western-style democracies to exhortations to resurrect the Russian empire. Within two years, however, "Russia had become Russia" to the point where most elites agreed that their country should preserve its great-power status in the

69

form of a Eurasian state distinct from the West, concerned more with restoring its influence over the territory of the former Soviet Union than on integrating itself into the West European system.[3]

Unfortunately, because most constructivists do not look at domestic politics, they provide no mechanism to explain this movement. In this chapter I attempt to provide such a mechanism by examining the politics of national identity. Since the early nineteenth century, states have legitimated themselves with the doctrine of popular sovereignty—the notion that states represent and protect the interests of their citizenry. This formula presumes that the citizenry shares a common identity, that the citizens believe that their individual destinies are linked to the fate of a self-conscious community whose boundaries are somehow linked to the governance of the state. However, individuals perform many different roles in many different social settings and they rank or interpret the values informing the "national" identity in different and even contradictory ways. The politics of national identity, therefore, refers to how politicians maneuver to mobilize popular and institutional resources toward their own more particular goals.

Foreign policy plays a critical role in the politics of national identity. As Astrid Tuminez notes, in Chapter 3 of this volume, national identity depends on the creation of common criteria distinguishing members of the community from "others" outside the community and the principles by which that community organizes itself in respect to these others. Such criteria make sense, however, only when they are embedded in a vision of a larger system organized along similar principles. Competing constructions of national identity, therefore, entail correspondingly competing images of the international system. Foreign policy can lend credence to these images by making them concrete, demonstrating through state practices how "we" distinguish ourselves from "them" and how "we" should behave toward "them."[4]

Russia's interaction with the international environment influences the politics of national identity, then, insofar as it helps to reinforce or undermine competing images of the national identity. Politicians can legitimate the demands they make upon citizens in the name of national identity only to the extent that the state's foreign policy can realize this identity. As the constructivists would argue, therefore, politicians must consider not only indigenous symbols of national identity but also the practical constraints confronting them as participants in global structures. The authoritative, institutionalized definition of the state polity emerges from a continuous negotiation between the traditions, symbols, and institutions specific to the polity on the one hand and the repertoire of state forms and behaviors recognized by the international system on the other.

In this chapter I concentrate on how Russian elites represent Russian identity to harness the resources of the state rather than on how Russians themselves feel. Since politicians seeking to harness the resources of existing state institutions must rely on symbols and accounts of national identity compatible with these institutions, such an emphasis allows us to concentrate on the three tendencies in this debate that had the most substantial claims to state authority during this pe-

Three major players for state authority - liberals / statists / Red-Brown.

POLICY AND THE POLITICS OF IDENTITY   71

riod: the liberals, who favored rapid market reforms in a Russia fully integrated into the West; the statists, who also favored reforms but called for a more interventionist state; and the extremists of the Red-Brown coalition, who favored authoritarian policies to restore Russia's (or the Soviet Union's) former glory in the face of Western hostility.[5]

In addition to providing an empirical basis for the constructivist agenda, the politics of national identity provides a profound insight into the relation between domestic and foreign policy realms. First, whereas most studies treat domestic and foreign politics as two separate if interrelated realms, the politics of national identity concentrates on the principle through which these realms define and organize each other. Second, because national identity organizes all social interaction involving the state, this approach stresses that the interaction between the domestic and foreign policy occurs at every level of society, not only among decisionmakers at the apex of the political system. I begin this analysis with a general treatment of the politics of national identity. I then examine how images of national identity inform views on domestic and foreign policy in the Russian debate and how Russia's interaction with this environment affected the outcome of political competition over foreign policy.

National Identity and Institutions

Oran Young defines institutions as "recognized practices consisting of easily identifiable roles, coupled with collections of rules or conventions governing relations among the occupants of these roles."[6] By coordinating social interaction to generate resources and perform tasks that individuals cannot accomplish by acting alone, institutions have concrete effects. But they are abstractions that exist only so long as the individuals constituting them perform their assigned roles in a more or less consistent manner. In doing so, people reinforce the institutions themselves.

Individuals who conform to institutionalized definitions and expectations of citizenship gain access to resources; those who do not are denied access. So the relative strength of competing institutional claims on individual or state identity resides first in the resources they bring to bear. Institutions command more resources and are more easily sustained the more broadly and deeply they are embedded in an interlocking framework. Deeply institutionalized accounts recede altogether from the conscious calculations determining people's behavior and are accepted as part of the natural world upon which these calculations are based.[7] For example, the industrialized state has become so effective in capturing the identity of its citizens because it represents a network of interlocking institutions with enormous resources available to survey, reward, and discipline the behavior of citizens.[8]

Still, the fate of the Soviet Union shows that even a highly intrusive regime systematically allocating rewards according to political reliability can be fragile. If state structures rely upon symbols and social expectations that overlap with the symbols and norms already found within the culture, citizens are more likely to consider the expectations associated with these symbols as authentic.[9] Communist regimes failed in part because they aimed to transform the indigenous culture—thereby highlighting the unnatural character of the regime's expectations and forcing them to rely more heavily on a transparent system of rewards and punishments to ensure compliance.

The symbols of national identity provide both the background and the raw materials for the domestic political debate. Some serve as the backdrop because all politicians claiming the authority to speak for state institutions must deploy fundamental symbols to present their policies as serving the common good. Because practices and symbols embedded in existing state institutions command so many resources, even politicians with differing agendas are likely to include them in their own rhetorical arsenal. In the United States, for example, the normative principles regulating state-society relations embodied in the Bill of Rights are so deeply embedded in domestic practices that all politicians profess to hold these principles sacred.

Yet politicians do have room to maneuver. Although the state's exclusive claim to authority rests on a more or less unified citizenry, the territorial boundaries of the state contain innumerable potential groupings with different interests and identities. These provide politicians with a wealth of symbols, rituals, and histories they can use to put together an image of the polity that will win institutional support for their goals. The Bill of Rights may limit debate in important ways, but politicians drawing on different constituencies and different institutional resources may offer quite different interpretations of what these rights entail and who has access to them.

How does the international environment influence the politics of national identity? Most obviously, politicians can draw upon the resources, ideas, and symbols associated with transnational and supranational organizations and practices to bolster their position in the domestic competition: Human rights activists seek support from the United Nations and nongovernmental organizations such as Amnesty International; Soviet enterprise managers adopt the language of the market to attract foreign investors.[10] In addition, politicians frequently invoke the more successful or more efficient practices of other countries as examples to support their own political preferences, claiming that they can reproduce this success at home. Appeals to the marketplace and its association with Western affluence proved nearly irresistible to populations in Eastern Europe after 1989. Even so, "ideas do not float freely," and popular conceptions of the marketplace were interpreted very differently in different institutional contexts.[11] All things being equal, reference to such transnational practices will translate more easily into domestic influence the more they can be made compatible with the symbols of national identity already embedded in state institutions. If they cannot, they can be ignored or stigmatized by opponents as alien, oppressive, and even traitorous.

The impact of the international environment on the politics of national identity is even more pervasive, because politicians also must define and organize this identity within the context of larger, global structures.[12] By defining the polity and its role in terms of globally sanctioned accounts and symbols, politicians can more easily win the recognition and respect for these claims from actors outside the state, and recourse to global symbols demonstrates to citizens that the domestic order is not merely the artifice of the regime itself.

The symbols of national identity, then, embed states within a network of global practices that recognize and sanction that identity. The international system also contains an enormous repertoire of symbols, accounts, and practices that politicians can refer to in seeking support. In the Soviet Union, for example, symbols that defined the Soviet polity as the vanguard of the international proletariat linked the mobilizational and propaganda functions of the Party apparatus with Communist regimes and parties that recognized the Soviet Union's ideological leadership. Symbols emphasizing Soviet nationalism located the military and defense industry—designed to preserve Soviet security—within the balance of power system that included the military-industrial complexes of other states as well.[13]

The relative success of competing representations of national identity, therefore, depend not only on the state resources but also on global resources. In the Soviet case, both revolutionary and nationalist identities were firmly embedded in domestic structures, and consequently most politicians sought to incorporate both of them in their own rhetoric. However, the tension between these accounts remained an axis of political competition throughout the Soviet period, and the Soviets' repeated failures to fulfill the revolutionary tasks prescribed for Soviet foreign policy by the class-based definition of the Soviet polity finally led to the success of politicians accepting a state-centered approach more in keeping with the dominant practices of the sovereign state system.[14]

Under most circumstances, the dual embeddedness of national identity in the domestic and international spheres inhibits change. Since the practices embedded in the polity reflect the accumulated history of its interaction with the outside world, one would expect on most occasions that they would complement prevailing practices in international politics. As patterns of foreign policy become institutionalized in one country, they also inform the institutionalized expectations and decisionmaking procedures of other states that interact with it. Politicians seeking to change their state's international role not only encounter resistance at home, but they also experience incomprehension, misinterpretation, and even hostility among leaders of other countries.[15] In such circumstances, the practice of foreign policy will help to maintain the status quo.

Still, savvy politicians will always be able to link the competing and contradictory accounts found in both domestic and global practices in new ways. Politicians will use the practice of foreign policy to affect the politics of national identity on issues where the elites disagree on what that identity entails. Where they agree on fundamental identity, they will disagree on the means to perform that role rather than on the advisability of the role itself. External pressures had a much smaller effect on Soviet politics in the 1950s than in the 1920s, partly because Stalin's revolution from above had created an enormous bureaucratic edifice around his image of the Soviet polity as an embattled island of socialism encircled by hostile capitalist powers.[16]

Consensual images and practices in domestic society can be shaken by external practices. Decisionmakers in weaker states are more likely to adjust their practices, and hence their identity, to the demands and opportunities provided by the international system than decisionmakers in stronger states. John Ikenberry and Charles Kupchan, for example, show how imperial Britain and the United States after World War II provided resources to the respective elites of colonial India and postwar Germany and Japan to shape the institutional structures of these states and "socialize" them to accept the hegemonic rules of the game.[17] International pressures that challenge consensual images of the polity's international role create opportunities for dissenters. Internal divisions within the polity magnify the impact of external practices on domestic politics. The ability of the United States to socialize the West German government after World War II, for example, reflected the willingness of many Germans to distance themselves from the Nazi regime as much as it reflected U.S. power.

In the case of the Russian Republic, the collapse of domestic institutions, the ambiguities over boundaries, and the need to redefine Russia's status as a nation-state broke down many of the meanings and practices associated with the old regime and made the Russian state particularly susceptible to external influences. Yet the legacy of the intrusive Soviet state and the absence of autonomous social organization supported images of Russian national identity embedded in state institutions. This was manifested in a consensus among the Russian elite that the Russian state should maintain its status as a great power in the international arena, play a central, if not dominant role on the territory of the Commonwealth of Independent States, and accept some responsibility for the fate of ethnic Russians living in non-Russian states in Eurasia.

National Identity, Domestic Order, and Foreign Policy

In the previous section, I argued that the symbols of national identity refer not only to institutionalized practices within domestic state and society but also to wider, global practices. National identity serves as the crucial organizing principle justifying and providing coherence to the state's domestic order, yet the boundaries defining this identity can be formulated only with reference to the external environment.

At the most basic level, the definition of national identity entails the state's territorial boundaries. These boundaries are the object of close scrutiny and control by the international community and they acquire concrete significance through maps, border patrols, and customs officials. As a result, when geographic boundaries are contested, the contests are often violent. However, boundaries are not only physical. Forms of nationalism use different principles to demarcate the members of a given community from outsiders.[18] Civic nationalism establishes membership on the basis of residence and willingness to conform to the laws of the land. Cultural nationalism establishes membership in the community based on common cultural ties and practices, such as allegiance to a common religious faith or proficiency in a common language. This form is more exclusive than civic nationalism, but it allows into the polity those individuals who are willing to assimilate. Ethnic nationalism determines membership on the basis of ascribed characteristics such as heredity or race.

How a politician defines the boundaries of the polity has important consequences for the politician's prescriptions for domestic order. Proponents of civic nationalism not only sanction the existence of different cultural identities within the polity, but they also are likely to favor policies that incorporate multilingual or multicultural practices. Proponents of more exclusive forms are likely to relegate individuals who do not share designated cultural or ethnic characteristics to the status of second-class citizens and justify exclusion by identifying members of the outgroup as "foreign" if not subversive. In extreme cases, political leaders advocate eradicating elements from within the territorial boundaries of the state.

The principles politicians use to draw boundaries around the polity affect foreign policy insofar as these boundaries coincide or conflict with the territorial boundaries recognized by the state system. For proponents of civic nationalism, these boundaries coincide by definition. Advocates of cultural or ethnic nationalism, by contrast, are more likely to claim some responsibility for the fates of people sharing the same culture or ethnicity outside the state's territorial boundaries, and they define the national interest toward other states in part on the basis of how these people are treated. Not surprisingly, politicians who claim a responsibility for people living outside state borders, even when such claims fall well short of irredentism, are likely to arouse suspicion and fear among the officials in the state where those populations reside.

In Russia, the dispute over boundaries is particularly divisive.[19] Elites in Russia agree that Russia is the successor to a truncated empire and that Russia should retain its dominant influence over the territory of the former Soviet Union. They disagree on where the formal political boundaries of Russia should be drawn. The imperial dynasty relied on Russian Orthodoxy rather than ethnicity as the defining principle of its polity, and it distinguished between the adjectives *rossiiskoe,* which pertains to the state encompassing all ethnic groups, and the more particular *russkoe,* which describes the ethnic identity.[20] In the current era, politicians use the adjective *rossiiskoe* to refer to a more inclusive definition of the polity approaching civic nationalism; however, since most politicians accept some responsibility for Russian speakers in all the republics of the former Soviet Union, the distinction between civic nationalism and cultural nationalism is unclear.

In addition to marking the boundaries between the polity and its "others," political leaders also must define how the polity should relate to these others.

Leaders identifying others as inferior to the official polity in the domestic realm are likely to have that stance affect their foreign policy. The United States refused to recognize the Haitian republic in the early 1800s in part because the racial construction of the U.S. polity that allowed the existence of slavery demanded that the former slaves of Haiti be denied the status of potential political subjects.[21]

An image of the international environment also depends upon the principles used to assign and organize individual identities within the polity. Is society a collection of individual actors or an organic whole made up of corporate, functional groups?[22] Politicians who make individuals the subjects of the state are more likely to advocate a form of civic nationalism and to respect competing loyalties to state, ethnic group, religion, and occupational status. Since many of these loyalties are likely to extend beyond the country, these politicians are more likely to stress global interdependence and the need for international cooperation. Politicians who refer to the nation as an organic unit consisting of corporate, functional groups are more likely to make an exclusive claim to individuals' identity. They are more likely to favor authoritarian policies at home and emphasize the distinction between "us" and "them" both inside and outside the state's boundaries. They are more likely to see the outside world as threatening.

The organization of friends/enemies and equals/subordinates depends as well upon how politicians situate their polity within larger divisions. Divisions may be based on religion, culture, or ethnicity (the "clash of civilizations");[23] domestic organization (the alliance of "fraternal" socialist countries, the "free world"); or geographical location. Although most politicians give priority to the immediate interests of their own polity, supranational communities frequently are indicators of where politicians seek allies in the international system and where they expect conflict. Moreover, the principles that politicians use to demarcate these larger groups and the ones they use to demarcate the citizenry of the state frequently overlap and reinforce each other.

The most pervasive discourses defining Russia's collective identity center on the east-west and north-south geographical axes. These discourses borrow heavily from global understandings of these terms, but they are loaded as well with other, more specific meanings gleaned from Russian history. Russian elites have long been obsessed about their relation to the West, reflecting in part the country's persistent geopolitical dilemma as a latecomer into the European state system competing with more economically advanced countries in Western and Central Europe.[24] The language they use represents the West as synonymous with rationalism, materialism, individualism, and empiricism, and Eastern culture as emphasizing intuition, spirituality, and collectivism combined with an experiential epistemological tradition.[25] In the Russian empire, however, this dualism between East and West also overlapped and reinforced a rigid class hierarchy: This discourse identified the aristocracy with the practices of the West and identified the peasantry as the custodians of authentically Russian practices.[26]

The East-West discourse overlaps with discussions about Russia's position on the north-south axis. The North represents the richer, more powerful, largely white countries of Europe, North America, and Oceania, whereas the South tends to be associated with weaker, poorer, and nonwhite countries everywhere else. The Russian foreign policy elite locates Russia in the North, as a great power, but fears that the country's economic and political decline will relegate it to a status similar to the countries of the South. In Russia the discourses of East-West and North-South intersect in a singular configuration, however. Slavophiles often depict Russian civilization as culturally and racially closer to Asia than the other imperialist powers. One Russian colonel in Central Asia, for example, wrote in 1870: "We are not Englishmen who in India do their utmost to avoid mingling with the natives. . . . Our strength on the contrary lies in the fact that up to the present time we have assimilated subject races, mingling affably with them."[27]

National Identity in Modern Russia

To understand how internal and external pressures converge upon the politics of national identity in Russia, I examine how liberal, statist, and extremist images of Russian identity served to organize politicians' preferences for domestic and international order.

The Liberals

The fundamental line guiding Russian foreign policy during the first year of the Russian Federation is generally associated with the liberals. The principle advocates of this line were officials of the Foreign Ministry and the Finance Ministry within the government, particularly Foreign Minister Andrei Kozyrev and then Prime Minister Yegor Gaidar, as well as the growing class of entrepreneurs, the "free" trade unions, and a large portion of the intellectual and journalistic elites. The most visible proponents of this line at present include the supporters of the party Russia's Choice.

The liberals organized their image of Russia's identity around the claim to a shared identity with the United States and the countries of Western Europe. They believed that Russia should return to the "civilized community of nations," build liberal institutions at home, and act as a "normal" power in the international arena. To establish this identity, they favored accommodating the demands of the United States and Western Europe. During his first year in office, Yeltsin accepted arms agreements with the West that most Russians believed to give a one-sided advantage to NATO, and he frequently supported, albeit reluctantly, Western positions on Yugoslavia and Iraq in the United Nations.

The underlying motives for their preferences are complex. The principled opposition to Yeltsin's attack of Chechnya indicated that many sincerely subscribe to liberalism's ethical claims, yet there is no doubt that many liberals clearly hoped that their rhetoric would gain them access to the efficiency, wealth, and power associated with the liberal states of the North and West. To frame these claims within consensual images of Russia's identity, for example, the liberals presented integration with the West as the surest route to preserving Russia's great-power status. Some even intimated that the West could confer great-power status on Russia simply by including it into such international institutions as the G-7 or granting it a special status in NATO. In July 1993, for example, Yeltsin's press secretary, Vyacheslav Kostikov, remarked that the Western countries should "recognize that Russia is already not a Communist country, but a state having the main characteristics of a democracy with a market economy" and added that "the logic of Russia's democratic, political and economic development brings all closer to an understanding that the big eight should become a reality sooner or later."[28] In addition to recognition, many advocates of the liberal line hoped their rhetoric and conduct would gain them access to more tangible resources, either directly in the form of foreign aid, foreign investment, and foundation grants or indirectly through the marketplace. By emphasizing Russian's shared destiny with the West, the liberals also hoped to justify their receipt of such resources as enhancing Russia's interest.

Liberals were far more willing than others to accept the truncated territory of the Russian Republic sanctioned by the international community and to recognize the sovereignty of the other republics. They complemented this image of Russia's territorial boundaries with support for a civic nationalist state that conferred equal rights on each individual regardless of ethnicity.[29] In defining Russia's boundaries in this way, the liberals clearly hoped to establish Russia in Western eyes as a "responsible" member of the international community, but they also reflected the liberals' domestic preferences for a Western-style democracy.

Complementing their preferences for a civic nationalist order, the liberals' programs in domestic and foreign policy stressed the individual rather than the group. Gaidar's emphasis on free prices, privatization, and a stable currency all intended to protect the individual property holder in relation to state institutions. Their liberal vision of world politics, moreover, presented the international system as an interdependent world where individuals held competing identities that frequently cut across or transcended state boundaries. Consequently, their foreign policy was far more likely to emphasize international norms of individual human rights than that of their competitors.

The similarities between the liberals' assumptions about the social organization at home and their interpretation of world politics were striking. Paralleling their image of the individual as a self-contained, rational unit in the domestic economy, they also regarded states as unitary, self-contained units in the international arena. Kozyrev expressed no interest in relinquishing Russian sovereignty: "Universal democratic values do not mean general unification and the loss of national specificity."[30] But at the same time, he argued that Russia should reject all claims to a special identity and become a "normal great power." In particular, the liberals distinguished between "ideological" interests in foreign policy and the rational pursuit of some objective, utilitarian national interest. The liberals argued that differences between reasonable individuals can be mediated through the institutions and laws of the state whereas the differences between governments can be mediated through such formal international institutions as the OSCE and the United Nations.[31]

Despite these affirmations of good liberal principles, however, the liberals' rhetoric contained an important tension between their protestations of individual sovereignty and their overriding interest in locating Russia as a great power. Kozyrev maintained that Russia should return "to that natural milieu where Russia ought to be by rights . . . even geographically Russia appears . . . as the one still unfulfilled link in the democratic profile of the northern hemisphere."[32] Their perception of threat reflected this assertion of Northern identity. The liberals regarded Russia's surroundings as relatively benign and when they did speak of threats to Russia's security they fixed upon regional conflicts in the South, particularly within the new states of Eurasia, and the dangers they presented to the stability in the North.[33]

The liberals' embrace of hierarchy clothed in the rhetoric of equality could also be seen in their attitudes toward the "near abroad." Despite recognizing the sovereignty of these new states in Eurasia, the liberals did not relinquish all claims of influence within the territory of the former Soviet Union. They stayed within the constraints of the domestic consensus in accepting limited responsibility for the fate of Russian speakers in the former Soviet states. This stance enhanced the Russian state's identification as the guardian of a Russian nation defined by culture and rendered the liberal balancing act between the *russkoe* and *rossiiskoe* identities difficult to sustain. To reconcile these objectives with their image of Russia as a "normal" country respecting the sovereign rights of others, the liberals hoped to reassert their influence through institutional channels sanctioned by the West. They appealed to international organizations such as the UN and the Conference on Security and Cooperation in Europe (CSCE) to protect Russian speakers in accordance with international norms on minority rights, and they asked these institutions to recognize Russia's unique capacity to act as a stabilizing power in Eurasia.[34]

The Statists

Statists presented a program relying heavily upon the practices found among the institutions Stalin created during the 1930s to strengthen the industrial power of the Soviet state and defend it from external attack. The most visible proponents of statism were the enterprise managers and official trade union officials in large industrial enterprises, particularly in the defense industries, but they also could be found among the remnants of Soviet-era institutions ranging from the forces of the military to the Women's Councils.[35] They include a diverse group of officials ranging from more liberal *demokraty-derzhava* (democrats who emphasize Russia as a great power) such as Sergei Stankevich, Viktor Chernomyrdin, and Vladimir Lukin, who favored market reforms and extensive cooperation with the West short of integration, to more conservative statists such as Aleksandr Rutskoi, Nikolai Travkin, Yury Skokov, and Oleg Lobov, who hoped to slow down market reforms while maintaining Russia's status as a superpower balancing the United States.[36] The variation between these groups depended in large part on their willingness or ability to draw resources from the international economy as well as from the state. Representatives of the oil industry such as Chernomyrdin tended to accept market reforms more frequently than the managers of economic enterprises and military structures that had little prospect of surviving the rigors of the market. But the statists of all stripes shared a preference for greater state intervention in the domestic economy to shore up industrial production and to preserve Russia's status as a Eurasian great power distinct and independent from the West.

Not surprisingly, the boundaries that the statists drew around the Russian citizenry differed substantially from the boundaries drawn by the liberals. In general, the statists' closer attachment to the practices of the Soviet regime coincided with a nostalgia for Soviet borders, particularly among the conservatives. Most statists acknowledged in early 1992 that the forcible restoration of Soviet boundaries was out of the question, but they demanded that Russia assert its military and economic power over the new republics more aggressively.[37] They tended to advocate a variant of sociocultural nationalism that privileged the Russian population, even though they sometimes disagreed whether to characterize this social identity as Russian or Soviet. This image of Russia's boundaries clearly influenced their preferences for policy toward the near abroad. The assertion of Russia's sociocultural identity led them to assert the Russian state's special obligation to Russian speakers sharing that identity in the new republics and to argue that military measures to protect Russian speakers in those territories would not constitute illegal intervention.[38]

The statists portrayed the polity as a more or less organic whole. Although they accepted that there was no alternative to a market economy in the modern world, they criticized Gaidar's single-minded reliance on the market as the engine to reform. The marketplace, they argued, would pit "every man for himself" and cause a layering within the Russian polity between the rich and the poor.[39] They found the entrepreneurial activities of small business people particularly suspect. Chernomyrdin, for example, disparaged the "shopkeepers" [*lavochniki*] populating the kiosks in Moscow: "I am for . . . a genuine market, but not for a bazaar."[40] They sought to subsidize state enterprises, make their production more readily available to the state, and mitigate the social disruption of economic transition by keeping unemployment and inflation down.[41]

Identification of industrial production as a function vital to the national destiny remains incomprehensible without understanding as well the statists' conception of Russia's international role. Like the liberals, the statists drew upon transnationally recognized representations of international politics to define what it meant to be a great power in a way that would reinforce their conception of Russian national identity. However, the statists, because of their idea of a unique, organic Russian identity, envisioned the nation-state as the natural, ethical unit of international politics. In many respects, therefore, they interpreted the processes of international politicians much along the line of more traditional realists such as Hans Morgenthau.[42] Like these authors, the statists not only prescribed the mutual practice of realpolitik among states as a natural outgrowth of the international system, but they also invested it with moral worth as the only way to preserve distinct national identities. Given this image of international politics, preserving domestic industries represented the best way to preserve Russia's international role. Rutskoi, in particular, argued that "as long as wars go on in the world, as long as weapons are modernized, we also cannot forget that our Fatherland must have profound and considered conceptions of foreign policy and conceptions of defense policy."[43]

This image of a realist international system led statists to criticize the Yeltsin government's early accommodations to Western demands as damaging Russia's prestige as a world power.[44] They opposed efforts to integrate Russia into Western institutions: The West, they argued, would use such institutions to exploit Russia's weakness and limit Russian sovereignty.[45] The realist image of international relations also served to justify Russian claims to dominance over the new Eurasian states lest the West take advantage of a political vacuum.[46] Arkady Volskiy criticized proposals for international involvement in Nagorno-Karabakh with the warning that "territory doesn't remain empty. The sphere of influence that a temporarily weakened power leaves others will necessarily want to occupy."[47]

Yet the analogy with realism does not indicate how much the statists' differentiation from the West relied on the traditional distinctions between East and West found in Russian history. The statists defined the Russian polity as a unique cultural identity ordained to perform an international mission as mediator between the northern industrialized countries of Western Europe and the Islamic and Asian countries to the east and to the south. According to Stankevich, Russia could not be the "normal" power seeking its rational self-interests envisioned by the liberals: "A policy founded entirely on interests is quite indefensible and in Russia . . . simply fatal. Besides interests, Russia needs a mission."[48] Asserting Russia's unique mission bolstered the statists' arguments against radical reform by presenting the liberals' uncritical acceptance of Western ways and their enthusiasm for foreign models as an abdication of Russia's unique cultural and geopolitical status.[49]

The image of Russia's unique mission also bolstered the statists' claims to dominate the territory of the former Soviet Union. Like the Slavophiles of the nineteenth century, the statists argued that Russia's unique status made it a natural ally of weaker peoples trying to protect themselves from the predations of the West. Different elements of the statist tendency envisioned this role quite differently. Stankevich, for example, argued that "Russia's mission in the world . . . is to initiate and support a multilateral dialogue of cultures, civilizations and states." Russia, in his view, is "singularly capable of a harmonic unification of many different origins, of an historical symphony."[50] The more nationalist view, however, proposed that Russia build alliances among the countries of the East and South as a counterweight to Western power. Both variants present Russia as a paternalistic protector of weaker countries against Western cultural and political domination. Stankevich argued that Russia should be a "power of mercy, tolerant and open within limits defined by law and good will, but terrible beyond those limits."[51]

Although the statists relied on discourses from the nineteenth century to define their image of Russia's international role, one can see several points of similarity with Soviet institutional practices from which they derive their material support. Both the statists and the Soviet regime presented their respective polities as unitary entities requiring the protection of a strong centralized state, envisioned the state as a great power equal to the West in prestige, and sought to preserve the state's international stature through an emphasis on defense production at home and alliances with weaker countries of the South and East. Despite disintegration of the Party and the symbols of Marxism-Leninism, their ideas did not disappear from the Russian foreign policy debate completely.

The Left-Right Coalition

A third voice in the domestic debate consisted of the ultranationalists and the diehard Communists. The most notable representatives of these groups include Vladimir Zhirinovsky and his Liberal Democratic Party, the Russian Communist Party, and the Agrarian Party. These groups, despite their obvious differences, vehemently opposed market reforms, supported a highly centralized and authoritarian state that would restore social order, and sought to restore the Russian empire in the face of a conspiratorial alliance between Russia's external and internal enemies. Until the elections of December 1993, many observers of Russian politics regarded these groups as fading relics of the Communist era that enjoyed little popular support beyond an aging population of pensioners. During the elections, however, these parties received 43 percent of the vote, demonstrating that the popular appeal of these parties was broader and that the institutions of the old regime were much hardier than most analysts realized.[52]

The extremists' image of the Russian polity converged with the statist image in several respects. Extremists envisioned the legitimate boundaries of the Russian state extending at least to the boundaries of the former Soviet Union. They shared the statists' rejection of liberalism and its notion of universal values and the sovereignty of the individual, embracing instead an image of the Russian polity as an organic unit charged with a common mission. The nationalists, in particular, have defined the Russian nation's unique, organic quality in terms of *sobornost'*, "a mystical notion whereby the assembled people (sobor) are united by an apprehension of religious truth that molds them into a community united in harmonious variety."[53] Sergei Kurginyan explicitly linked this image with a vision of global order: "For centuries Russian philosophical thought has opposed the extreme individualism that underlies the current notion of 'human rights' and the extreme rationalism that underlies the notion of 'universal human values.' What it has offered as an alternative is not nationalism, not provincial isolationism, but a different idea and a different plan for building global civilization."[54]

The extremists differ from the statists in four ways. First, the extremists not only identified the Russian polity as separate and distinct from other entities, but they also insisted more strenuously on Russia's superiority. Second, the extremists generally insisted on restoring sovereignty over the physical boundaries of the Soviet Union rather than mere domination. Whereas the statists defined the polity in terms of a sociocultural identity, the extremist nationalists were much more likely to use more exclusive, hereditary characteristics such as Russian ethnicity or, on a global scale, race.[55]

Finally, the extremists perceived greater foreign threat than did the statists. Although they recognized that nuclear war with the West did not seem imminent, they also argued that the United States might initiate military hostilities with Russia in order to ensure access to natural resources or to secure its debts. Yury Slobodkin, a deputy in the Russian Congress before the 1993 elections, argued that "if we don't recognize all the danger hanging above the country and its future, it is only a matter of time before we must fight for our freedom as American green berets come to us under the guise of 'defending American property and American citizens in Russia.'"[56]

For the extremists, the threat extended beyond the military into the moral and philosophical. Similar to the Stalinist image of capitalist encirclement, the extremists saw an ideological enemy committed to the destruction of the Russian state. Kurginyan has argued, "the New World Order . . . cannot be carried out unless these [liberal] principles are regarded as absolute truths. And preserving their status as unchallenged, absolute truths requires, in turn, that the only serious competitor to these ideas, Russia, be removed from the world arena."[57] The extremists also shared with Stalinism an enthusiasm for conspiracy theories. To the extent that they saw the Russian polity as an organic unit marked by concrete boundaries called to perform a glorious mission, they attributed all failures to achieve that mission to a conspiracy of outside forces, usually the United States and the "Zionists."[58]

The extremists' prescriptions for foreign policy are predictable. Although some called for an isolationist policy to demonstrate Russia's uniqueness and protect it from contamination, most have demanded that the state actively demonstrate Russia's superiority by asserting its status as a great power. They have been much more likely than the statists to support using the military to regain the territory of the former Soviet republics. They have ardently supported the Serbs in the civil war in Yugoslavia, regarding the United Nations' support of the Bosnians as part of the West's conspiracy against the Slavic peoples. Finally, whereas the statists combined competition with the United States and Western Europe with pragmatic recognition that Russia must also deal with these powers and even emulate some of their ways, the extremists advocated a renewal of Cold War tensions.

Becoming Russia

This section examines the fates of these competing images of national identity during the first two years of the Russian Federation, concentrating on the declining influence of the liberal vision and the narrowing of the debate around something approaching the statist vision. In accordance with the above discussion of the politics of national identity, this analysis first examines how deeply these images are embedded in existing institutional practices in the Russian Federation and then observes whether interaction with the international environment acted to reinforce or subvert these practices.

In the first months after the Soviet Union collapsed, the liberals clearly dominated the foreign policy debate. Under Soviet rule, the affluent, powerful, capitalist United States had loomed large in official propaganda as an ideological antipode and as an object of emulation. When the Soviet model became discredited, therefore, it was quite natural for members of the elite, and not only the elite, to express their alienation from the old regime by embracing the ideals and principles of its most visible and more successful alternative. Moreover, many people, noting Russia's abundant natural resources, its educated, skilled population, and its historical role in world politics, assumed that Russia need only adopt the more efficient ways of its capitalist competitor to attain the wealth and status appropriate to its natural role.[59] This feeling reinforced an expectation that the United States, after its long competition with the Soviet Union, would recognize Russia's status as the successor to that great power and offer substantial assistance to Russia during its transition to capitalism. None of these expectations were realized.

Despite the popularity of the liberal vision, its emphasis on international interdependence and the individual pursuit of wealth bore little relation to the practices of Russian economic and governmental institutions or to the realities of most Russians' lives organized around those institutions. The liberals could continue to legitimate the introduction of such "foreign" practices only to the extent that they realized their vision of Russia as a prosperous great power. Instead, though the incomplete introduction of market practices did succeed in disrupting the patterns of daily life that informed the individual identities of Russians under the Soviet regime, it benefited only a relatively small segment of the population that either had access to resources in demand in the global marketplace or could adapt to the informal rules of an unregulated market.

These success stories soon came to be regarded negatively as speculators, members of the old *nomenklatura,* or members of the mafia, and not without reason. The corruption, legal confusions, high taxes, and other attributes of Russia's incomplete transition rewarded individuals who channeled their most productive activities in ways that evaded state regulations and punished those who tried to remain within the bounds of sanctioned behavior.[60] As a result, the winners from reform became perceived as having departed from the norms of social behavior in

Russia, adding credence to the statists' and extremists' claims that Western practices were alien and contemptible to the Russian character. Liberal rhetoric that identified Western practices as "civilized" and excluded people who would not adapt to these practices did little to blunt these impressions.

The liberal attempt to overturn the entrenched practices in Russia could succeed only if the liberals could mobilize sufficient resources to reorganize Russian lives in accordance to their own vision. They did not shy from using the coercive mechanisms of the state: Given the legacy of state domination over society, they may have had little choice. Soon after Yeltsin's successful assault on the Russian White House in October 1993, for example, his adviser Kostikov argued that "democracy has to be strict and professional" and maintained that "all the manifestations of nationalism and political localism . . . must be resolutely nipped in the bud."[61] Needless to say, recourse to the state presented the liberals with an intractable dilemma. Statements like this directly contradicted the liberals' expressed intention to create a civil society and lent credence to assertions from people like Vladimir Zarikhin, of the statist People's Party of Free Russia, that Russian liberalism was "a classic variant of . . . destroying everything for the sake of creating a new social order, a purely bolshevik thing which is not limited to communist ideology."[62] Since the institutions of the state are organized around corporate, functional actors, any attempt to use them to implement the liberal vision would undermine the liberal viewpoint. Yeltsin's most loyal supporters were found among individual, private, and unorganized businessmen. The organized economic interests that had access to state institutions tended to oppose him.[63] Yeltsin ultimately won the confrontation in October 1993 only with the reluctant support of the military.

The liberals' inability to mobilize the necessary resources from within Russian boundaries increased their dependence on the West. Although the United States and Europe clearly could not provide the credits and investment sufficient to reorganize Russian institutions, they might have buttressed the credibility of the liberal vision with symbolic gestures. Symbolic evidence came too slowly to have an impact: The importance of the CSCE in relation to the more exclusive NATO declined visibly, and Yeltsin gained no nominal standing within an expanded G-8 until July 1994. Meanwhile, as early as April 1992, efforts by the United States to prevent the sale of Russian missile engines to India alienated powerful members of the military-industrial complex from the Yeltsin government and prompted more nationalist forces to contend that the United States continued to be guided by the interests of its own military complex.

Expectations are key. Suzanne Crow notes that the Western governments in fact did provide substantial aid to Russia and offered key concessions to the Russian government on arms control and on Yugoslavia.[64] But since these concessions did not meet the inflated expectations for Western help excited by the liberals, Western actions aroused suspicion regarding Western intentions toward Russia, adding to the growing dissatisfaction with market reforms. Russian efforts to assert its interests as a great power damaged its efforts to gain recognition as a "normal" power in the West, whereas cooperative efforts aimed at allaying Western suspicions reinforced domestic claims that the liberals were abdicating its international position. As Andranik Migranyan notes: "For too long we have kept the West under the impression that a positive foreign policy in the case of the Soviet Union, and then Russia, is when we go along with everything the West does. That is why any sign of independence in Russia's foreign policy catches the West unawares and seems abnormal."[65]

These setbacks to the liberals' foreign policy, though probably not decisive, undoubtedly reinforced domestic opposition to the liberal program and accelerated the government's retreat from the foreign policy vision it had articulated in the early part of 1992. Yeltsin began as early as summer 1992 to insist that Russia had unique needs and a unique history that international financial institutions ought to respect when negotiating agreements. In October, Kozyrev proclaimed that the "romantic period" in relations with the West had ended.[66] As early as January 25, 1993, moreover, Yeltsin criticized the United States for its tendency "to dictate its own terms" in its policies toward Iraq and Yugoslavia and declared that Russian foreign policy toward the West "had to be balanced. After all, we are a Eurasian state."[67]

The widest gap between Russia's interactions with the international environment and the expectations aroused by the liberals occurred in the "near abroad." Instability on Russia's periphery and Russian military presence in the region reinforced statist and extremist arguments that Russia needed to exercise its prerogatives as a great power and impose a paternalistic peace over its sphere of influence. The liberals tried to accommodate such pressures within their vision of Russia by requesting special dispensation from international institutions for Russia to act as peacekeeper in the region. Western governments withheld such recognition on the grounds that it would sanction resurgent Russian imperialism. In doing so, the West nourished suspicions in Russia that it would never accept Russia as a great power. At the same time, however, the West did very little to prevent Russian involvement in Moldova, Tadzhikistan, Georgia, and elsewhere, reinforcing claims that Russia could assert this status unilaterally despite Western protests. Migranyan, for example, argues that the Foreign Ministry had opposed supporting the Russian-dominated Trans-Dniestr in Moldova on the basis that such a move would hurt relations with the West: "After the Western countries refrained from serious protests to Russia," Migranyan continued, "the Foreign Ministry's position began to change in the direction of unconditional defense of the Dniester republic."[68]

Perhaps the greatest difficulty facing the liberal government concerned the fate of Russian speakers in the new states of Eurasia. The liberals sought to balance advocacy of civic nationalism and willingness to accept responsibility for Russian speakers abroad by calling on the new states to observe internationally recognized standards of human rights. However, many Russians had inflated notions of what "fair treatment" meant and expected the enactment of laws that local nationalist elites believed would perpetuate Russian speakers' privileged access to power. Many of the new governments enacted language and citizenship policies that disproportionately benefited the sociocultural and even the ethnic identities of their nationalities, arousing the resentment and resistance of Russian speakers in those territories. Liberals tried to resolve these dilemmas by appealing to international institutions to enforce the rights of Russian speakers in the new states, but these institutions failed to meet the liberals' expectations. By February 1994, Yeltsin declared that Russia would protect Russian speakers in Eurasia "not by words, but by deeds."[69]

The most visible mark of liberalism's declining fortunes could be seen in its defeat in the elections of December 1993 at the hands of the extremists, particularly Zhirinovsky's Liberal Democratic Party. Analyses of the election concluded that Zhirinovsky received his strongest support from male middle-aged skilled workers in provincial cities dominated by heavy industrial plants and from younger male entrepreneurs in large urban centers who made their decision late in the election.[70] However, several factors suggest that he and ultranationalists like him cannot maintain their political strength over the long term. The Liberal Democrats have no concentrated institutional support they can rely upon to mobilize support between elections. Moreover, as Mary Douglas argues, groups that see the world in conspiratorial terms tend to find conspiracies within their midst as evidence for their fears.[71] As a result, Zhirinovsky and his Liberal Democrats have found it difficult to sustain the unified action necessary to make a difference in policy. The ultranationalists are unlikely to mobilize the necessary resources to enact their image of a restored Russian empire and can expect little international recognition or assistance toward that goal.

The Communist and Agrarian parties, which received approximately 20 percent of the vote in the 1993 elections, have fared much better. Unlike the nationalists, the Communist vision of the Russian polity had relied upon the support of an established network of Communist Party members as well as upon the institutional resources of the collective farms in sustaining their position between elections.[72] Like the ultranationalists, however, the Communists cannot expect to find much material or ideological support from the international environment, and they also do not have the resources at their disposal either to restore the Soviet Union to its former borders or to sustain an antagonistic policy toward the West. Therefore, although the Communists will remain an important force in Russian politics, one might expect them to follow the path of their counterparts in Poland and move their domestic and foreign policy rhetoric closer to the statists' program.

The most interesting development in Russian politics since the elections has been the Yeltsin government's general adherence to the statist program in domestic and foreign policy, despite the statists' miserable showing in the December elections. Although this turn of events emerged partly as a result of a compromise within the elite, it reflects more profoundly how institutions informed by statist assumptions still dominate Russian decisionmaking. They command so many social resources that all politicians must work through them in implementing their political program and so must adapt that program to the corporatist practices embedded in those institutions. Moreover, the advocates of statist policies who control these institutions (e.g., the enterprise managers, the military, and the traditional trade unions) are likely to maintain their privileged access to decisionmaking processes despite that they clearly do not have the support of the public. Russia's initial interactions with its international environment have tended to confirm the statists' image of a great power that can and must assert its influence over the new states of Eurasia while maintaining a cordial but cautious and essentially competitive relation with the West.

Conclusion

How has the practice of foreign policy helped Russia become Russia? The constructivist agenda centers on the possibilities of change: The practices of international politics depend upon socially constructed accounts of reality for their reproduction, so a critical examination of these accounts can open the space for political change. Yet the movement of Russian foreign policy back toward one informed by institutional forms and practices harking back to the Soviet and even imperial period—a movement reinforced by Western responses to Russian behavior—indicates how difficult it is to translate such critical thinking into practice.

However, the apparent consensus on Russia's assertive foreign policy remains fragile and may not endure over the next decade. The statists' control over Russian institutions still has not translated into popular support. Their vision of Russia's international role—Russia's initial interactions with the external environment notwithstanding—remains rooted in the national industrial practices of the late nineteenth and early twentieth centuries and seems oddly anachronistic in a world of globalized production. Growing interenterprise debt in the industries supported by the statists, Russia's national debt, and the strictures of the International Monetary Fund also indicate that the institutions and practices informing the statist vision cannot be sustained over the long run. Meanwhile, the liberals, despite their decline, are unlikely to go away. Their image of Russian national identity provides greater access to resources generated by such international organizations as the European Union, the International Monetary Fund, and the World Bank. As long as the Russian government depends upon these resources, Russian foreign policy will not completely disregard the demands of these organizations.

In sum, the contest over Russian national identity remains divided between the liberals, who despite their narrow domestic support can rely on resources and recognition from powerful international institutions, and the statists, who despite their ability to work with the existing institutions of the state are not likely to withstand the primarily economic pressures placed upon these institutions by the international economic system. This leaves three potential outcomes for Russia's future. In the least likely, and least desirable, outcome, the conservative statists ①　would prevail despite their inability to draw resources from the international system. Such an outcome would establish an authoritarian form of government in Russia that defines its international role in opposition to existing international institutions dominated by the United States and Western Europe. In a second, more ②　likely outcome, Russia would become a divided society in which an elite stratum conforming to international expectations and dependent on resources from the international environment would dominate a society organized along traditional lines and therefore excluded from the benefits of the international economy. Such an outcome would suit the needs of Western policymakers, at least in the short run, but would remain unstable. Finally, and most desirable, a synthesis could be ③　devised, perhaps under the leadership of the *demokraty-derzhava,* that would maintain a connection between the corporate structures of the Russian state and the demands of the international economy. Such a regime would continue to assert Russia's distinctiveness toward the West and its dominance over the new states of Eurasia but at the same time would preserve some elements of pluralism in domestic politics and keep the lines of communication open to the West.

What can the United States and other Western countries do to influence this debate? As the U.S. response to the Russian invasion in Chechnya suggests, the consensual Russian claim to great-power status presents Western decisionmakers with a dilemma. If the United States and other countries ignore this claim and attempt to limit Russia's influence in Eurasia, they risk discrediting even further the liberal vision of Russia's destiny as a Western country and reinforcing the advocates of a more exclusive, more chauvinist nationalism. Yet if they accommodate Russian leaders and ignore their efforts to reestablish dominance over Eurasia, they will not only doom these states to dependence on Moscow but may also encourage the nationalists to pursue this goal even further while alienating the principled liberal advocates who looked to the West for support in opposing such a policy. Furthermore, as long as state institutions in Russia have such a dominant position in domestic society, this dilemma is unlikely to go away and U.S. decisionmakers will have to negotiate as best they can. The policy that would do the most good while minimizing risk would encourage transnational ties, which would provide those social actors autonomous from the state enough resources to make their demands more forcefully.

Notes

1. Sergei Stankevich, "Derzhava v poiskakh sebya," *Nezavisimaya gazeta,* 28 March 1992.

2. The formulation of the relation between structure and agent found here is drawn largely on the structuration theory of Anthony Giddens, *Central Problems in Social Theory* (Berkeley: University of California Press, 1979). In particular, I draw on the appli-

cations of Giddens's work to international relations found in Alexander Wendt, "The Agent-Structure Problem in International Relations Theory," *International Organization* 41 (Summer 1987): 335–370.

3. Suzanne Crow, "Russia Asserts Its Strategic Agenda," *Radio Free Europe/Radio Liberty (RFE/RL) Research Report* 2 (17 December 1993): 1–8.

4. Richard Ashley, "Foreign Policy as Political Performance," *International Studies Notes* 13 (1987): 51–54.

5. In addition to my own research, my account of these three tendencies borrow heavily from similar typologies presented by other authors, particularly Aleksei G. Arbatov, "Russia's Foreign Policy Alternatives," *International Security* 18 (Fall 1993): 5–43; Aleksei K. Pushkov, "Russia and America: The Honeymoon's Over," *Foreign Policy* 93 (Winter 1993/94): 76–90; Douglas W. Blum, "Disintegration and Russian Foreign Policy," in *Russia's Future: Consolidation or Disintegration?* ed. Douglas W. Blum (Boulder: Westview Press, 1994), pp. 127–146.

6. Oran R. Young, "International Regimes: Toward a New Theory of Institutions," *World Politics* 39 (October 1986): 104–122 (cited in Paul J. DiMaggio and Walter W. Powell, "Introduction," in *The New Institutionalism in Organizational Analysis,* ed. Walter W. Powell and Paul J. DiMaggio [Chicago: University of Chicago Press, 1991], p. 8).

7. On institutionalization and embeddedness, see Ronald L. Jepperson, "Institutions, Institutional Effects and Institutionalism," in *The New Institutionalism,* ed. Powell and DiMaggio, pp. 149–153; Stephen Krasner, "Sovereignty: An Institutional Perspective," in *The Elusive State: International and Comparative Perspectives,* ed. James Caporaso (Newbury Park, Calif.: Sage Publications, 1989), pp. 77–80.

8. Anthony Giddens, *The Nation-State and Violence: Volume Two of a Contemporary Critique of Historical Materialism* (Berkeley: University of California Press, 1987).

9. See particularly Roger Friedland and Robert R. Alford, "Bringing Society Back In: Symbols, Practices, and Institutional Contradictions," in *The New Institutionalism,* ed. Powell and DiMaggio, pp. 232–263.

10. See especially Peter Haas, "Do Regimes Matter? Epistemic Communities and Mediterranean Pollution Control," *International Organization* 43 (Summer 1989): 377–403; Kathryn Sikkink, "Human Rights, Issue-Networks and Sovereignty in Latin America," *International Organization* 47 (Summer 1993): 411–441.

11. This idea is adapted from the central argument in Thomas Risse-Kappen, "Ideas Do Not Float Freely: Transnational Coalitions, Domestic Structures, and the End of the Cold War," *International Organization* 48 (Spring 1994): 185–214. See also Matthew Evangelista's contribution to this volume, Chapter 8.

12. James Mayall, *Nationalism and International Society* (Cambridge: Cambridge University Press, 1990), chap. 1.

13. See James G. Richter, *Khrushchev's Double Bind: International Pressures and Domestic Coalition Politics* (Baltimore: Johns Hopkins University Press, 1994), esp. pp. 21–24.

14. See William Zimmerman, *Soviet Perspectives on International Relations, 1956–1967* (Princeton: Princeton University Press, 1969); Allen Lynch, *The Soviet Study of International Relations* (Cambridge: Cambridge University Press, 1987).

15. James Richter, "Perpetuating the Cold War: Domestic Sources of International Patterns of Behavior," *Political Science Quarterly* 107 (Summer 1992): 271–301.

16. Jack L. Snyder, "International Leverage on Soviet Domestic Change," *World Politics* 42 (October 1989): 1–30.

17. G. John Ikenberry and Charles A. Kupchan, "Socialization and Hegemonic Power," *International Organization* 44 (Summer 1990): 283–315.

18. This typology is adapted from Charles F. Furtado, Jr., "Nationalism and Foreign Policy in Ukraine," *Political Science Quarterly* 109 (Spring 1994): 81–104.

19. Stephen D. Shenfield, "Post-Soviet Russia in Search of Identity," in *Russia's Future,* ed. Blum, pp. 5–16.

20. See Roman Szporluk, "The Imperial Legacy and the Soviet Nationalities Problem," in *The Nationalities Factor in Soviet Politics and Society,* ed. Lubomyr Hajda and Mark Beissinger (Boulder: Westview Press, 1990), pp. 1–4.

21. Robert Baril, "The Impact of Racial Constructions in the United States on US Foreign Policy Towards Haiti" (senior thesis, Bates College, 1994).

22. For the impact of the construction of individual identity on domestic politics, see Ronald L. Jepperson and John W. Meyer, "The Public Order and the Construction of Formal Organizations," in *The New Institutionalism,* ed. Powell and DiMaggio, pp. 204–231.

23. Samuel P. Huntington, "The Clash of Civilizations?" *Foreign Affairs* 72 (Summer 1993): 22–50.

24. Liah Greenfeld, *Nationalism: Five Roads to Modernity* (Cambridge: Harvard University Press, 1992).

25. Contemporary examples of this dichotomy can be found in B. Grois, "Poisk russkoi natsional'noi identichnosti," *Voprosy filosofii,* no. 1 (January 1992): 52–60; Vadim Kortunov, "Istina v iskusstve: russkii mistitisizm v sisteme mirovozzrenii Vostoka i Zapada," *Scholarly Reports of the Russian Scientific Fund* (Moscow), no. 2 (1992). For evidence of a similar discourse in India, see Partha Chatterjee, *The Nation and Its Fragments* (Princeton: Princeton University Press, 1993).

26. Sidney Monas, "'Self' and 'Other' in Russian Literature," in *The Search for Self-Definition in Russian Literature,* ed. Ewa M. Thompson (Houston: Rice University Press, 1991).

27. Milan Hauner, *What Is Asia to Us?* (Boston: Unwin and Hyman, 1990), p. 43.

28. ITAR-TASS Report of 9 July 1993, cited in *FBIS-SOV-*93-131, pp. 5–6.

29. A relatively recent statement of this position can be found in Aleksei Arbatov, "Real Integration: With Whom and What Kind?" *Nezavisimaya gazeta,* 24 June 1994, cited in *Current Digest of the Post-Soviet Press* 46 (3 July 1994): 5–7.

30. Andrei Kozyrev, "Vystuplenie na praktickeskoi konferentsii 'Preobrazhennaya Rossiya v novom mire,'" Moscow State Institute of International Relations (MGIMO), 26–27 February 1992, pp. 2–3.

31. Steven Foye, "Yeltsin Interviewed by Army Newspaper," *RFE/RL Daily Report,* 23 February 1993.

32. A. Kozyrev, "Vystuplenie," p. 3.

33. Suzanne Crow, "Kozyrev on Maintaining Conquests," *RFE/RL Daily Report,* 8 October 1993.

34. On the liberal strategy toward Russian speakers in the near abroad, see Nikolai Rudensky, "Russian Minorities in the Newly Independent States," in *National Identity and Ethnicity in Russia and the New States of Eurasia,* ed. Roman Szporluk (Armonk: M. E. Sharpe, 1994), pp. 69–76. For the liberal's request for special status, see Suzanne Crow, "Russia Seeks Leadership in Regional Peacekeeping," *RFE/RL Research Report* 2 (9 April 1993): 28–32.

35. The support that the statist tendency found among the members of Russia's Women's Councils is based in part on interviews I conducted with members of the

Women's Council in Ivanovo-Vosnesensk on 20 June 1994, as well as on the positions taken by the political party, Women of Russia, as summarized in Wendy Slater, "Female Representation in Russian Politics," *RFE/RL Research Report* 3 (3 June 1994): 27–33.

36. Pushkov, "Russia and America," pp. 78–80.

37. Valentin Larionov, "Geostrategiya nas obyazyvaet," *Krasnaya zvezda,* 4 December 1992.

38. A. Rutskoi, "Osleplenie," *Rossiiskaya Gazeta,* 20 May 1992; also A. Rutskoi, "Rech' A. Rutskogo," *Rossiiskaya gazeta,* 8 April 1992; Sergei Stankevich, Radio Moscow World Service, 28 November 1992, in *FBIS-SOV*-92-230, 30 November 1992.

39. Nikolai Travkin, Speech at 26 November Meeting of the Russian Supreme Soviet, in *FBIS-SOV*-92-230, 30 November 1992, pp. 46, 47. See also A. Rutskoi, "Rech' A. Rutskogo," *Rossiiskaya gazeta,* 5 December 1992.

40. "Chernomyrdin prodolzhaet reformy," *Rossiiskie vesti,* 16 December 1992. The term "bazaar" in itself clearly indicates that Chernomyrdin did not consider such activity as properly Russian.

41. Rutskoi first outlined an economic plan in an article in *Pravda,* 8 February 1992. See also the economic program of the Civic Union announced in November, summarized in *FBIS-SOV*-92-229, 27 November 1992, p. 28; *FBIS-SOV*-92-230, 30 November 1992.

42. My interview, 3 November 1992, with Sergei M. Rogov, who played a leading role in the formulation of Civic Union's foreign policy program. Rogov explicitly described the Islamic world as a more or less unitary actor.

43. A. Rutskoi, "'Rech' A. Rutskogo," *Rossiiskaya gazeta,* 5 December 1992.

44. Larionov, "Geostrategiya nas obyazyvaet"; Keith Bush, "Chernomyrdin Sees a Western Plot," *RFE/RL Daily Report,* 20 August 1993.

45. Oleg Cherkovets, "A Meager 'Aid' Package," *Federatsiya* 77 (13 July 1993), cited in *FBIS-SOV*-93-132, July 1993, p. 9.

46. Larionov, "Geostrategiya nas obyazyvaet."

47. Arkady Volskiy, "Karabakh, My Anguish (Bloodshed in Armenia and Azerbaijan)," *Moscow News* 40 (4 October 1992): 3.

48. Stankevich, "Derzhava v poiskakh sebya."

49. See speech by Travkin cited in *FBIS-SOV*-92-230, 30 November 1992, p. 47.

50. Stankevich, "Derzhava v poiskakh sebya," p. 4. See also the writings of Dmitry Likhachev, as summarized in Dmitry Shlapentokh, "Russian Nationalism and Soviet Intellectuals Under Gorbachev," in *The Search for Self-Definition,* ed. Thompson, pp. 120–137.

51. Stankevich, "Derzhava v poiskakh sebya."

52. Vera Tolz, "Russia's Parliamentary Elections: What Happened and Why," *RFE/RL Research Report* 3 (14 January 1994): 1–9; Darrell Slider, Vladimir Gimpelson, and Sergei Chugrov, "Political Tendencies in Russia's Regions," *Slavic Review* 53 (Fall 1994): 711–732.

53. Michael Urban, "The Politics of Identity in Russia's Postcommunist Transition: The Nation Against Itself," *Slavic Review* 53 (Fall 1994): 733–765.

54. Sergei Kurginyan, "Counteraction," *Nash sovremmenik,* no. 7 (July 1992): 3–15 (cited in "Kurginyan Outlines Political 'Counteraction,'" *Current Digest of the Post-Soviet Press* 44 [14 November 1992]: 13). See also Sergei Kurginyan, "Esli khotim zhit'" *Den',* no. 1 (January 1993).

55. The efforts of contemporary Communists to justify a specifically nationalist version of communism, as well as an excellent account of Communist positions generally, can be

found in Wendy Slater, "The Russian Communist Party Today," *RFE/RL Research Report* 31 (12 August 1994): 1–6.

56. Yury Slobodkin, "Ne nuzhna burzhuaznaya konstitutsiya," *Narodnaya pravda,* October 1992.

57. Kurginyan, "Counteraction," p. 13.

58. Moscow Interfax, 24 November 1992, in *FBIS-SOV*-92-238, 25 November 1992. See also the speech by Aman-Geldy Tuleev, *Rossiiskaia gazeta,* 11 April 1992. Other examples can be found in almost every issue of the newspaper organ of the National Salvation Front, *Den'.* I would also like to acknowledge Tatyanna Shakleina, "American-Russian Relations: Confrontation or Cooperation: A Review of the Nationalist Press" (unpublished manuscript, Moscow, October 1992).

59. Pushkov, "Russia and America."

60. See Vladimir Gimpelson, "Russia's New Independent Entrepreneurs," *RFE/RL Research Report* 2 (10 September 1993): 44–48.

61. Kostikov in *Rossiiskie vesti,* cited in Russian Press Digest, Russica Information, Inc., 16 October 1993.

62. Urban, "The Politics of Identity," p. 735.

63. "Business Circles Propose Simultaneous Early Elections," Russian Press Digest, Russica Information, Inc., 25 September 1993.

64. Suzanne Crow, "Why Has Russian Foreign Policy Changed?" *RFE/RL Research Report* 3 (6 May 1994): 1–6.

65. Pushkov, "Russia and America," p. 87.

66. Andrei Kozyrev, "Partnership with the West: A Test of Strength," *Moscow News,* no. 43 (25 October 25–1 November 1992): 3.

67. Fred Kaplan, "Yeltsin Hits US Policy on Iraq, Yugoslavia," *Boston Globe,* 26 January 1993. See also Suzanne Crow, "Yeltsin Wants Partnership with Asia," *RFE/RL Daily Report,* no. 20 (1 February 1993).

68. *Nezavisimaya gazeta,* 12 January 1994, cited in Suzanne Crow, "Why Has Russian Foreign Policy Changed?" p. 6.

69. Yeltsin speech before the Federation Council, 24 February 1994, cited in Suzanne Crow, "Why Has Russian Foreign Policy Changed?" p. 3.

70. Elizabeth Teague, "Who Voted for Zhirinovsky," *RFE/RL Research Report* 3 (14 January 1994): 4–5.

71. Mary Douglas, *How Institutions Think* (Syracuse, N.Y.: Syracuse University Press, 1986), pp. 39–40.

72. Slater, "The Russian Communist Party Today."

CHAPTER 5

The Foreign Policy Preferences of Russian Defense Industrialists: Integration or Isolation?

Kimberly Marten Zisk

Russia is faced with a major choice in the direction of its future foreign policy. Should it strive to belong to the group of Western developed states, integrating its economy into the trading and investment system dominated by wealthy countries and tying its security interests to those of Western Europe? Or should it strike out on its own as an independent great power, refusing to allow Western concerns to influence its policy choices and seeking to reestablish the clout the Soviet Union once held as a military powerhouse? Regardless of which foreign policy question Russia is considering at the moment, from the activities of its military troops in the "near abroad" to the sale of advanced weaponry to Iran, the questions of how these actions will affect Russia's relationship with the West, and of whether the West matters, are repeatedly raised in political debates in the parliament and the press.[1] Russia has throughout history been split philosophically between Westernizers and Slavophiles, and the decline of the Soviet Union was directly connected to Cold War competition against the West. Therefore, Russian political figures tend to align themselves on one side or the other of a Manichean view of the Western world.

Clearly, it is in the interests of the West to be able at least to predict which vision will prevail and at best to determine whether there is anything the outside world can do to convince Russia to choose a Westward-leaning path. This chapter is an attempt to contribute to both of those goals by examining the foreign policy preferences of a key set of Russian domestic actors: managers of the remnants of Soviet defense industrial firms.

The study of Russian defense industrialists is important from the standpoints of both policy and theory. In policy terms, the defense industry may turn out to be the keystone of whatever political edifice is built in Russia today. This industry must of course compete with other economic actors for access to the policy agenda. The preferences of its managers alone will not determine Russian actions. Yet this industry has been the source of significant tension and pressure in Russian politics. Defense industrial lobbying over the state budget and subsidies contributed to the violent rift between the Supreme Soviet and the Russian government in 1993[2] and to President Boris Yeltsin's election-eve promises of additional subsidies to the defense industry in November of that same year.[3] Angry political battles on those issues continue.[4] The number of Russians employed by the defense industry is quite large, especially in many major cities (including the three largest—Moscow, St. Petersburg, and Nizhni Novgorod, where the percentage of the population involved in defense production at one time ranged from 40 to 75 percent). The views of defense industrial workers thus matter in both regional and national elections, and protest activity organized within the industry could engender general destabilization in certain key regions. In fact, Prime Minister Viktor Chernomyrdin, who has become one of the harshest critics of defense industrial managers, sees their lobbying efforts as directly tied to the ongoing power battle between regions and the central government.[5] The preferences of defense industrial managers thus could play a significant role in Russia's decision for or against Western integration.

From a theoretical standpoint, the Russian defense industry is interesting because it is a newcomer to the developed world market, and its managers thus lack well-developed expectations about asset value. This makes the international economic interests of the sector both opaque and potentially malleable. Although some pundits have portrayed the sector as a whole as a lost cause, lacking useful business skills and physical resources,[6] the evidence indicates that the performance of the sector is variable, especially in terms of firms' ability to attract Western investment and trade contracts. As I will elaborate below, this means that the kinds of determinate predictions about coalition formation that political economists can make from an analysis of established factoral or sectoral interests are impossible in this case. The interests of Russian defense industrialists vary greatly by firm. Although a sectoral coalition is likely to coalesce eventually, the choices made now by Western states will help to define which direction that coalition will take. Economic interests at the firm level can be manipulated for political purposes.

It is currently not feasible to measure the foreign policy preferences of Russian defense industrial managers directly. These managers rarely express their opinions publicly about what Russia's future world role should be. Furthermore, fieldwork conditions in Russia now discourage successful, probing survey research of the sector by Westerners. Sometimes analysts treat certain political figures, such as Arkady Volskiy, leader of the Civic Union faction, as representatives of the opinion of defense industrialists. Yet this is unreliable, since we lack evidence that defense managers as a bloc support all of Volskiy's views. In fact, a young Russian sociologist (whose work has gained much respect among Western specialists) interviewed a variety of Russian defense research institute managers between 1991 and 1993 and found diversity in the political candidates and parties that these managers said they preferred.[7]

Therefore, some indirect means to determine the foreign policy preferences of Russian defense industrialists is needed. In this chapter I will attempt to deduce the preferences of Russian defense industrialists for either a pro- or anti-Western set of foreign policies from an analysis of their economic interests. I identify these economic interests based on evidence gathered from an in-depth search of a variety of recent Russian press sources, which often summarize in detail the economic circumstances facing individual firms. The argument is as follows.

It is a well-established tenet in the field of international political economy that one can assess the trade policy preferences of economic actors by examining their structural economic circumstances. I will extend this approach—what Peter Gourevitch has termed the "economic explanation" for state trade policies[8]—to argue that the foreign economic policy preferences of Russian economic actors should be further correlated with their general preferences for integration into or isolation from the dominant world economy. In today's world, those preferences should translate into foreign policies that are either cooperative or antagonistic toward, for example, member states of the Organization for Economic Cooperation and Development.

If an economic actor has an interest in maintaining an open economy—for example, if the actor's production relies on imported materials, on the availability of an export market, or on integrated activities within a multinational corporation—then the actor also has an interest in maintaining the goodwill of the foreign states that control the availability of these trade flows. It would not be in this actor's interests for the home state to become involved in any major political conflict with foreign states that could lead to trade wars or other protectionist policies abroad. Although conflict between states does not always engender economic closure, and amity does not guarantee economic exchange, open trade and investment are nonetheless most likely to occur when conflict is minimized.[9] Those who value openness are therefore likely to prefer not to risk confrontation.

Of course, in some cases, such investment and trade might occur merely among a limited number of states that are not integrated into the world economy as a whole. If this is the case, then the economic actor may be indifferent to the general foreign policy line followed by the home state, as long as good relations are maintained between the relevant trading states. (For example, a Russian economic actor whose well-being is dependent on only one foreign tie, with Iran, may not care what the United States thinks about that tie.) But if the economic actor depends on open markets in states that are well integrated into the dominant world economy, then the actor's interests point in the direction of a generally cooperative and integrationist foreign policy.

Conversely, if an economic actor's interests are threatened by imports from the dominant world economy, or by export competition in a market not yet firmly dependent on the rest of the world (a concrete example might be competition between a Russian economic actor with few export markets and a German exporter for control over a market in China), the actor will prefer protectionist policies against the competitor state. To make protectionist policies politically feasible, and especially to prevent other domestic actors from developing an interest in free trade with the target state, it will be in the interests of the protectionist actor to have its home state perceive the competitor as a general threat to the state's economic well-being or security. To portray one state in the integrated world economy as a threat risks alienating the trading and security partners of that integrated state. Protectionism against the West is thus most compatible with a foreign policy isolated from the West.

In the case of the defense industry, where production and sales are closely tied to questions of defense and potential violence, the link between economic preferences and general foreign policy preferences should be even stronger than usual. For example, the sale of significant arms by Russia to a pariah state would be a direct challenge to Western security interests and would likely result in an immediate decline in the Western economic relationship with Russia. Conversely, supporting the West's counterproliferation efforts leads inexorably to lost markets for Russian weapons that could bring in much-needed hard currency. Furthermore, the more hostile that Russia believes the West to be, the more weapons the Russian state is likely to buy; the more cooperative the West appears, the less justification there is for weapons acquisition.

The task is thus to determine, based on their current economic situations, whether Russian defense industrial managers are likely to prefer free and open trade and investment relationships with the West or whether instead they prefer protectionist measures against the West in either domestic import-competing markets or in foreign markets where export competition is the issue.

In order to use models from the literature on open economies to assess the preferences of managers, it is necessary first to specify what economic role managers occupy within their firms. I will assume that Russian defense industrial managers can be treated for analytic purposes as owners of their firm's capital. In Russian firms that have already privatized, most managers have either bought or finagled ownership of a significant share of their firm's stock, approximately equivalent to the levels owned by managers of U.S. firms. On average the management team of a privatizing enterprise has acquired 17 percent of the enterprise stock, with the individual chief executive officer (CEO) on average acquiring 7 percent of the total.[10] That they lack complete control of the stock, and that they have a separate interest in maintaining their own employment, means that their interests as agents differ from the interests of an ideal owner-manager.[11] The problem is complicated by the fact that privatization has been accompanied by huge state subsidies to the industry, shielding managers from the real market and allowing firms to survive in the absence of market profit. Nonetheless, since most managers of privatized firms do have something to gain from the firm's well-being, it makes sense to treat them as having at least partial ownership interests. According to authoritative Russian government sources, 1,550 of Russia's approximately 2,100 defense industrial enterprises were to have been privatized by 1995; as of March 1994, 700 were reported to already be private.[12] Evidence from Poland indicates that managers who expect privatization in the future act as if their firms were already privatized.[13]

For enterprises that do not face privatization (the Russian government maintains a list of strategic enterprises forbidden to leave state control), the assumption that managers are capital owners is less intuitive. Some might view the state as the capital owner, with managers, like other employees, treated as part of the labor pool. Yet economists who specialize in the study of socialism agree that ownership rights over property (i.e., capital) in state-owned firms are split between high-level state bureaucrats who set prices, wages, and profit levels and those managers on the ground in the firm who decide in practice how the property should be utilized.[14] Managers should thus be considered at least partial capital owners, since their power over capital utilization exceeds that of run-of-the-mill workers, even though they must bargain with bureaucrats up the line in order to wield that power. Jan Winiecki notes that these utilization property rights are often used for the personal ends of the managers (e.g., using company workers on company time to build private dachas).[15] The agency interests of managers of state-owned firms are particularly strong. Managers still have an interest in the appreciation of their capital investment in this case, but such appreciation might involve resources other than profits for the firm (e.g., increased opportunity for borrowing to expand the manager's stock of cash or increased barter for scarce goods that the manager can sell for personal enrichment).

Once it is accepted that defense industrial managers can be treated as owners or partial owners of their firm's capital, the next step is to determine what interests capital ownership entails. The literature on open economies provides three economic actor categories that can be used to describe those interests: Managers could be treated as owners of a factor (capital), as members of a sector (the defense industry), or as representatives primarily of their individual firms.[16] All of these models assume that actors' preferences are based on their position in the international economy. Any of these three categories would fit most standard definitions of rational interest, since factor owners, sectoral members, and firm representatives are all interested in their own economic well-being. Yet each of the models makes different predictions about how political coalitions form. I will discuss the models in detail below, but an encapsulation of their predictions first will set the stage for my major argument.

The factoral model pictures capital owners as having the freedom to move their assets between sectors. In this case, the interests of Russian defense industrial managers would be determined by the relative scarcity or abundance of capital (as opposed, for example, to labor and land) in the country's economy and would not be based on any common interests within the specific industry. Ronald Rogowski has used the Stolper-Samuelson theorem[17] to argue that political coalitions within countries will thus form along factoral lines. If capital is abundant, its holders will support free trade alongside holders of other abundant factors and against those who hold scarce ones. If capital is scarce, its holders will favor protectionism. If this model were correct, then the interests of Russian defense industrial managers would be determined by the preexisting balance of factors within the Russian economy.

The sectoral model assumes, in contrast, that assets are not transferable across industries. As a result, it pictures industries acting as political units and sees capital owners and laborers within an industry as sharing common interests. Different industries within a country will have different international interests since they will have different degrees of vulnerability to a cutoff of foreign trade and investment opportunities. Coalitions will therefore split along industry lines. Both Jeffry A. Frieden and Eduardo Silva have applied the sectoral perspective to less-developed economies in Latin America,[18] demonstrating that the model's utility is not limited to developed capitalist countries.

The firm-based model, finally, sees the international interests of actors varying within individual industries. Certain firms are more vulnerable to a cutoff of foreign ties than are others within the sector.[19] Because firms within a state are often each other's biggest competitors, they are likely to view any change in state trade policy in terms of their own advantage against each other rather than in terms of the effect on their industry as a whole. As Helen Milner has noted, whether capital owners in a particular sector act in concert with each other or as firms competing against each other depends on the commonality of their interests. The range of their possible interests can be treated as a continuum,[20] and within a particular industry, the degree of sectoral versus firm identification can vary over time. Capital owners will join sectoral coalitions only if their firms' interests coincide with those of other firms and will leave such coalitions if their firms' interests are no longer met.

The firm-based model therefore predicts much more variability over time in the directions that industrial coalitions take than either the sectoral or factoral models do. Although factor and sector interests change over time (such change is a major theme of most international political economy works on those subjects), for example, in reaction to changes in technology, consumer taste, and market openness,[21] those interests are aggregated at a higher level than are the interests of firms. A firm's interests, and thus its political preferences and activities, can change from day to day as its contracts, customers, and investors change.

This means that in cases where factor and sector interests are not well established, then, outsiders can influence how the firm's interests develop and thereby work to shape the development of political coalitions. As Silva notes, domestic and international actions outside the control of capital owners can influence the shifting coalitional activities of those owners.[22] In the following sections, I will argue that the Russian defense industry is one such case where the definition of owners' interests is flexible. As a result, Western actions can help to determine the international economic preferences (and resulting foreign policy preferences) of Russia's military-industrial complex.

Model One: Russian Defense Industrial Managers as Factory Owners

Classical international economists might recommend an analysis based on factor ownership, arguing that in the long run there is no reason why defense industrial managers could not transfer their capital ownership stake from their current firms to some other use. Rather than viewing defense industrial managers as tied to their industrial sector or firm, we should see them as having mobile financial interests dependent on relative factor abundance.

Several problems arise, however, in trying to apply this model to the world of the Russian defense industrialist. First, it is not clear whether we should treat capital in Russia as being abundant and therefore at a comparative advantage internationally or as being scarce and therefore at a disadvantage. At some level, capital has a clear quantitative comparative advantage in the Russian economy, since Russia's raw supply of fixed capital stock (factories, machines, and so on) and human capital (advanced training and education) is certainly above the world per capita average.[23] As Jeffrey Sachs notes, the Soviet Union was overindustrialized[24] and thus capital-heavy. However, much of the capital stock in Russia is not useful. It was designed to make products that were demanded by a Soviet state that no longer exists; the output of this capital stock does not appear to be in high demand at present. The type of capital that is in most demand worldwide—fixed capital that is useful for flexible high-technology consumer goods production and liquid capital (i.e., money for investment)—is very scarce in Russia. Thus, the capital factor is not a useful analytic category unless it is differentiated,[25] and such differentiation makes measurement very difficult.

Yet the capital that managers of formerly Soviet-state-owned industries control is not "scarce," if we use standard definitions from international economics that are based on pricing. The capital available is not in particular demand for production at home, even in the absence of imports, since there is a dearth of domestic consumer goods production industries demanding investment. Thus capital owners will not be able to raise their factor's price if borders are closed. Open borders are in fact advantageous since they make capital flight to more productive investment possible—a situation that undercuts the fundamental fixed-border assumption of the factor model.[26] The fact that good-quality capital is in short supply in Russia does not bring capital owners a clear protectionist advantage.

A second, related problem with using the factor model to analyze the political economy of Russia is that industrial capital there is not convertible between sectors. Given the absence of developed financial markets, capital ownership in Russian factories primarily means ownership of the physical plant involved in production. Although the physical plant of a defense industrial factory can be quite diverse, including consumer goods production facilities, farmland, power plants, worker housing, and so on, each component tends nonetheless to be geographically specific, integrated into the whole, and based on equipment that is narrowly designed for specific purposes. The only way for managers to liquidate their capital would likely be to sell most of it as a bloc to another purchaser. Since much of this capital is in poor repair and was designed for purposes under the Soviet system that now lack economic relevance, the adjustment costs involved in such capital movement are likely to be immense. The agency interests of managers would also be jeopardized by an investment transfer, since the connections they use to gain personal power and favors tend to be long-established personalistic ties within particular industrial branches.

Such sectoral specificity makes the cost of capital movement very high. As Albert O. Hirschman discovered, unhappy economic actors face two choices: They may opt for exit (adapting to the current situation by moving their factors to another sector) or voice (engaging in political activity that is designed to change current policy).[27] When the adjustment costs of capital movement are high, the costs of political activity are likely to seem a bargain in comparison. Since defense industrial managers who sell their capital stocks will likely take huge losses, there is reason to expect that they will define their political interests in terms of their industry or firm, rather than as factor owners, and will engage in voice to protect those interests. The factor model does not provide an adequate description of the political-economic interests of Russian defense industrial managers.

Model Two: Russian Defense Industry as a Unified Sector

There are a wide variety of possible common interests for industries to have in regard to free trade and protectionism. Frieden suggests two that could be easily applied to the current situation of the Russian defense industry: (1) A reduction of government investment in a particular sector (e.g., a decline in state subsidies) can lead that sector to search for new foreign investment and therefore to favor an open economy and (2) a stagnation of domestic sectoral demand (e.g., a decline in state purchases) can lead the sector to search for new foreign markets and again to favor openness.[28] The drastic decline in Russian state weapons orders, beginning in 1992, and current increasing state threats to cut off easy access to credit should lead managers to search for foreign markets and foreign investment. Such a search may also be undertaken to replace the broken networks of firms located on Russian soil that used to receive imports from Eastern and Central Europe or that used to be engaged in joint production with enterprises elsewhere on Soviet territory.[29]

At the same time, opposing factors could apply in this case. The fact that many Russian weapons systems and most Russian high-technology consumer goods are of relatively poor quality by world standards means that the sector should fear foreign competition. Although the Russian state seems unlikely at present to consider buying foreign weapons for its own defense needs (although many developed states, including the United States, are becoming increasingly dependent on foreign suppliers for weapons components), foreign competitors are stealing both the previous domestic consumer goods market of the Soviet defense industry (including its former domestic monopoly production of such items as television sets, radios, and washing machines) and its former arms sales markets (particularly in East-Central Europe and the Third World).

To maintain a unified sectoral model, these opposing interests must somehow be reconciled, since otherwise firms within the sector would find themselves at loggerheads. The logical conclusion for the sector theorist is thus that the sector as a whole will favor different degrees of protectionism and openness toward different countries or in different markets.[30] If new investment and new input and export markets are needed, the sector as a whole may turn to the West in search of opportunity. At the same time, the sector as a whole may favor protectionist measures designed to maintain its advantage in existing arms markets (e.g., Russian state refusal to purchase foreign weapons components, the Russian state's unique willingness to accept barter of goods for weapons, or Russian pressure in the United Nations to lift sanctions against states where it has a traditional arms market advantage) and export subsidies to assist Russian foreign arms sales. H. Richard Friman notes that empirical studies indicate that export subsidies are the type of protectionist measure least likely to incite retaliation from other states.[31] The sector may thus not perceive any contradiction between open markets in general and arms export subsidies.

The sectoral perspective further argues that the most concentrated industries (i.e., those with a few large firms rather than a multitude of smaller firms) have the greatest chance of having real political impact.[32] By combining small numbers with economic heft, they will have an easier time coordinating and maintaining their government lobbying activities, thereby overcoming the collective action problem. The logical extension of this argument—one not usually made, however—is that if industrial sectors wish to act as units, it is to their policy advantage to concentrate themselves as much as possible. If assets are sectorally specific but not firm-specific, they may be more profitably invested in an industrial consortium rather than serving to keep a firm independent.

If the sectoral model describes this case well, then we should find evidence of three effects in particular. First, Russian defense industrial factories (which are saddled with a vast amount of fixed capital and appear to lack asset liquidity) should be trying to take political action as a unit, or at least as subindustrial sector units. Second, to be particularly effective, they should attempt to concentrate themselves as much as possible. Only through unified action and sectoral concentration can they succeed in marshaling the pressure needed for effective political action. Finally, the particular policies they should favor as a sector include the freedom to search for foreign markets, the encouragement of foreign investment, and state subsidies to improve their own cost competitiveness.

How does the evidence match the hypotheses? On many political-economic issues, Russian defense industrial workers and managers do in fact seem to be acting as a unit, rather than in opposition to each other, to voice their current political demands. For example, in two recent temporary work stoppages to protest government policy toward the defense industrial sector (on July 29 and September 17, 1993), labor and management demands—for more subsidies, for payment of back wages owed by the state on orders already filled, and for a clearer state military doctrine and arms procurement policy—were obviously coordinated.[33] It is also clear that management and labor are working in tandem to take inside control over privatizing enterprises.[34] Both sets of actors fear corporate raiders, especially outsiders who might destroy the firm and lay off current employees to use the property the firm currently occupies.

There is further evidence of unity not merely between managers and workers but also among firms within the sector. Russian government leaders are said to believe that defense industrial labor unions, along with coal miners, are one of the only groups strong and unified enough to be able currently to wage a successful national strike.[35] One-day protest work stoppages have become common. Although the economic impact of a serious nationwide strike would be negligible, given the current low production levels of the Russian defense industry, the political impact could be staggering, especially among parliamentarians representing defense-heavy regions. A sectorwide managerial union is also active. It submitted its own draft version of privatization legislation to the government in May 1993. The draft focused on closed stock sales, which allow managers and employees together to buy out virtually the entire company.[36] Its chief later threatened to sue the Russian Defense and Finance ministries for the Russian government's failure to pay for military orders that were already delivered in 1993.[37] At an industrywide level, then, both workers and managers seem to have achieved an unusual degree of unity surrounding the questions of their domestic economic interests.

There is also evidence of unified, sectoral action in the field of arms exports. On this foreign policy issue, many managers have expressed their opinions forcefully. Throughout 1993, managers argued that the Russian government failed to grant them a sufficient number of export licenses quickly enough, and they lobbied for more export opportunities. Lobbying activities were reported in a wide variety of firms, including those undertaken by the manufacturers of a fast and accurate surface-to-air missile, the S-300, considered to be a competitor of the American Patriot missile;[38] by the makers of a self-propelled artillery mount;[39] and by the producers of a sniper rifle.[40]

This lobbying effort appears to have worked. In June 1993 the first official arms export license was issued under new rules, to makers of the AK-47 automatic rifle.[41] In October and November, additional licenses were given to the manufacturers of a heavy transport plane[42] and to the company that lobbied for S-300 exports (for sales to Kuwait, reinforcing the S-300's image as a Patriot competitor).[43] Finally, in February 1994 a new umbrella organization was created in an attempt to streamline the arms export process. It took over from the three previous overlapping bureaucracies, which were infamous for their red tape and unwillingness to share information and profits with enterprises.[44] As in the case of its more general economic concerns, then, it appears that the Russian defense industry is acting as a unified sectoral group when it has clear common interests.

Further support for the model is provided by the fact that attempts have been made to concentrate industrial efforts at a subsectoral level, presumably to augment the industry's political weight. The desire to give the sector more power against the government has led to a tendency toward horizontal integration among similar firms. This has occurred largely under the aegis of the supposedly defunct defense industrial ministries, many of which have been constituted under new form in the Russian government apparatus and some of which have turned themselves into private holding companies. Examples of such efforts have occurred in the areas of space and missile technology,[45] gas weaponry (which includes production of mace and tear gas),[46] and aviation (both civil and military).[47]

Those who claim to represent the interests of the defense industry have argued for even further amalgamation of effort. Georgii Kostin, one of the rare outspoken plant directors, has argued that Russia needs a "managed economy"[48] and decried the regionalization of conversion efforts in Russia as a phenomenon that will fragment well-laid existing plans.[49] Oleg Soskovets, first deputy prime minister with responsibility for the defense industry, has proposed that Russian defense industrial factories be united into industrial blocs so that the strong performers can bail out their weaker comrades.[50] Viktor Glukhikh, chairman of the Russian State Committee for the Defense Sectors of Industry, has suggested that a "pooling [of] efforts" by producers is needed, citing the People's Republic of China as a successful example of such an experiment.[51] Among this group, concentration appears to be the preferred political strategy.

When examining the evidence, however, it is important to keep in mind that government ministers who claim to be speaking for defense industrialists may not actually represent their interests, and individual enterprise directors may not speak for all directors. It is difficult to imagine that successful managers of competitive firms would welcome proposals that they bail out failed colleagues. Furthermore, there is evidence that at least some firms very much resent the power of the old ministries over their activities.

A prime example of efforts by individual firms to get out from under the control of the ministries was the wide extent of lobbying in favor of defense industry privatization in 1992. As mentioned above, the Russian government maintains a list of enterprises forbidden to privatize because of their strategic significance. Well-publicized efforts to get taken off the list, or to get permission for independent civilian production contracts, were undertaken by the Sukhoi Design Bureau aviation complex,[52] the "Impuls" satellite and communications equipment factory in St. Petersburg, and the "Bolshevik" tank factory of the same city.[53] The lobbying efforts of these firms have paid off, since privatization of the defense sector is proceeding rapidly (as noted above), in spite of reports that some firms are trying to get themselves added to the not-for-privatization list to ensure continued state financing.[54]

Further calling the sectoral model into question, there are disagreements about foreign economic issues among those who supposedly represent the defense industry. Soskovets, who suggested that the strong should bail out the weak, has complained about the growth of foreign investment in the Russian defense industry, arguing that domestic technology should be used instead of foreign imports.[55]

Volskiy, the man who reputedly defends the interests of those managers who want absolute control over the enterprises they headed,[56] has made exactly the opposite complaint. He has argued that Russia needs new laws to encourage more foreign investment, and he fears that potential partners may instead turn to Kazakhstan, which apparently has a more liberal legal climate.[57]

Thus in this case the sectoral approach has a high degree of analytic power: It explains concerted action by defense industrial labor and management to further their joint economic interests where agreement on those interests is easy. But the level of disagreement among firms and among those who supposedly represent their interests suggests that another perspective is needed for a complete understanding of the situation. Where the Russian defense industry has common interests, it is acting as a sectoral bloc: No rational defense firm would object to more state subsidies or easier arms export rules. As the issues become more complex and immediate, however, the power of the sectoral model breaks down, at least in the short term.

It must be remembered, however, that since Russian defense industrialists must compete with other economic actors for access to the policy agenda, it remains in the long-term interests of managers to attempt to form a unified sectoral coalition to strengthen their political voices. In turning to the firm-level model, then, it is important to consider whether eventual sectoral cooperation (and thus political influence) will be possible and, if it is, which of two competing directions it will take—toward openness in search of investment and markets or toward protection that allows an uncompetitive industry to survive.

Model Three: Russian Defense Industrial Firms as Competitors Among Themselves

This model obviously describes some industries better than others. Barbara Spencer points out, for example, that the less concentrated a sector is, the more likely it is that other firms will lose from a single firm's trade advantage, since strategic coordination becomes harder.[58] Currently, tension clearly exists between defense managers' desire for control over their specific firms and their desire for the kind of political influence that can be achieved only through collective action. We would not expect a firm-level model to be the best predictor of political action indefinitely.

The firm-based perspective provides a concrete checklist that can be used to predict the foreign policy preferences of the owners of each firm. Any firm with a significant foreign tie, especially one that cannot be replaced with a domestic tie in the event of a trade war, will favor free trade. Any firm whose market, investors, and suppliers are primarily domestic, while its competitors have foreign ties, will favor protectionism. Each firm will act in a way that maximizes its competitive advantage.

Although it is not possible at the moment to reliably connect individual Russian defense industrial firms with particular lobbying efforts, and thus to demonstrate in practice the utility of the political predictions of this model, there are two structural conditions that should hold if this model is valid. First, Russian defense industrial managers should own assets that are not easily transferable to other firms within their industry, since otherwise the political power provided by sectoral unity should attract them to amalgamate their assets. Second, the international ties of Russian defense industrial firms should be unevenly distributed within the sector, including within subsectors, and should subject firms to varying degrees of vulnerability to foreign cutoff.

The skills (or human capital) that Russian defense industrial managers own (arguably their primary assets in the firm, since the transferable economic value of their ownership shares is likely to be low) are in fact very likely to be specific to their firms' production. These managers did not attend business schools; instead, they tend to be engineers who have spent most of their professional lives inside a single factory.[59] It would be extremely risky for them to move elsewhere, since there is no reason to believe that their skills would bring them benefit in a new context. In some cases, it is possible that the successful problem-solving skills of a manager in one factory undergoing privatization and conversion could be usefully applied to a similar factory in another location. There are some isolated cases where such movement has occurred in the Russian defense industry, for example, when a firm undergoing bankruptcy has an outside manager appointed to oversee restructuring.[60] In practice, however, even such intersectoral relocation seems to be rare, regardless of the sector considered.[61] Most managers of defense industrial firms today have been at their firms for years; if one manager is removed from his position (for example, by an election held by the worker collective), a more junior member of the existing management team takes his place.[62]

There is a solid structural reason why this should be the case. The personal ties that managers have built up over the years are what currently allow them to obtain supplies for their production, consumer goods for their workers, as well as favors from local officials. The firm would thus be disadvantaged by hiring an outsider. Managers would simultaneously have their interests as agents compromised by moving to a new firm, since those same specific personal ties now bring them side benefits that would be lost with movement away from their factories. Identification with the firm is rational.

At this point, then, we need a description of the current international interests of Russian defense industrial firms to see if they differ significantly from each other. The development of numerous joint ventures and trade relationships between Russian defense industrial firms and firms from wealthy capitalist countries has been well publicized. Particularly noteworthy in this regard are the successes of Russian aerospace firms.[63] Other examples include a tank factory now selling four-wheel-drive mountain vehicles throughout the Americas,[64] a major

St. Petersburg shipyard making civilian freighters for West European con-sumers,[65] and a communications equipment factory now making videocassette recorders in cooperation with Japan's Sharp Electronics company.[66] A striking example is that of Leninets, a huge aviation electronics concern in St. Petersburg, now producing 1.2 million razor blades and shaving kits per year for the Gillette company.[67]

Perhaps the most remarkable example of success in the Western market is that the British Royal Air Force (RAF) has agreed to buy twenty-five A-40 Albatross amphibious combat aircraft from the Taganrog Aviation Scientific-Technological Complex. This is the first time that a NATO country's military organization has bought Russian equipment.[68] There are other examples of Russian firms express-ing interest in NATO military deals. The Russian Antei firm has begun discus-sions with the French firm Matra for joint production of a new antiballistic mis-sile system based on the S-300 technology.[69] The potential of this deal was undoubtedly strengthened by a February 1994 arms industry cooperation agree-ment signed between the Russian and French defense ministers.[70] In a surprise move for any leftover U.S. cold warriors, Mikhail Simonov, general designer at the Sukhoi Design Bureau, says that he has approached Yeltsin directly and has lobbied other officials in the Russian government with his idea for joint U.S.-Russian production of a new, heavier fighter bomber based on the SU-27.[71]

It thus appears that international ties in armaments production may sometimes actually work in the same direction as civilian sales from the defense industry, connecting individual firms to the Western-oriented world economy. Some Russian arms deals with foreign countries, especially those with China, Iran, and India, have been very disturbing to Western policymakers concerned about con-ventional arms proliferation and regional power balances. Yet a manager whose firm's well-being depends on military sales to a NATO country is likely to be a very strong supporter of cooperation with the West. Military sales and joint ven-tures, like their civilian counterparts, have impacts that vary by firm.

Examples of joint venture achievement number in the dozens, in an industry whose firms number in the thousands, and some firms are clearly doing better than others. One clear example of potential intra-industry political conflict over trade policy is found in military shipbuilding. The Amur Shipyard, formerly the largest defense enterprise in the Russian Far East, has signed an agreement with McDermott International for joint construction of civilian ships and coastal shelf oil extraction equipment. The U.S. government has, in an unprecedented step, agreed to certify that the new production lines meet international standards. The venture intends to produce primarily for the export market.[72] The manager of an-other shipbuilding company, Sevmash, a huge nuclear submarine plant, lost hope in his ability to form any foreign joint ventures. He therefore formed a domestic joint-stock company with the former Soviet Gas and Oil Ministry (Gazprom), called "Rosshelf," to engage in coastal shelf development. According to an *Izvestiia* correspondent, "Severodvinsk and the enormous 'Sevmash' territory are a kind of ideological reserve where an incredible number of busts of Lenin and other visual agitation has been preserved and [opposition figure Aleksandr] Rutskoi's expose articles are pinned to the stands."[73] (The correspondent expressed surprise that even a domestic joint-stock deal could have grown out of this environment.) Without foreign cooperation, this firm lacks international certification for its products.[74] Given that the Amur Shipyard has not only formed a foreign joint venture for coastal development equipment but has also received a promise from the U.S. government for international sales certification, it would seem that Sevmash's general director, D. Pashaev, is a good candidate for joining a protectionist coalition since his firm finds itself unable to keep up with similar firms in Russia in efforts to capture the world market.

This may explain why First Deputy Defense Minister Andrei Kokoshin recently announced that Sevmash would receive priority funding from the government for the construction of a new multipurpose military nuclear submarine.[75] Those who cannot join the world market may be convinced through domestic protection to refrain from anti-Western political activity. In other words, at the firm level, economic interests and thus the likelihood of political activity can be manipulated by outsiders.

Even among those firms with established foreign joint ventures, the money-making potential of these ventures varies. Some have been extremely successful. For example, Russian missile firms have broken into the Western-dominated commercial satellite launch market. A joint venture between Lockheed, the Russian Khrunichev Space Center, and the Russian firm Energiia edged out the French-based Ariane consortium to win a five-launch deal with a Luxembourg television broadcasting company.[76] Multiple launches for the Space Systems/Loral and Motorola companies had already been arranged by LKEI (Lockheed-Khrunichev-Energiia International). This joint venture's potential to take over a significant market share was so great, because of Russia's low labor costs, that the U.S. and Russian governments signed an agreement to limit Russian firms to no more than eight commercial launches involving U.S. payloads, with bids that cannot undercut the lowest Western bid by more than 7.5 percent.[77]

Yet some very active foreign joint ventures, including both civilian and military producers from the Russian defense industry, face profitability problems that may limit their long-term potential. Even in the one area where Russian technology is almost universally recognized to be at world standards, aerospace, international competition is stiff and the eventual profitability of joint ventures remains open to doubt. For example, the Iliushin Design Bureau has "firm orders" for five of its new 96-M passenger jumbo jets, with Pratt and Whitney engines and Collins Air Transport/Rockwell International avionics, from the Dutch company Partnairs N.V. An additional twenty planes have been ordered by Aeroflot.[78] Yet even though the 96-M will be significantly cheaper than its Airbus, Boeing, and McDonnell Douglass counterparts because of low Russian labor costs,[79]

Aeroflot's new Russian airline competitors are not turning to Iliushin. Air Russia, for example, a joint venture between Aeroflot and British Airways, is building a new international terminal at the Domodedovo Airport in Moscow that is designed specifically to accommodate its forthcoming purchases of Boeing 767s.[80] As recently as May 1993, the Il-96M was reported to have insufficient funds for large-scale production,[81] and indeed, Iliushin was still relying on the Russian state for 65 percent of its revenues.[82] World experience indicates that only those firms able to generate orders in the hundreds are likely to break even (much less realize a profit) on a new civilian aircraft design.[83] Similar situations have been reported by other Russian aircraft manufacturers.[84]

Even those Russian firms with clear quality and reliability and low prices may therefore have difficulty finding a niche in the market. They lack the decades-long reputation for service reliability and the international reach of their Western competitors, and domestic political instability in Russia makes many Western businesses wary of long-term commitments. In foreign arms sales, cash-strapped Russian firms may find it hard to compete against the low-cost financing packages offered by U.S. dealers.[85] And the one comparative advantage that Russian firms have had, in labor cost, may be lost soon. As Clifford Gaddy and Melanie Allen point out, many of the best workers have now left the Russian defense industry, and to keep quality high, managers may have to raise salaries to lure these workers back.[86]

In those firms that are making money off of joint venture or trade relationships, the level of vulnerability to the cessation of the Western relationship varies. Some firms, such as the Kamov Helicopter Aviation Factory, publicize their relief at finding Western ties. Kamov managers attribute their ability to maintain their previous markets in East-Central Europe and the Third World to the fact that their "traditionally weak, domestically-made engines and avionics have been replaced with foreign ones thanks to successful contacts with the producers of similar equipment in the USA, France, and Israel."[87] Part of this dependence may be due to the fact that many countries are now significantly tightening their noise pollution standards for aircraft, changing the world helicopter market by forcing manufacturers to pay more attention to ecological concerns. Kamov managers appear to see themselves as dependent on healthy Western ties and are likely to favor economic openness toward the developed world.

Other deals with Western firms appear to be somewhat trivial, filling the gap until something better comes along. One example may be the deal that the Coca-Cola Corporation signed with the Research and Production Association "Nauka," a space equipment firm that is now manufacturing aluminum kiosks for Coca-Cola street sales.[88] (Coca-Cola kiosks in Moscow are made to look like giant Coke cans.) Another is the service offered by MiGs, Etc., Inc., a joint venture of the Sukhoi factory and a Sarasota, Florida, firm, which for $90,000 offers individuals a two-week training course in aerial combat. Two paying customers engage in a judged mock dogfight at the end of the course, and "the winner receives a video tape of the dogfight—set to either classical or heavy metal music—along with a silver-plated Russian flight helmet inscribed with the names of the victor and the accompanying Russian pilot."[89] Although MiGs, Etc. has had 150 customers so far,[90] such arrangements do not appear to create dependency relationships.

Vulnerability becomes a key issue when considering the foreign policy preferences of managers. Managers whose future is tied to an economic relationship with a particular country are much more likely to support cooperative relations with that country than managers whose ties to another economy are ephemeral at best. If firms such as those producing cola kiosks and MiG lessons find a better deal, even if it is one that aggravates Western world opinion toward Russia, they will be unlikely to be swayed by their existing foreign economic ties.

An interesting example of where such vulnerability might become a key issue is found in firms that have diversified foreign product lines, balancing Western partners in civilian production against arms sales directed toward Third World markets. General arms exports might be seen as commodity deals that favor a militaristic, anti-integrationist view of Russia's foreign policy interests, but in fact arms sales to the Third World and civilian product sales to the West may occur simultaneously within the same Russian company. For example, the Smelchak company is a manufacturer of highly accurate, laser-guided smart artillery units. As state orders fell in 1990 and 1991, talented weapons designers left the firm to form their own company, Ametech, which manufactures small food and agricultural machinery. Ametech is said to have attracted the interest of German and Czech beer companies with its inexpensive, high-quality, computer-monitored breweries. Meanwhile, it is combining with sixteen other military factories and research and development (R&D) centers to form an arms export association called Dinamika. According to a Russian news report, "the objective is to increase annual output of equipment for civilian use to 15 billion rubles and resume production of Smelchak and Centimeter [artillery]."[91]

A cynic might look at such an arrangement and deride it as diversification that merely finances arms sales. A political economist might, however, note the crosscutting international interests such an arrangement creates within the firm. If Ametech succeeds in developing a significant civilian export market in Western or Westward-leaning countries, its managers will have an interest in pursuing integrationist policies in order to keep that market open. Although this will not stop Dinamika's arms sales, it may ensure that those sales are limited to countries acceptable in the eyes of the West. In 1993, the United States demonstrated its willingness to impose sanctions against specific Russian firms—those that were planning the sale of rocket technology to India in what the United States considered to be a violation of the Missile Technology Control Regime.[92]

Diversification in arms production companies may therefore be a tool for Western integration. It is not reasonable to expect Russia to disappear from the world arms market. It may nonetheless be possible to keep Russia's weapons markets limited to those that are acceptable to the community of nations.

Merging the Models

At present, the firm-based model seems to describe well the conflicting international economic interests of Russian defense industrial managers and, by association, their foreign policy preferences. Yet the sectoral model also has some validity. Defense industrialists have been taking some concerted lobbying action, particularly on the issues of state payment of back wages, continuing state loan credits, and the loosening of the state arms export bureaucracy. At least at the moment, however, the economic situations and experiences of individual firms seem to have varied drastically from each other. Despite efforts by some industry representatives to concentrate sectoral activity, managers of firms are acting independently in search of Western investment and sales, and some have discovered on their own that no such contracts are forthcoming. (Table 5.1 summarizes and compares the predictions of the models.)

Since sectoral unity and integration are, at the moment, mixed at best, competition within the Russian defense industry and the absence of a single economic platform among its members are likely to be harming the sector's ability to influence policy. Budget hearings in spring and summer 1994 tend to bear this out, since despite the support of several factions within the Duma and of President Yeltsin, defense industrialists failed to obtain the level of increase in subsidies that they sought. In response to this circumstance, it has been reported, powerful groups of managers are seeking ways to exert more pressure on policy—for example, by creating a single sectoral party to support their interests against the more unified blocs of agricultural and energy sector managers.[93]

Given that firms do not currently share a variety of international interests, it is likely that a choice will have to be made between the two competing pressures now affecting the sector: the lure of Western investment and markets and the threat facing a largely uncompetitive industry. Two scenarios are possible.

First, the majority of Russia's 2,000-odd defense industrial firms, those whose managers share a common interest in survival but not in Western relationships, could band together. The proportion of firms currently reporting successful

TABLE 5.1   Sector and Firm Models: Predictions and Results for the Russian Defense Industry

	Sector Model Prediction	Firm-Level Model Prediction	Empirical Evidence
Asset specificity	High	High	High
Concentration of industry	High	Low	Mixed (high within ministerial holding companies; low for independent, privatized firms)
Commonality of economic interests	High	Low	Mixed (high in favor of state subsidies and arms export promotion; low on issues of foreign trade and investment)

Western relationships is low. If intra-industry competition is in fact a key factor in explaining political action, then the success of only a few firms in the world market may galvanize the rest to act together to defeat them. These firms, characterized by an inability to compete on world markets, have a clear interest in gaining government subsidies and other forms of protectionism. If their managers believe that they cannot transfer their investment and skills elsewhere in the economy, then they will attempt to soak the state budget to ensure their firms' continued operation and will lobby to keep Western competitors out of any of their potential markets (including traditional Soviet arms markets). They are likely to favor policies hostile to Western interests, including high tariffs on imported consumer goods (especially the durable goods that they once sold), arms sales to pariah states, and a general state perception of external hostility that would necessitate additional arms purchases.

Some might argue that it would not be in state interests to respond to such pressure. At a minimum, the state should protect only a sector whose imperfect competition advantage (e.g., a technology lead in an industry with high entry barriers) promises net economic gain.[94] The Russian defense industry has no such obvious advantage. Free trade economists would go further, arguing that protectionism in the real world never leads to net economic gain and is therefore always against state economic interests.[95] Nonetheless, it is in Russian state interests to maintain a viable and cooperative domestic military industry for the sake of state defense. The state's failure to act on defense industry demands may also complicate reform efforts by encouraging retaliatory tax evasion and other disruptive economic behavior. Furthermore, political actors, especially those dependent on regional support, are likely to have an interest in suppressing unrest within the defense industry, even if this means supporting economic inefficiency. Certainly, the defense industry might line up behind those Russian politicians whose rhetoric is currently hostile toward the West.

An alternative scenario is also possible. The few large firms that seem to be succeeding in attracting lucrative Western investment may emerge as the politically dominant faction within the sector, especially if continuing and growing Western investment seemed possible. They could then lobby the government to use contracts to buy the support of other large firms that might be potential protectionists, such as what already seems to have been done for Sevmash. Milner notes that large firms can often win political battles over trade policy against smaller firms within their industry.[96] In this case, by outmaneuvering less powerful firms that lack integrationist interests, larger firms could convince the sector to favor openness toward the West, leading to a cooperative tone in Russia's overall foreign policy choices.

The consequences of such actions could be viewed passively, through the lens of the international system: A web of ties between individual Russian and Western firms might lead to their continuing cooperation[97] and eventually to their working to overcome potential conflicts between the involved states. Alternatively, the West could choose to view the situation in realist terms, using the dependence of Russian defense industrial firms on Western openness to influence indirectly Russian foreign policy. Hirschman has argued that the "influence effect" of dependency can lead one state to gain political power over another.[98] Analysis at a lower level of aggregation suggests that the same principle can be applied to those representatives of firms and sectors who engage in lobbying activities within the state.

The likelihood of the West's ability to achieve significant results here is bolstered by the fact that significant players in the current Russian government are trying to pull the sector as a whole in the direction of integration into the capitalist world economy rather than merely reacting to sectoral demands. Andrei Kokoshin, first deputy minister of defense with responsibilities for the defense industry, has formed a new Council on Military-Technical Policy, which links defense industrial managers, scientists, General Staff officers, the Interior and Security ministries, and independent analysts to exchange opinions and to reach consensus about current policy issues.[99] He is apparently trying to repeat the success he helped achieve in the Gorbachev era, when General Staff officers were convinced to communicate with civilian analysts interested in defensive defense military doctrine and appeared to be influenced by them.[100] His goal this time seems to be to convince defense industrialists to redefine their interests in ways that are more in accord with the Russian government's economic reform policies while convincing the government to meet the pressing concerns of industrialists (e.g., by paying off government debts to firms on state defense orders and encouraging foreign arms sales). One of his aims is to create a Russian National Industrial Policy, which would encourage defense industrial cooperation in dual-use technology manufacture to serve as a mechanism both for economic growth and for Western integration.[101]

Political pressures thus move in both bottom-up and top-down directions. Interests are not predetermined when situations within the sector differ but may instead be influenced by powerful or persuasive outside actors. Both Russian government officials and foreign economic actors can attempt to manipulate the beliefs of defense industrialists about where their interests lie.

If most managers believe that the prospects for Western trade and investment are dim, then they will lobby the sector to support their goals of protectionism. If, however, managers with political clout—those with personal ties to government circles (e.g., Yeltsin began his career as Communist Party boss in Yekaterinburg, a major defense industrial city) or who employ large numbers of people in defense-heavy regions that lack other economic opportunities—can be convinced that the road to survival lies in Western connections, then they may be able to exert sectoral pressure in favor of openness. Most Russian firms lack the marketing expertise and resources to attract international trade and investment on their own. It is thus in the interests of the developed world economy to target economic assistance toward any Russian defense industrial firm that seems to have an ability to produce something that a Western firm would find useful or profitable, cementing integration through joint ventures and trade.

What the analysis here suggests is that the West should view such investment not only in economic terms but also in terms of Western security interests, particularly in light of current concerns about conventional weapons proliferation. Western states could decide to assume the risk of joint venture activities based on a security calculus rather than on pure economic considerations. Working at the firm level now could lead the sector to favor an integrationist foreign policy in the future. A Western choice to dismiss Russian defense industry as a whole as a behemoth of the past could become a self-fulfilling prophecy, as managers with no economic alternatives take political action designed to restore the former health of their firms. If, however, free trade interests can become established within the sector, the conservative power of Russia's military-industrial complex will be broken. Such an outcome is far from assured, but policymakers in the developed world economy may be able to tip the balance toward its achievement.

Notes

The work leading to this chapter was supported by funds provided by the National Council for Soviet and East European Research and by the Social Science Research Council/MacArthur Foundation Program on International Peace and Security. Support was also received from the John M. Olin Foundation Critical Issues Series at the Russian Research Center, Harvard University, and a supportive working environment was provided by the John M. Olin Institute for Strategic Studies, Center for International Affairs, Harvard University. Earlier versions of this chapter were presented at the Ford Foundation Workshop on Defense and Foreign Policy Issues in the Russian Federation, St. Antony's and Wolfson colleges, Oxford University; at the Harvard University Russian Research Center; and at the 1994 Annual Meeting of the International Studies Association, Washington, D.C. This version benefits from comments received at those meetings. None of these organizations is responsible for the findings or content of this report. I am grateful to these organizations; to Sharon Shible for her valuable research assistance; and to Jeffrey Checkel, Christopher Davis, Matthew Evangelista, Vladimir Gimpelson, David Holloway, Ethan Kapstein, Jeffrey Knopf, Lisa Martin, Ronald Rogowski, David Rowe, Randall Schweller, Randall Stone, Celeste Wallander, and three anonymous readers for their thoughtful and insightful criticisms and suggestions.

1. For a sophisticated treatment of the question of how the West fits into Russian foreign policy decisions at present, see Aleksei G. Arbatov, "Russia's Foreign Policy Alternatives," *International Security* 18 (Fall 1993): 5–43.

2. See, for example, Stephen Foye, "Parliament Defies Government on Defense Budget," *Radio Free Europe/Radio Liberty (RFE/RL) Daily Report,* 19 July 1993.

3. Keith Bush, "Boost for Defense Industry," *RFE/RL Daily Report,* 9 November 1993.

4. For examples, see Sander Thoenes, "Increase in Defense Spending Proposed," *Moscow Times,* 5 June 1994; and Stephen Foye, "Parliamentary Hearings on 1995 Defense Budget," *RFE/RL Daily Report,* 26 July 1994.

5. "Russian Premier Savages Regions over Reforms," Reuters, 15 July 1994.

6. See Kenneth L. Adelman and Norman R. Augustine, "Defense Conversion: Bulldozing the Management," *Foreign Affairs* 71 (Spring 1992): 26–47.

7. Leonid Kosals, "Military R&D Institutes in the Context of Demilitarization in Russia," Working Paper 94–002, International Institute for Applied Systems Analysis, Laxenburg, Austria, January 1994, p. 5.

8. Peter Alexis Gourevitch, "International Trade, Domestic Coalitions, and Liberty: Comparative Responses to the Crisis of 1873–1896," *Journal of Interdisciplinary History* 8 (Autumn 1977): 281–313.

9. The positive relationship between trade levels and alliance has been demonstrated by Joanne Gowa, *Allies, Adversaries, and International Trade* (Princeton: Princeton University Press, 1993).

10. Maxim Boycko, Andrei Shleifer, and Robert W. Vishny, "Privatizing Russia," paper prepared for the Brookings Panel on Economic Activity, Washington, D.C., September 1993, pp. 34–35.

11. For a clear discussion of the theory of agency, see Thrainn Eggertsson, *Economic Behavior and Institutions* (New York: Cambridge University Press, 1990), pp. 40–45, 128–138.

12. Alfred Koch, Deputy Chair of the Russian State Property Committee, and the person with chief responsibility for overseeing the privatization of defense industry, as cited by Keith Bush, "Most Defense Enterprises to Be Privatized by End 1994," *RFE/RL Daily Report,* 1 March 1994. These figures seem consistent with others reported by the Russian government, since it was said that by 1 January 1994, 488 enterprises had already had their privatization plans approved. See "Razreshenie na Privatizatsiiu Poluchili 8% Predpriiatii, Proizvodiashchikh Boepripasy i Spetskhimiiu," *Segodnia,* 1 February 1994.

13. Brian Pinto, Marek Belka, and Stefan Krajewski, "Transforming State Enterprises in Poland: Evidence on Adjustment by Manufacturing Firms," *Brookings Papers on Economic Activity* 1 (1993): 213–270.

14. Janos Kornai, *The Socialist System: The Political Economy of Socialism* (Princeton: Princeton University Press, 1992), pp. 64–66; Gertrude E. Schroeder, "Property Rights Issues in Economic Reforms in Socialist Countries," *Studies in Comparative Communism* 21 (Summer 1988): 175–188; and Frederic L. Pryor, *Property and Industrial Organization in Communist and Capitalist Nations* (Bloomington: Indiana University Press, 1973). For a more general discussion of similar issues, see Eggertsson, *Economic Behavior and Institutions,* pp. 34–35.

15. Jan Winiecki, "Large Industrial Enterprises in Soviet-Type Economies: The Ruling Stratum's Main Rent-Seeking Area," *Communist Economies* 1, no. 4 (1989): 363–383.

16. I am following Gourevitch's conceptualization of this task in his "International Trade, Domestic Coalitions, and Liberty," p. 283.

17. Ronald Rogowski, *Commerce and Coalitions: How Trade Affects Domestic Political Alignments* (Princeton: Princeton University Press, 1989). A clear explanation of the assumptions, significance, and shortcomings of the Stolper-Samuelson theorem is found in Charles P. Kindleberger and Peter M. Lindert, *International Economics,* 6th ed. (Homewood, Ill.: Richard D. Irwin Publishers, 1978), pp. 85–97.

18. The most complete statements of these arguments are Jeffry A. Frieden, *Debt, Development, and Democracy: Modern Political Economy and Latin America, 1965–1985* (Princeton: Princeton University Press, 1991); and Eduardo Silva, "Capitalist Coalitions, the State, and Neoliberal Economic Restructuring: Chile, 1973–88," *World*

Politics 45 (July 1993): 526–559. For variations, see Jeffry A. Frieden, "Sectoral Conflict and U.S. Foreign Economic Policy, 1914–1940," *International Organization* 42 (Winter 1988), as reprinted in *The State and American Foreign Economic Policy,* ed. G. John Ikenberry, David A. Lake, and Michael Mastanduno (Ithaca: Cornell University Press, 1988); and idem, "Winners and Losers in the Latin American Debt Crisis: The Political Implications," in *Debt and Democracy in Latin America,* ed. Barbara Stallings and Robert Kaufman (Boulder: Westview Press, 1989).

19. Helen V. Milner, *Resisting Protectionism: Global Industries and the Politics of International Trade* (Princeton: Princeton University Press, 1988). Also see her "Resisting the Protectionist Temptation: Industry and the Making of Trade Policy in France and the United States During the 1970s," *International Organization* 41 (Autumn 1987): 639–665.

20. Milner, "Resisting the Protectionist Temptation," pp. 646–647.

21. John S. Odell, "Understanding International Trade Policies: An Emerging Synthesis," *World Politics* 43 (October 1990): 143–144.

22. Silva, "Capitalist Coalitions."

23. This is based on the definition of comparative advantage provided by Edward E. Leamer, *Sources of International Comparative Advantage: Theory and Evidence* (Cambridge: MIT Press, 1984), p. 15.

24. Jeffrey Sachs, *Poland's Jump to the Market Economy* (Cambridge: MIT Press, 1993), pp. 74–75. Rogowski, *Commerce and Coalitions,* pp. 98 and 121, shares this capital-abundant view of the Soviet economy.

25. For an in-depth critique of Rogowski's work on this point, see Paul Midford, "International Trade and Domestic Politics: Improving on Rogowski's Model of Political Alignments," *International Organization* 47 (Autumn 1993): 535–564.

26. Leamer, *Sources of International Comparative Advantage,* p. 22.

27. Albert O. Hirschman, *Exit, Voice, and Loyalty: Responses to Decline in Firms, Organizations, and States* (Cambridge: Harvard University Press, 1970).

28. Frieden, *Debt, Development, and Democracy,* p. 247.

29. See Christopher Mark Davis, "The Exceptional Soviet Case: Defense in an Autarkic System," *Daedalus* 120 (Fall 1991): 113–134.

30. Helen V. Milner and David Yoffie provide the theoretical justification for such an example, in "Between Free Trade and Protectionism: Strategic Trade Policy and a Theory of Corporate Trade Demands," *International Organization* 43 (Spring 1989): 239–272.

31. H. Richard Friman, "Rocks, Hard Places, and the New Protectionism: Textile Trade Policy Choices in the United States and Japan," *International Organization* 42 (Autumn 1988), pp. 689–690 n. 2.

32. Mancur Olson, *The Logic of Collective Action* (Cambridge: Harvard University Press, 1965); and J. J. Pincus, "Pressure Groups and the Pattern of Tariffs," *Journal of Political Economy* 83 (August 1975): 757–778.

33. Sheila Marnie, "Warning Strike at Defense Industry Plants," *RFE/RL Daily Report,* 30 July 1993; and Yurii Konorov, "The Defense Sector Has Stopped Work," *Rossiiskaia Gazeta,* 17 September 1993, as reported in *Foreign Broadcast Information Service Daily Report, Central Eurasia (FBIS-SOV),* 22 September 1993, pp. 19–20.

34. Boycko, Shleifer and Vishny, "Privatizing Russia," p. 35.

35. Elizabeth Teague, "Gaidar Warns Insolvent Firms," *RFE/RL Daily Report,* 15 November 1993.

36. "U VPK Svoi Vzgliad na Privatizatsiiu," *Segodnia,* 28 May 1993.

37. "'Oboronka' Pred'iavila Isk Minfinu," *Rossiiskaia Gazeta,* 3 July 1993.

38. "Arms Exports Will Save Severny Zavod," *Moscow News,* 3 September 1993.

39. Viacheslav Shchepotkin, "Volley of Bans Against Missiles," *Rossiiskaia Gazeta,* 19 June 1993, as reported in *FBIS-SOV,* 23 June 1993, pp. 15–20.

40. "Large Circle" program, Russian Television Network, 5 May 1993, as reported in *FBIS-SOV,* 6 May 1993, pp. 43–45.

41. John Lepingwell, "Arms Export License Granted to Kalashnikov Factory," *RFE/RL Daily Report,* 3 June 1993.

42. V. Prunov and V. Myznikov, "Vesti" newscast, Russian Television Network, 16 October 1993, as reported in *FBIS-SOV,* 21 October 1993, pp. 43–44.

43. John Lepingwell, "Russia, Kuwait, Sign Defense Agreement, Discuss Arms Sales," *RFE/RL Daily Report,* 30 November 1993.

44. The charges are laid out by Clifford Gaddy and Melanie Allen, "Dreams of a Salesman: The Russian Drive to Increase Arms Exports," *Brookings Review* (Fall 1993): 36–41; announcement of the new organization was noted by Keith Bush, "Controls Tightened on Arms Exports," *RFE/RL Daily Report,* 21 February 1994.

45. Russian Television Network, 16 June 1993, as reported in *FBIS-SOV,* 18 June 1993, pp. 31–32.

46. "Entrepreneurs Dispute Weapons for Civilian Use," *Moscow News,* 10 September 1993, p. 10.

47. Valentin Rudenko, interview with Aleksandr Voinov, director of the Russian section of the V.O. Aviaeksport joint stock company, "Russian Aircraft Builders Leaving for Dubai Not for Sensations but for Contracts," *Krasnaia Zvezda,* 19 October 1993, as reported in *FBIS-SOV,* 20 October 1993, p. 16.

48. Georgii Kostin, "Reforms Yes, but Not the President's Way," *Rossiiskaia Gazeta,* 4 August 1993, as reported in *FBIS-SOV,* 5 August 1993, pp. 30–32.

49. Georgii Kostin, "Thoughts on Conversion," *Krasnaia Zvezda,* 30 July 1993, as reprinted in *FBIS-SOV,* 3 August 1993, pp. 22–23.

50. Irina Savvateeva, "Young Oligarchies Want to Be Legalized," *Komsomolskaia Pravda,* 20 July 1993, as reported in *FBIS-SOV,* 21 July 1993, pp. 26–28.

51. Viktor Glukhikh, "Can a Tank Plant Be Privatized?" *Rossiiskie Vesti,* 17 June 1993, as reported in *FBIS-SOV,* 22 June 1993, pp. 27–28.

52. "Firme Otkazano v Privatizatsii," *Kommersant-Daily,* 4 November 1992.

53. Steven Erlanger, "Capitalists Short of Capital, Russian Managers Privatize at a Time of Scarcity," *New York Times,* 19 August 1992.

54. Gherman Lomanov, "Military-Industrial Complex: Privatization Partially Suspended," *Moscow News,* 15 October 1993. Also see the comments of enterprise director Kostin, "Thoughts on Conversion."

55. Sergei Podiapolskii, quoting Soskovets, ITAR-TASS, 28 June 1993, as reported in *FBIS-SOV,* 30 June 1993, p. 45.

56. For example, see Vladimir Gimpelson, "Novoe Rossiiskoe Predprinimatel'stvo: Istochniki Formirovaniia i Strategii Sotsial'nogo Deistviia," *Mirovaia Ekonomika i Mezhdunarodnye Otnosheniia,* no. 6 (1993): 36–37.

57. Vladimir Kondratev, quoting Volskiy, Ostankino First Channel Television Network, 15 May 1993, as reported in *FBIS-SOV,* 17 May 1993, p. 23.

58. Barbara J. Spencer, "What Should Trade Policy Target?" in *Strategic Trade Policy and the New International Economics,* ed. Paul. R. Krugman (Cambridge: MIT Press, 1986), pp. 73–74.

59. Peter Almquist, *Red Forge: Soviet Military Industry Since 1965* (New York: Columbia University Press, 1990), p. 46.

60. Anatolii Yershov, "Bankrotami Stali po Sobstvennoi Vole," *Izvestiia,* 10 February 1994. I am grateful to Yevgenii Gorkov for this citation.

61. Katharina Pistor, "Privatization and Corporate Governance in Russia: An Empirical Study," in *Privatization, Conversion, and Enterprise Reform in Russia: Selected Conference Papers,* ed. Michael McFaul and Tova Perlmutter (Stanford: Stanford University Center for International Security and Arms Control, 1994).

62. For an example, see Oleg Kotov, "Aerokosmicheskaia Firma Namerena Zhit' po Zakonam Rynka," *Kommersant-Daily,* 22 April 1993.

63. "East/West Aerospace Ventures on the Rise," *Aviation Week and Space Technology,* 23 August 1993, pp. 51–59.

64. Anatoly Tkachenko, "Ulyanovsk Cross-Country Vehicles Conquer America," *Moscow News,* 6 August 1993.

65. "Military Shipbuilding Will Be Frozen at the Baltiisky Plant," *Moscow News,* 4 June 1993.

66. N. Zvereva and I. Stanovov, "Vesti" newscast, Russian Television Network, 5 May 1993, as reported in *FBIS-SOV,* 6 May 1993, p. 45.

67. Irina Usyumenko, "Leading Concern in St. Petersburg to Become a Holding Company," *Moscow News,* 5 March 1993.

68. Radio Rossii, 14 September 1993, as reported in *FBIS-SOV,* 15 September 1993, p. 35.

69. Craig Covault, "Russian SA-12 Missiles Eyed for European ABM," *Aviation Week and Space Technology,* 13 September 1993, p. 99.

70. Stephen Foye, "Franco-Russian Military Accords," *RFE/RL Daily Report,* 7 February 1994.

71. Craig Covault and Boris Rybak, "Sukhoi May Seek U.S. Partner for New Fighter," *Aviation Week and Space Technology,* 27 September 1993, pp. 47–48.

72. Boris Reznik, "Far East Conversion with U.S. Government Participation," *Izvestiia,* 4 August 1993, as reported in *FBIS-SOV,* 5 August 1993, p. 3.

73. Sergei Leskov, "They Are Building Submarines in Severodvinsk but Thinking of Developing Sea Shelf," *Izvestiia,* 13 July 1993, as reported in *FBIS-SOV,* 14 July 1993, pp. 39–40.

74. Ibid.

75. Cited in Stephen Foye, "Russian Ship-Building to Continue," *RFE/RL Daily Report,* 18 January 1994.

76. Louise Kehoe, "Satellite Venture Wins $600m Contracts," *Financial Times,* 18 March 1994.

77. Ibid.

78. Richard W. Stevenson, "A New Course for Russian Aerospace," *New York Times,* 26 November 1993.

79. Ibid.

80. Victor Belikov, "Boeing Soars into Russian Sky," *We/My,* 1–14 November 1993.

81. "Russian Airlines Are Being Equipped with Boeings," *Moscow News,* 7 May 1993.

82. Stevenson, "New Course for Russian Aerospace."

83. Milner and Yoffie, "Between Free Trade and Protectionism," p. 257.

84. Vladimir Kulikov and Boris Antsiferov, "Novosti" newscast, Ostankino First Channel Television Network, 12 June 1993, as reported in *FBIS-SOV,* 17 June 1993, pp. 41–42.

85. Ethan Kapstein, *The Political Economy of National Security: A Global Perspective* (Columbia: University of South Carolina Press, 1992), p. 155. This is an application of the full argument that he made concerning the Brazilian defense industry, in "The Brazilian Defense Industry and the International System," *Political Science Quarterly* 105 (Winter 1990/91): 589–590.

86. Gaddy and Allen, "Dreams of a Salesman."

87. Andrei Baranovsky, "Helicopter Company Kamov Introduces New Models," *Moscow News,* 24 September 1993.

88. Natalya Komina, "Coca-Cola Cooperates with Defense Plants," *Moscow News,* 20 August 1993.

89. Jonathan Broder, "You, Too, Can Fly a MiG Fighter," *We/My,* 1–14 November 1993.

90. "11-Year-Old American Flies MiG," Associated Press, 13 July 1994.

91. Gherman Lomanov, "Russia Can Earn Millions of Dollars Exporting Unique Armaments," *Moscow News,* 4 February 1993.

92. For a Russian perspective on the consequences of this move, see Natalia Kalashnikova, "Vashington Vvel Sanktsii v Otnoshenii Rossisskikh Eksporterov Raketnykh Tekhnologii," *Kommersant-Daily,* 30 June 1993.

93. Gleb Cherkasov, "The Military-Industrial Complex's Generals Want to Have Their Own Political Party," *Segodnia,* 15 March 1994, as reported in *Current Digest of the Post-Soviet Press (CDPSP),* 13 April 1994, pp. 4–5; and Pavel Felgengauer, "Day of Judgment for the Military-Industrial Complex," *Segodnia,* 15 March 1994, as reported in *Current Digest of the Post-Soviet Press (CDPSP),* 13 April 1994, p. 5.

94. James A. Brander and Barbara J. Spencer, "Export Subsidies and International Market Share Rivalry," *Journal of International Economics* 18 (February 1985): 83–100. Also see Spencer, "What Should Trade Policy Target?" pp. 70–71.

95. See the literature review critiquing the Brander-Spencer findings in Paul R. Krugman, *Rethinking International Trade* (Cambridge: MIT Press, 1990), pp. 250–253.

96. See Milner, "Resisting the Protectionist Temptation," pp. 649–650, for some examples.

97. For an analysis supporting the notion that webs of connections between firms can contribute to the building of open markets regardless of how states behave, see Susan Strange, "Protectionism and World Politics," *International Organization* 39 (Spring 1985): 233–259.

98. Albert O. Hirschman, *National Power and the Structure of Foreign Trade* (Berkeley: University of California Press, 1945).

99. Andrei Naryshkin, ITAR-TASS in English, 28 May 1993, as reported in *FBIS-SOV,* 2 June 1993, p. 40.

100. For an in-depth discussion of this process, see Kimberly Marten Zisk, *Engaging the Enemy: Organization Theory and Soviet Military Innovation, 1955–1991* (Princeton: Princeton University Press, 1993), chap. 5.

101. Julian Cooper, "Transforming Russia's Defense Industrial Base," *Survival* 35 (Winter 1993): 147–162. Also see the early position paper written by Kokoshin's group, "Osnovy Natsional'noi Industrial'noe Politiki Rossii: Kratkii Variant Programmy," *Rossiia,* 7–13 October 1992, pp. 1–8.

CHAPTER 6

Russia and Europe After the Cold War: The Interaction of Domestic and Foreign Policies

Bruce D. Porter

During the Cold War, Western observers of Soviet foreign policy typically couched their analyses in terms of the strategy, objectives, intentions, calculations, and ideological tenets of Soviet leaders. A rational actor approach dominated the study of the Soviet Union's foreign policy, and with a few notable exceptions, this approach worked well. The state- and party-centralized bureaucratic apparatus, bolstered by Marxism-Leninism, produced a Soviet foreign policy marked by a degree of strategic coherence and purpose that made a rational actor approach both logical and theoretically useful.

The collapse of communism has made this approach largely obsolete, and it will remain so as long as Russian government and society remain in a state of internal turbulence and uncertainty. By every possible measure, Russian foreign policy from 1991 until at least fall 1993 was sorely lacking in coherence, design, and a sense of strategy. Nor did post-Soviet Russia have any well-defined bureaucratic or political mechanism for imposing order on the policymaking process. No single person dominated the policy process, and leaders' views were strongly influenced by changing winds of domestic opinion and pressure. Russia's foreign policy toward the West during this period was marked by ad hoc and poorly coordinated efforts to maintain good relations with the West and to attract desperately needed capital. Although such a foreign policy cannot be described as irrational, it reflected neither a sophisticated strategic plan nor a determination to defend the prestige and prerogatives of a great power in Europe.

At the same time, two other trends developed that are important for Russian foreign policy: the evolution of Russian elite thinking on the new international environment and the evolution of the post-Soviet Russian political system. The Russian political elite after 1991 gradually divided into three intellectual and informal groupings: an "Atlanticist" bloc; a "Russia First," or extreme nationalist bloc; and a "Eurasianist" grouping that sought to forge a middle course between Europe and Asia as well as between the first two tendencies. The struggle over who will govern Russia in the future—and how they will do it, in both the domestic and the foreign realm—has played out largely among these three tendencies. This chapter will argue that the post–Cold War security environment has profoundly influenced this internal struggle for power and that Russian foreign policy since 1989 has developed at a critical nexus between mounting internal cleavages and a rapidly evolving external environment.

A Theoretical Digression: External Conflict and Internal Strife

The German historian Otto Hintze wrote in 1902 that students of politics frequently overlook "the development of the state in relation to its neighbors." According to Hintze, a state's rivalry with foreign powers has as much impact on its internal structure as do domestic rivalries among class and interest groups.[1] Charles Tilly, Max Weber, Theda Skocpol, and other scholars have similarly argued that the external environment of states substantially determines their internal structure and affects their evolution.[2] By the impact of the external environment on a state's foreign or domestic politics, we mean more than mere bureaucratic politics or the influence on policy formation of interest groups and lobbies that have foreign ties.[3] The external environment of states influences their entire formation, evolution, and nature. It has an impact not only on individual leaders and interest groups but also on the whole development of the state as a semiautonomous *collectivity of actors,* an entity whose whole is greater than the sum of its parts. The billiard ball to which the state has sometimes been likened by structural realists in fact possesses a complex interior, whose structure is heavily shaped by the interaction of the balls on the table of world politics.

This point is best illustrated by an unlikely case: Stalinist Russia. In the early 1930s, the USSR was perhaps as isolated from the outside world as any large power could be: Communications and travel were highly restricted, diplomatic contacts with the West were fraught with suspicion, and any contact with foreigners was probable grounds for charges of treason. One might suppose that such extreme isolation would have vastly reduced the impact of the external environment on internal Soviet affairs, that the Soviet state would have developed with little impact from the outside world: no contact, no influence. In fact, the opposite was true. The totalitarian structure and extreme repression of the Stalinist regime were intimately linked to its isolation and to Stalin's perception of an external environment of profound threat. The linkage between the external environment and Stalin's forced-pace industrialization campaign was captured in his oft-repeated slogan *"dognat i peregnat"*—"to overtake and to surpass"—the Western industrial powers "in the shortest time possible." The unspeakable sacrifices and deprivations of the collectivization and industrialization drives were justified—indeed could *only* be justified—by reference to an all-powerful, imminent foreign threat.[4] An external environment of threat was also evoked as the primary rationale behind the Great Purge that took place a few years later.

The potential contribution of an environment of threat to reinforcing the internal cohesion of a given state has long been recognized by political philosophers and analysts.[5] Foreign threats tend to generate "internal rallying" within states, as regimes and their internal oppositions close ranks in order to deal with a perceived foreign enemy. The exigencies of dealing with such adversaries cause cooperation to increase at home, factionalism and partisanship to decline, and national unity to solidify. As Jean Bodin wrote at the beginning of the modern era, "the best way of preserving a state, and guaranteeing it against sedition, rebellion, and civil war is to keep the subjects in amity one with another, and to this end, to find an enemy against whom they can make common cause."[6] The rallying effect of external adversaries is powerful enough to tempt rulers and governments to fabricate or exaggerate such threats (or to promote aggressive designs) in order to unify a fractious state. They may be tempted to engage in *divergence,* promoting unity by resorting to foreign adventure—"to busy giddy minds with foreign quarrels" in the words of Shakespeare's Henry IV.[7]

The phenomenon of divergence suggests the advisability of categorizing external threats into at least three categories: objective, perceived, and contrived. *Objective threats* would be the existence of actual military forces deployed in such a manner as to be capable of attack coupled with an adversarial relationship that gives such an attack a significant degree of probability. Outside observers who are not a party to the potential conflict would generally recognize, if given adequate intelligence, the existence of objective threats. *Perceived threats* would be those that a given party perceives as existing, regardless of whether they objectively do. A perceived threat may derive from an objective threat or it may be largely in the imagination, a product of suspicion and doubt. Finally, *contrived threats* would be those deliberately invented by rulers, governments, or internal factions, intended to accomplish a certain political effect at home (unifying the populace, discrediting a given political line, and so on) even though the contriver is fully aware that the threat is not real. By definition, contrived threats cannot also be objective threats, though they may well become perceived threats if the fabrication is successful.

If threats and enemies can potentially unify states, what happens when threats suddenly disappear or enemies become friends? This is a question of utmost importance for all of post–Cold War Europe and especially Russia, which for the first time in its history lacks objective enemies (at least great-power enemies). Quincy Wright observes in his classic *A Study of War* that "communities without an enemy have tended to divide," and Michael Desch has similarly argued that as war contributes to state formation, peace may tend to threaten state deformation.[8]

The aftereffects of a preceding period of war or rivalry also may make peaceful eras a time of domestic stress. The national mobilization that occurs during great wars is a searing, revelatory experience for any political system: Like some vast social audit, it unmasks the weaknesses and defects of a given polity more starkly than any peacetime processes could ever do. This has been termed the "audit of war" or the "inspection effect" since pressure for reform inevitably mounts as large numbers of individuals audit and inspect the flaws of their state during periods of national mobilization.[9] This may be one reason why revolutions, revolts, and civil wars so often follow in the wake of great wars.[10]

The Cold War was a protracted rivalry that fell short of an all-out war, but it shared many features of a great war, including high levels of national mobilization and widespread perceptions of constant threat. In the case of the USSR, it provided the Communist elite with a legitimizing raison d'être for policies of extreme internal repression and intense social mobilization. The question logically follows: How will the Russian state fare now that it is no longer faced with a well-defined external threat? Will its termination exacerbate latent internal cleavages in the Russian polity? Will Russian leaders seek to contrive threats in order to unify a fractious polity?

Threats, Myths, and the Dilemma of Military Modernization

Russia's external environment has helped shape its political development throughout history. For Russia, the forging of national unity and identity has always been an immense challenge, given that it was a larger and more far-flung country than any in Europe or indeed the world. Yet a coherent national identity, as well as a sense of national unity, are essential conditions for the exercise of political authority and the mobilization of military power; hence, they are integral components of successful nation building. From Ivan the Terrible on, three classic methods were brought to bear in the shaping of a unified Russian state: first, the evocation of external threats (many of them wholly objective) as a means of achieving internal mobilization; second, the construction of a powerful, centralized government capable of enforcing order and imposing unity; and finally, the promulgation of legitimizing national myths.

All three of these were closely linked. An external environment of profound threat provided both motivation and rationale for the construction of a highly authoritarian, militarized Russian state—the classic Hobbesian solution to internal division, which Ivan the Terrible fixated on a full century before Hobbes was born. The centralized state in turn required legitimizing myths to justify its existence and its excesses. Those myths helped shape the self-image of the Russian people as a great nation with a unique and special mission, a self-image that in turn contributed to the rise of the xenophobic nationalism that characterized so much of Russian thinking.

The external environment of both tsarist and Soviet Russia was not only fraught with military threats, both objective and perceived, but with military opportunities as well. From the late fifteenth century onward, the threats emanated primarily from Europe and were exacerbated by Russia's intrinsic geographical insecurity (indefensible borders, vast territory, open plains). The opportunities, however, lay primarily to the south and east. The existence of vast, lightly populated frontiers in Central Asia and Siberia helped shape the political-military machinery of the Russian state almost as much as the mind-concentrating threats emanating from the west and north. A state that faced profound threats from the west could hardly resist enhancing its resources and population by expansion to the east, where nomad-populated steppes posed no serious obstacle.[11]

As Russia expanded, it developed a set of national myths that undergirded state formation and justified territorial expansion. Russia's legitimizing and unifying myths were never solely national in nature but always aspired to a kind of universalism, a reflection of the deep-rooted idealism of the Russian people. They initially derived from Russian Orthodoxy and the concept of Moscow as the Third Rome; eventually, the sense of Russia's destiny came to encompass Pan-Slavism as well. In our century, both were integrated into a new, yet more grandiose myth: communism. Russia's territorial expansion seemed to corroborate the myths: Surely the largest country in the world, which sat astride the heartland of both Europe and Asia, must have a unique destiny and mission.

Despite these three unifying factors—external threats, a powerful state, and a national myth—Russia was never a fully unified nation-state. This was true not only of the larger, multiethnic imperium under the dominion of Moscow but also of the inner Russian heartland. The problem was a seemingly unbridgeable gulf between the aristocracy (and later the Communist apparat)—the backbone of the political state—and the peasantry and working classes, which together constituted the bulk of the Russian ethnic nation. The historian Geoffrey Alan Hosking observes: "Russia constitutes a remarkable, perhaps unique case of a nation which has taken [two] paths together, in parallel with one another, building at the same time an aristocratic, imperial nation and a demotic, ethnic one."[12] It is significant that only in periods of profound threat, usually meaning actual invasion, did the two nations come together as one, and even then only temporarily.

Russia and the Two "Wests"

In the modern era, most of the nation-unifying threats faced by Russia emanated from the West, as when the armies of Napoleonic France, Wilhelmine Germany, and Nazi Germany invaded deep into the Russian heartland. Yet the impact of the West as a factor in Russian state formation was not always or even primarily unifying. In fact, *except* during periods of great wars and invasions, the almost inexorable tendency of Western influence was to divide Russia politically. This was a central problem of Russian state development, a problem that arose because there were really two different "Wests" that interacted with Russia throughout modern history and to whom the Russians looked in their search for a model of national development.

The first West was the liberal, democratic West of the Enlightenment, the West that embodied high principles of individual worth, human liberty and dignity, rationality, dialogue and tolerance, the rule of law, representative government, and constitutionalism. This was the Western world of parliamentary assemblies, free elections, bills of rights, Roman law, popular sovereignty, and national self-determination. This was the core of Western civilization that appealed to the highest of human instincts and that had profound attraction to the idealistic side of liberal Russian intellectuals. This was the West that the Westernizers of old (and those of today) thought they were following.

The other West was the militarized, regimented, technological juggernaut embodied by the armies of Charles XII of Sweden, Frederick the Great of Prussia, Napoleon Bonaparte of France, Kaiser Wilhelm of Imperial Germany, and Adolf Hitler of Nazi Germany. This was the West that time and again sparred with or invaded Russia, that dazzled Russian leaders with its technical-military superiority, and that acted as a constant spur to military modernization and bureaucratic reform. *This* was the West that Russia actually emulated. The attractions of Western humanism, liberalism, and Enlightenment philosophy aside, it was the military prowess of the West that served again and again as a profound shock to traditional Russia and later Soviet Russia. Russia's perennial inability to maintain qualitative parity with Western military power forced it into state-driven, state-strengthening efforts at military reform and modernization, even though in the end it always (and quite successfully) relied on its quantitative superiority and sheer mass to defeat Western invaders.[13]

The often unrecognized contradiction between the two Wests—and the difficulty Russians had in discerning any logical connection between the two—meant that Western influence and Russian pursuit of Westernization very often proved to be divisive factors in Russian politics. Military modernization and reform invariably required that the state mobilize talent and resources. Nothing but a top-down approach seemed feasible, but this meant that the pursuit of military parity with the West strengthened only the autocratic, and later totalitarian, Russian state. The pursuit of military modernization mandated extreme centralization of state power. Conversely, efforts to undertake liberal reform invariably weakened the state and thus were seen as threatening Russia's internal cohesion as well as its capacity to maintain pace with the West. There were, in effect, two paths Russia could take, as shown in Figure 6.1.

Russia almost always remained on the first path, in part because it objectively faced an environment of high threat, in part because whenever it veered even

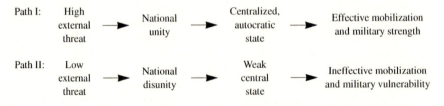

FIGURE 6.1   Historical Paths from Security Environment to Domestic Effects

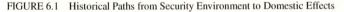

briefly onto the second, the sense of internal disunity and military vulnerability rapidly became so great as to encourage a reassertion of central power. For centuries, Russia in its relationship with the West has found itself trapped in this Sisyphean cycle, wanting to emulate the West but forced to do so primarily in the military sphere because of the imminence of both the objective and perceived threats that the latter posed.

Russia in the New Europe

With this theory and historical background in mind, let us now examine how the European security environment has changed and how Russia is responding to those changes. The truly radical feature of the immediate post–Cold War era for Russia is the absence of a great-power threat that Russian leaders could evoke as a rationale for their policies and the exertion of their power internally. This decline in the objective threat to Russia was a result of reduced defense spending by the Western powers, the limitations placed on Germany's armed forces during its unification, and the withdrawal of large numbers of U.S. troops from Western Europe. An emerging Sino-Russian rapprochement simultaneously has reduced the sense of threat from the Far East, while Russia's continuing possession of a large and robust arsenal of nuclear weapons further contributes to a sense of fundamental security. All these factors make it difficult for Russian leaders to plausibly argue that Russia faces a serious threat of invasion from abroad.

More specifically, and confining our focus to Europe, at least five fundamental changes have taken place in Russia's external security environment.

The End of an East-West Division of the Continent

Political, physical, and ideological walls no longer divide Europe. Russia is no longer treated as a pariah or an overt enemy of the West. To the contrary, it is a member of the North Atlantic Cooperation Council (NACC) and the Council of the Baltic Sea States, and it has reluctantly joined NATO's Partnership for Peace (amid much hesitation and failed attempts to gain special status). It has conducted talks on joining the Council of Europe, negotiated on cooperation with the European Union, and requested observer status in the Paris Club. Boris Yeltsin participated as a full partner in summit-level talks with the leaders of the G-7 in Naples in July 1994. Moscow has signed bilateral treaties of friendship with several West European countries, and it is the recipient of billions of dollars in aid from the West and from international institutions such as the IMF. For a country that less than a decade earlier was vilified as an "evil empire," these steps represent dramatic progress. With large numbers of U.S. ground troops withdrawn from Europe, tactical nuclear weapons drastically reduced, and the overall military spending of NATO Europe down by about 3 percent since 1989, Russia faces the least degree of threat from the West since the 1920s.

Yet for all this, there remain significant obstacles to Russia's full acceptance by the West. The largest of these is its reassertion of influence in the former Soviet republics, an issue that Western states initially treated cautiously but has led to growing alarm and formal protests.[14] Russian trade and diplomatic initiatives toward Serbia, Iran, Iraq, and North Korea are also viewed with increasing concern. East-West differences still exist over the security architecture of postwar Europe. Russia has sought strenuously for renegotiation of the Treaty on Conventional Forces in Europe (CFE) in order to accommodate its peacekeeping activities in the Caucasus and elsewhere; NATO has repeatedly rebuffed this initiative. Partly in response, Russia has argued that an expansion of NATO into Eastern Europe would violate the CFE Treaty.[15] The Western powers likewise have been unreceptive to Russia's proposal of July 1994 to subordinate NATO and other European organizations to an enhanced OSCE. Russia inevitably interprets Western responses to its initiatives as evidence that it is still not trusted by the West. The chief of staff of the Russian General Staff, Mikhail Kolesnikov, complained in May 1994 that Western refusal to make even minor concessions on the CFE treaty proved that Russia was not regarded as a true partner.[16] Russia is thus left with a conundrum: The West is not yet prepared to accept Russia as a full partner, with all the benefits that might entail, but at the same time, the "West" as a collective entity no longer serves as an adversarial counterpoint against which Russian national identity and pride can coalesce.

The Withdrawal of Soviet Power
from the Heartland of Europe

Russia is not threatened by the West; in addition, it cannot in any plausible short- to mid-term scenario pose a credible threat against the West. When Soviet troops stood on the inner German border, astride the heart of Europe, Russia had to be taken seriously by the West. It might be loathed, feared, mistrusted, or resisted, but its thirty-three divisions, half million ground troops, and nearly two thousand combat aircraft could not be ignored. The withdrawal of these forces—accomplished in August 1994—means that Russia arguably no longer exerts the influence it once did in West European affairs. It has become instead a benign bystander, a spectator, on the sidelines of a unifying Western Europe. Without the capacity to threaten the West, Russia simply is not taken as seriously as it once was. As one Russian scholar, Andrei Zagorsky, observes: "There is no getting away from the impression that every further visit abroad ends in relations between Russia and European countries returning as it were to a state of lethargy, or almost."[17]

A New "Buffer Zone" Between Russia
and the Rest of Europe

Russia's waning influence in Europe is compounded by its increased physical separation from the West in consequence of the independence of Belarus, Ukraine, the Baltic states, and Moldova. In 1992, Sergei Stankevich, then Yeltsin's state counselor, observed, "We are now separated from Europe by a whole chain of independent states and find ourselves much farther from it, which inevitably involves a . . . substantial redistribution of our resources, our potentialities, our links and interests in favor of Asia."[18] The rise of this new buffer zone does not supplant the original one—the former Warsaw Pact states of Eastern Europe—but only adds an additional layer.

The emergence of this inner ring adds an increased degree of complexity to Russia's relations with all states to its west, forcing Russian leaders to deal with a whole new set of bilateral and multilateral issues, many of which were previously domestic issues that could be resolved from a position of sovereign strength. Such issues include borders and tariffs, the status of the oblast Kaliningrad, the citizenship status and rights of ethnic Russians living in this buffer zone, access to seaports, military bases, economic links and cooperation among formerly integrated industries, and the division of Soviet assets. At the same time, events such as Lithuania's participation in NATO's Baltic Sea exercises (BALTOPS '93) make it difficult for Russia to regard the states of the region simply as weakling upstarts whose policies can pose no threats to its security.

A Reunified Germany

Less than a decade ago, most Western observers believed that the Soviet leadership would never tolerate a unified Germany allied with NATO. The moderate Soviet resistance and ultimate acquiescence to reunification from 1989 to 1991 suggest that by then the Soviet leadership had come to believe the benefits of ending the division of Europe far outweighed the potential threat of a unified Germany. Since 1991, post-Soviet Russia has maintained a generally friendly relationship with Germany. Several issues have rippled the relationship; they have been primarily linked to larger European, rather than bilateral, concerns. These include a handful of espionage cases; the status of Kaliningrad Oblast; the extension of NATO into Eastern Europe; the withdrawal of Russian troops from the Baltic states; and the conflict in former Yugoslavia. None of these have been allowed to derail the momentum of post–Cold War rapprochement, however.

The two world wars of this century too easily cause us to forget that the historical pattern of relations between Germany and Russia has been one of cooperation, trade, and affinity. That pattern—which even in the rivalry of our century produced both the Treaty of Rapallo and the Molotov-Ribbentrop Pact—now seems to be reasserting itself. Russian politicians have resisted the temptation to regard Germany as an enemy or to fret publicly about possible German revanchism. Given the small size of the Bundeswehr, the security guarantees linked to reunification, the Russian possession of nuclear weapons, and the simple fact that Germany has provided more aid to Russia—more than $50 billion in grants and credits—than all other Western countries combined, it is difficult for even the most nationalistic Russians (Zhirinovsky aside) to see Germany as an imminent threat. There have been concerns voiced about its future potential in the Russian media, but such worrying has not become a trend.

The Continuation of West European Unification

The Soviet leadership wanted to end the Cold War in part to end the USSR's isolation from the West, an isolation that was costing it dearly in terms of trade and technical development. Yet now that the Cold War is over, Russia finds itself still isolated from a Europe continuing on the path of political unification affirmed at Maastricht. That process of unification—soon to be joined by the Scandinavian states and in all probability eventually to extend to Poland, the Czech Republic, and Hungary—threatens to leave Russia isolated once again. Part of the motivation for Russia's strenuous opposition to the latter three states joining NATO may arise not only from basic security concerns but also from fear that it will be a first step toward their entering the European Union. Russia would thus be shut out of trading on equal terms with most of the continent and hence be more isolated than ever before. This isolation, however, is largely economic and political in nature. Although in the long term the European Union may become a formidable military force, in the short term its military potential is both declining and locked up in the structure of NATO, where the United States exerts heavy influence.

The Implications of a Low-Threat Environment

Given the crucial role of the external environment in the historical development of Russia, these five transformations of European politics are inevitably of great consequence for the future of the Russian state. The most significant shift, as noted earlier, was the decline of objective threats to Russian security—which meant that the external environment no longer promoted a unifying and rallying effect within the Russian polity. This is turn contributed to the decline of two other sources of national unity: the power of the central state and the legitimizing myth of ideology. Although both of these declined for reasons wholly indigenous to Russia, that decline was abetted by the new international environment, the threatening nature of which previously had always been held up as a justification for centralized power and the pursuit of empire.

To say that Russia faces no great-power threat at the present juncture is not to argue that it faces no threat at all. Although the objective threat from Western Europe has diminished, a perceived threat continues, epitomized in Russian concerns over the possible extension of NATO into Eastern Europe, worry over its technological backwardness vis-à-vis the West, and awareness of its continuing separation from the mainstream of Western life. The conflict in Bosnia especially has aroused Russian concerns, since it pits a Slavic people under a once Communist government against Western-supported secessionist states. The analogies and the allies involved evoke uncomfortable parallels and stir pan-Slavist sentiments. The disintegration of the Soviet Union has also presented the Russian leadership with a new threat (new, at least as an *international* threat), namely, the emergence of fourteen newly independent states on its borders. The new Russian military doctrine announced in fall 1993 reflected a preoccupation with potential threats from these new states—the "near abroad." Ethnic conflict in Eastern Europe, the Caucasus, and Central Asia further intensified a general sense of insecurity on the part of the Russians. Once surrounded by powerful but predictable enemies, they are now surrounded by much weaker but less predictable potential enemies.

Yet the perception of threat in all of these instances is of a different order of magnitude than Russia has faced throughout most of its history. The threats are ambiguous and diffuse enough that they have not served to unite a fractious Russian polity (except briefly in the case of Bosnia, as will be discussed below), but for the most part they have only intensified differences. This is a critical shift from past Russian responses to threat, demonstrating that the new set of Russian threat perceptions, centered on Central Europe and the newly independent states, will not simply become a substitute for the old threat environment centered on Western Europe. Russia really has entered a new and largely unprecedented phase of its history, in which the outside environment provides no ready justification for internal repression.

The end of communism and of Russia's ideological rivalry with the West also means that for the first time in hundreds of years Russia lays claim to no such universal mission. The obvious course left is for Russia to behave as a "normal country" pursuing nothing more than peace and prosperity. But this is a fate that increasing numbers of the Russian elite resist. The loss of empire and the stark evidence of national failure evident on every side have left a deeply wounded sense of national pride, including contradictory feelings about Russia's role in the world.[19] Russia historically has sought to overcome its inferiority complex vis-à-vis the West by claiming a special, universal mission—either divinely ordained or historically determined. As a kind of compensation for immense loss, Russian political leaders and intellectuals today are already searching for new myths.

Internal Cleavages and the Search for Unifying Solutions

In the absence of the three unifying factors mentioned earlier, Russia in the aftermath of the Cold War has suffered from multiple internal cleavages. Although those cleavages stemmed partly from domestic factors, they were reinforced and aggravated by the altered external environment, both in Europe and in Asia. Most of the fault lines that emerged, and that continue to exist today, had direct implications for the shaping of Russia's national identity and the course of its relations with the West.

The most serious of these splits, as to its potential to have international repercussions, is the political schisms among Russia's three principal political groupings: the new Westernizers, or "Atlanticists"; the new Slavophiles, or "Eurasianists"; and the "Red-Brown coalition" of extreme nationalists and Communists.

The Westernizers want Russia to follow a clearly Western path of development, similar to the course they believe it had embarked on successfully between 1905 and 1914. They favor liberal democracy, Western-style capitalism, and a broad-reaching partnership with the West. The Eurasianists, in contrast, believe that Russia must follow its own course, sometimes characterized as a "third way" between West and East. Although not necessarily anti-Western, this tendency looks to the Russian interior, and especially to Siberia and the Far East, for the future development of Russia. The third group, both in its left-wing (Communist) and right-wing (neo-Fascist) tendencies, is highly reactionary in its politics, seeking a restoration of the former Soviet empire and the reemergence of that empire as a militarily strong, global superpower. Its foreign policy pronouncements are blatantly anti-Western; this plays well in the outlying provinces, rural areas, and small cities, which view with distrust the expansion of Western influence in Moscow and St. Petersburg.

It is important to recognize that these three groupings are imprecise in constitution, fluid in organization and adherents, and themselves divided into numerous factions. They nevertheless represent the principal political fault lines along which Russian society is divided today. But Russia is divided not only along these political-ideological lines but along other important lines as well. A second source of internal cleavage is its multiethnic population. Although its most urgent problem with minority nationalities was in theory resolved by the breakup of the Union (in theory only, since conflict between Russians and non-Russians continues throughout the former USSR), rump Russia itself contains numerous ethnic minorities, some of which constitute a majority of the population in specific enclaves and political units. Demands for autonomy from Tatarstan, Chechnya, and other ethnic enclaves within the Russian Federation have bedeviled the central leadership almost constantly since 1991.

A third schism is between central authority, now shakily embodied in Yeltsin's government and the new constitution, and a host of assertive local political units, whose leaders in many instances have openly defied Moscow's will. The refusal of nearly half of Russian's republic and regions at one time or another to remit taxes to the central government is indicative of this problem. This division is not necessarily along ethnic or even sectional lines, for many of the most adamant opponents of central power are ethnic Russians situated in regions long under Russian control. But local opposition to central rule often merges with or reinforces ethnic opposition to Russian rule. As a result, the Russian Federation is threatened by powerful centrifugal forces that could even cause it to break up if central authority should further diminish.

There is, finally, a continuing split between Russia's ruling elite and the Russian population (the faceless "masses" of Bolshevik lore)—the "imperial nation" and the "ethnic nation," to use Geoffrey Hosking's terminology. A problem that has plagued Russia throughout the modern era still plagues it today: It has never achieved a genuine fusion of nation and state. This problem of achieving a long-overdue fusion of nation and state is the defining challenge of Russian political life today.

Given the magnitude of that problem and the serious cleavages that afflict the Russian society and polity, Russia is today searching for new unifying principles—legitimizing myths—around which its national identity can be shaped. In addition, it is searching for a new conception of national interest that can serve as the basis for future foreign and domestic policies. The three main alternatives coincide with the three political tendencies noted above: a liberal solution, a "Russia First" restoration of empire, and a "Eurasianist" alternative.

The Liberal Solution

The collapse of communism and the consequent disintegration of the Soviet Union brought to power a new generation of leaders, self-styled "democrats" who saw liberal democracy and free market capitalism as principles capable of midwifing the national rebirth of Russia. Boris Yeltsin, Andrei Kozyrev, Yegor Gaidar, and the coterie of young intellectuals who supported them and staffed senior positions in the new Russian government hoped that by pursuing democratization and privatization—that is, Westernization—vigorously, they could ensure prosperity, political freedom, and national security for their smaller Russia. For the first time in Russian history, security would be based not on military power but on a broad-reaching accommodation with the West. Russia would permit, even invite, a Western strategy used before in post-1945 Germany: entangle it in a web of institutional strands, cooperative arrangements, and economic interdependency that would reduce its autonomy but enhance its security (and eventually its prosperity).

This strategy accounts for the vigorous, at times almost blatantly sycophantic, manner in which Russian diplomacy since 1989—and with increased vigor since 1991—has sought to enter Western organizations and to sign cooperative agreements and treaties with Western partners, including participation in the OSCE, cooperation with NATO, and participation in UN peacekeeping. More reluctantly, Russia has also sought to be a good neighbor toward the former Warsaw Pact states and even toward the Baltic states—whether out of a belief that opportunities for positive gains beckoned here also or simply out of a belief that benign behavior in this region was a prerequisite to overall good relations with the West. Despite Russia's quarrels with Estonia over troop withdrawals and the treatment of ethnic Russians, and with Latvia over the Russian presence at the Skrunda radar base, the fact remains that Russia continued to withdraw troops gradually and in July 1994 reached agreement with both states on the major disputed issues.

The Atlanticists failed to foresee the strong nationalist backlash that would occur at home in response to the loss of the larger Soviet empire, the decline of Russian military power, and perceptions of Russian humiliation before a Western world that refused to accept Russia as a full partner. The depth of that backlash contributed to the debacle of the first Russian Congress of People's Deputies, which Yeltsin forcibly disbanded in fall 1993, and to the strong anti-Yeltsin electoral currents of the December 1993 national election. It also led both Yeltsin and Kozyrev, by fall 1993, to begin taking a much more nationalistic, hard line on a variety of foreign policy issues.

At the core of the Westernizers' inability to sustain their strategy of accommodation was the familiar dilemma pointed out earlier: the contradiction between liberal reform and military modernization. As early as 1982, the farsighted military reformer and chief of the General Staff, Nikolai Ogarkov, saw that Soviet Russia could not match the West in an emerging generation of high-tech, silicon-based weaponry: a military-technical revolution threatened to leave the USSR far behind. Ogarkov saw no hope but to pursue a more Western model of social and political development, and he openly called for "perestroika" of "the entire economy [as well as] political, social, scientific, and other institutions" in order to lay a foundation for enhanced military strength.[20] But, as we know, the result of perestroika, as well as of the more radical reforms that followed it, was not enhanced Russian military power but military decline and social disarray.

This contradiction remains at the heart of the crisis of liberal reform facing Russia today. The liberals can make Russia free, but only by allowing it—at least temporarily—to become weak. By comparison with its centralized, totalitarian predecessor state, the new Russian state is too weak, too disorganized, and too unstable to act as an effective mobilizer of physical and human resources. Liberal democracies mobilize military power at least as effectively, or even more effectively, than centralized autocracies—but only if they are well established, have a high degree of popular legitimacy, and possess stable political institutions. Until Russian democracy develops to this point—a process that may take a generation or more—it will have to settle for relative military weakness or revert to more authoritarian forms of resource mobilization. The liberal solution thus implicitly requires that Russia obtain its security by diplomatic means—through compromise and accommodation with the West. The burden that rests upon Russia's new Westernizers is to persuade an increasingly skeptical, nationalist-minded population that drawing near to the West will both ensure Russia's security and make possible its economic and social revitalization.

The Atlanticist case has been difficult to make for several reasons. First, the process of accommodation with the West is proving to be slow, and the course of internal reform is even slower. But the "Yeltsin Revolution" generated expectations for change well out of proportion to its real possibilities. Second, whereas the objective Western threat to Russia has declined, as noted earlier, the emergence of new threats (perceived, if not objective) both from the former Soviet republics and from a NATO-infatuated Eastern Europe gives fodder to nationalist-minded critics of the new regime, who charge it with having sacrificed Russia's superpower status. Finally, national pride prohibits Russian leaders of any persuasion from becoming junior partners in a U.S.- or German-dominated Europe.

As press spokesman Vyacheslav Kostikov stated during Yeltsin's December 1993 visit to Brussels, "Russia considers itself to be a great power and the successor to the Soviet Union and all its might. Everybody clearly understands that Russia cannot and does not want to wait in the entrance hall of 'the European house' and ask permission to enter."[21]

Despite these problems, the Atlanticist line had managed to prevail in the foreign policy arena by making concessions to nationalist sentiment at home while still pursuing a general line of accommodation with the West. Whether Russia's leaders can or will continue with this approach depends on three factors: the continuation of an external environment of relatively low threat, the success of Atlantic-oriented leaders in making their case domestically, and the strength and prowess of the opposition forces arraigned against them. It is to this third factor that we will now turn.

"Russia First": The Restoration of Empire

The surprising electoral showing of the ultranationalist Vladimir Zhirinovsky's Liberal Democratic Party (LDP) in Russia's December 1993 national elections was a stark reminder to both Russian and Western leaders that Yeltsin's pro-Western orientation faces a formidable challenge at home. Equally or more significant than Zhirinovsky's success was the even larger combined vote of Russia's two Communist parties: the Communist Party of the Russian Federation, headed by Gennadii Zyuganov, and its rural counterpart, the Agrarian Party. Together these two parties won 112 seats in the new State Duma, more than any other party or bloc. They announced their intention to cooperate with Zhirinovsky's LDP—thus reincarnating the infamous "Red-Brown coalition" of extreme Russian nationalists and reactionary Communists that had first emerged in October 1992.[22] Although Zhirinovsky may be the most colorful of politicians from this tendency, its more natural electoral leader on the right is Aleksandr Rutskoi, the former vice-president under Yeltsin, who briefly served time in prison following his unsuccessful coup attempt in October 1993; and on the left, Zyuganov, head of the Communist Party. The Atlanticist line of trading autonomy for security is anathema to both the Zhirinovskyites and the Communists.

The uniting of left and right that this coalition represents is obviously of only short-term stability; it would likely break up quickly if it actually came to power. On broadbrush issues of foreign policy, however, the extreme nationalists share a number of common views. Their top priority is a restoration of the former Soviet empire, both within the pre-1991 boundaries and with the same superpower status and standing it enjoyed during the Cold War. This demand was raised explicitly by Rutskoi, and he has since continued to raise this demand, announcing the formation of a "Great Power" movement, a new political party whose agenda is the restoration of "the great power of Russia" within the borders of the former USSR "by means of the freely expressed will of its peoples."[23] Zhirinovsky made a similar appeal at almost the same time, calling for a restoration of former Soviet borders and the acquisition of additional territory in the south for the sake of

Russian security.[24] Zhirinovsky has been explicit about linking the restoration of Russia's Soviet-era borders to a foreign policy of expansion (primarily toward the south) and aggressive nationalism. In counterpoint to the Atlanticist line, he has also generally opposed Russian membership or involvement in Western organizations.[25]

A phalanx of extreme nationalist and neo-Fascist writers and newspapers trumpet a similar agenda daily before the Russian public. Western researchers have identified more than seventy-five organized extreme right-wing groups in Russia today.[26] The domestic political agendas of these groups vary widely, but with respect to foreign policy, they are uniformly anti-Western and most favor a rebuilding of the Russian empire and of Russian influence in the world. Publications by or sympathetic to this point of view include *Sovetskaia Rossiia, Den', Liberal, Pamyat', Pravda Zhirinovskogo,* and *Molodaya gvardiya;* together, their circulation runs into the millions.[27]

The neo-Fascist program for a restoration of empire and great-power status is echoed by the Communist left. In May 1994, a Council of Union of Communist Parties from many of the former Soviet republics called for restoration of the USSR, an appeal seconded a few days later by Zyuganov at a public meeting in Samara.[28] Other more extreme Communist organizations—such as Nina Andreeva's All-Union Communist Party of the Bolsheviks, the Russian Communist Workers Party of Viktor Anpilov, or the Union of Communist Parties under Oleg Shenin—all share a similar agenda of imperial restoration. The numerous cleavages within the Red-Brown coalition thus almost disappear when the focus is on foreign policy and security issues.

The Communist-nationalist alliance clearly sees the advantage of an external environment of threat in rallying the public behind its agenda. As such, it has sought repeatedly to vilify the West, to target Japan and Germany as potential enemies, and to stress the magnitude of risks Russia faces from instability on its southern borders. The interesting question, perhaps impossible to answer, is whether this is a genuinely *perceived* threat on the part of the extreme nationalists or whether it is a consciously *contrived* threat, evoked for political advantage. Most probably, it is a combination of the two—perceived as a threat but exaggerated in its public manifestation for the sake of obtaining leverage in the internal struggle for power.

The Eurasianist Alternative

The Slavophiles of today, "Eurasianists," as they have been called, have come to see the West not merely as an unsuitable alternative but as the very source of Russia's problems. Consider the following ruminations from academician Elgiz Pozdnyakov of the Russian Academy of Natural Sciences, written in 1993:

> One result of [Peter the Great's turn to the West] was the appearance in Russia of "Europeanism" or "Westernization," a malady that has infected a sizable section of

the Russian cultural community. This malady was fed before and is still fed . . . by superficial admiration of the wonders of European civilization coupled with an utter inability to tie in ideas discovered abroad with the driving forces of Russian life.[29]

The outcome of Westernization, according to Pozdnyakov, has been "superficial borrowings, deceptive changes, useless luxury and a moral decline." Westernization has brought more harm than good; indeed the West, he argues, is the source of virtually all that has afflicted Russia since Peter, including communism (an indictment reminiscent of that of Aleksandr Solzhenitsyn). Pozdnyakov's solution to Russia's woes is the creation of a strong, centralized state, which, he argues, has always been the source of national unity in Russia.[30]

Pozdnyakov is a highly influential scholar, whose published works on foreign policy and political science are widely read and admired.[31] They reflect a deep-rooted anti-Western attitude, a belief that Russian must make out its own course in the world between East and West. Although he is only one scholar, his views are representative of a large and growing number of Russian thinkers and government officials today. A May 1994 opinion poll showed that nearly 70 percent of State Duma members (from all factions) and 69 percent of the Moscow public supported the position that Russia should try to follow its own road rather than that of the West.[32]

In effect, the Eurasianists of post-Soviet Russia, even when they do not posit a specific threat emanating from the West, are casting "the West" as a generic, cultural enemy of Russia, making it a focal point to unite *against*. Their success in doing this is based also on the regrettable, but only human, resentment rising in Russia over the dependency and loss of sovereignty associated with aid. Until recently, the West forced its civilization on Russia by means of guns; today, it is by means of capital. Yet the tendency of Western leaders to attach numerous strings to their assistance—often seeking leverage far out of proportion to the actual amounts given—has fed Russian resentment and stoked anti-Western sentiments.

Contemporary Russian nationalists also proclaim the need for Russia to fulfill a unique national "mission," reflecting the sense of destiny and predestination that has run like a thread through Russian history. In its search for a unifying principle, Russia is sifting among many possibilities. Konstantin Pleshakov of the USA and Canada Institute writes that Russia has time and again played the role of saving Europe from would-be invaders and hegemons (Mongols, Tatars, Napoleon, Hitler). He argues that Russia today should serve the role of a bridge between East and West and that its special mission is to provide "continental stability" to all of the Eurasian landmass. This includes of course enforcing order among the unruly nationalities of the near abroad states.[33] There is also more than one group pushing the less idealistic notion of "Russian state power," its cultivation and advancement, as a unifying principle independent of any particular end toward which that power should be directed.[34] What is common to almost all such Eurasianist visions of a special Russian mission is the belief that Russian military power must be restored. Because in their eyes the contradiction between liberal reform and military modernization seems intractable, the solution is to abandon liberal reform.

The Interplay of External and Internal Factors

Russia's foreign policy, and indeed its entire political future, are being shaped by the struggle among these three factions. That struggle in turn is heavily influenced by the external environment. This is best illustrated by looking at the course of Russian foreign policy during the period from fall 1993 to late summer 1994, a period during which three primary issues engaged the attention of the foreign policy community in Russia: the Russian role in the former Soviet republics, the conflict in Bosnia, and the issue of NATO's extension into Eastern Europe. Concern over the security implications of these three issues caused a brief coming together of the three factions described above. For a short time in spring 1994, it appeared that Russia was regaining a measure of political cohesion based on opposition to the West with respect to all three issues. Once Russia had a falling out with its Serbian allies, however, and once it became apparent that the West would not seriously challenge Russia's assertive role in the former republics and did not intend to move rapidly with respect to NATO's extension into Eastern Europe, that cohesion began to disappear and the internal debate resumed in earnest.

Beginning in fall 1993, Andrei Kozyrev, previously the most liberal-minded of high-level Russian politicians, made what appeared to be a sharp turn toward a more nationalist, "Russia First" position. This shift was interpreted by some Western observers as a tactical concession to the strength of the Eurasianist and Red-Brown coalitions—a response to domestic pressures such as the December 1993 election and the subsequent formation of a powerful opposition bloc in the State Duma.[35] It appeared that Kozyrev and Yeltsin had bowed to the anti-Western line of their opponents, concluding that the only unifying principle that would work for Russia was opposition to the West. But Kozyrev's shift was not purely a tactical maneuver; it was also a response to a perception of emerging threats in the external environment. German defense minister Volker Ruehe had stated publicly in May 1993 that the Visegrad countries should be allowed to join NATO, and in September 1993, Foreign Minister Klaus Kinkel had urged an extension of NATO into Central Europe. Chancellor Helmut Kohl had endorsed their recommendations publicly, and NATO capitals were alive with talk of how to accomplish such an extension. Shortly thereafter, in December 1993, Western foreign ministers meeting under the auspices of the CSCE in Rome had protested Russia's military involvement in Moldova and other former Soviet republics. The unsettled conflict in former Yugoslavia was also pulling NATO nearer to direct involvement in defense of the Bosnian Muslims, a tendency that troubled Russian leaders whose sympathies tended to lie with their fellow Slavs, the Serbs.

As the conflict in Yugoslavia intensified in the first months of 1994, it emerged as an ideal issue around which the fractious Russian polity could unite. The ardor with which Russian political leaders and intellectuals initially fixated on the Bosnian crisis as a test of Russian will, especially after the shelling of the Sarajevo market in February 1994, illustrated this. All factions of the parliament condemned NATO's threat to conduct air strikes, as did Russian officials in the foreign and defense ministries and the United Nations.[36] On March 11, 1994, the day NATO conducted its first ever air strike against Serbian forces near the Bosnian city of Gorazde, Yeltsin's chief spokesperson, Vyacheslav Kostikov, told reporters that Russia's romantic embrace of the West was over, that Russia increasingly saw itself as a great power with strategic interests different from those of the United States and Europe. "It has started saying this loudly," he reportedly said.[37] Virtually all parliamentary factions from Russia's Choice to the LDP denounced the NATO action.[38] The Russian State Duma condemned the air strike by an overwhelming vote. The subsequent decision in April to send 600 Russian paratroopers to Serbia and Sarajevo to participate in peacekeeping operations generated considerable enthusiasm across all Russian political factions—a stunning example of a resurgent pan-Slavism seized upon largely for want of other unifying factors in Russian life.

Aside from the question of how seriously the course of events from fall 1993 through April 1994 *objectively* threatened Russian security, there is no question that they were *perceived* as threatening by large cross sections of the Russian elite. Already by December, there were signs of a consensus on foreign policy in Russia for the first time in over two years, a consensus centered around the importance of maintaining strong Russian influence in the near abroad and in the Slavic regions of Central Europe.[39] This consensus spanned the various ministries and offices of the executive branch, including the office of the president, as well as all three major factions of the Russian polity. The subsequent crisis in Yugoslavia strengthened this consensus dramatically. By May 1994, even Zhirinovsky had positive things to say about the direction of Yeltsin's foreign policy.[40] The successful signing on April 28, 1994, of the Treaty on Social Accord by almost all of the major political parties in Russia, as well as a large number of regional leaders, was a manifestation of this growing internal accord, which flowed in part from the external challenge. Even Gennadii Zyuganov, head of the Communist Party of the Russian Federation, though he did not sign the document, spoke favorably of the process and dialogue that had led to greater domestic unity.[41]

By late spring 1994, it appeared that Russia might be veering back into its historical pattern of national unity through the evocation of external threats, the building of a strong state, and the creation of legitimizing myths. It appeared to be heading toward the first path outlined earlier. Prominent foreign policy specialists in the West raised questions about the possible resurgence of this traditional Russian pattern, of the advent of a new "bad Russia" on the world scene.[42]

Already by August 1994, however, it had become clear that the tendencies that had seemed so ominous in Russia's foreign policy in the first half of the year were—with one exception—temporary anomalies. In the case of former

Yugoslavia, the Bosnian Serbs proved virtually intransigent to any outside influence, snubbing Russian efforts to mediate in the conflict almost as firmly as they had snubbed U.S. efforts. By August, even Slobodan Milosevic of Serbia had broken with them over their refusal to countenance a negotiated compromise with the Bosnian Muslims. Russia officially froze its relations with the Bosnian Serbs and announced in the United Nations on August 4 that it endorsed the Serbian government's decision to cut off relations with them.[43] At the same time, Western policy in the Balkans proved to be far more cautious than Russia had at first feared; NATO conducted only one additional air strike after March, emphasizing dialogue and diplomacy instead. The White House made greater efforts to consult with Russia on the situation in the Balkans. The "objective threat" to the Slavic peoples in the Balkans thus turned out not to be a threat at all; Western and Russian policies in former Yugoslavia came closer into alignment. The Atlanticist line thus vindicated its potential to defend the national interest by means of a co-operative relationship with the West.

Russian relations with NATO also found a happier medium than appeared possible early in the year. Instead of expanding NATO eastward, the Partnership for Peace program, announced by NATO in January 1994, enabled closer ties between NATO and Eastern Europe but did not exclude Russia, as a true extension of the alliance would have. This gave Russia a fig leaf for acquiescing in closer ties between NATO and the former members of the Warsaw Pact while allaying Russian perceptions of a newly emerging threat from the West.

There was only one issue on which a harder line continued to prevail—that of Russia's relations with the near abroad. The Russian leadership made clear its commitment to an economic—and partially political—reintegration of the former Soviet states and pressed for strengthened economic and political ties within the CIS. Vladimir Shumeiko, speaker of Russia's Federation Council and chairman of the CIS Interparliamentary Assembly, even proposed the transformation of the CIS into a confederation as a first step toward "political unity."[44] But even here the Russian leadership attempted to address Western concerns by insisting that any reintegration of the Russian empire would take place only voluntarily and primarily on the basis of an economic union of some kind. Russia reached agreements with both Estonia and Latvia on key military issues, and it continued negotiations on outstanding issues with most of the other former republics.

How are we to interpret these developments? In the case of Russian relations with the former Soviet republics (the so-called near abroad), Russia faced what virtually all internal factions agreed was a genuinely objective threat to its security and the security of its 25 million nationals living outside the borders of Russian proper. Consequently, an internal consensus emerged on the need to defend Russian interests vigorously in this part of the world—and that consensus held despite moderate protests from the West and resistance from some of the former Soviet republics. That the NATO powers did not choose to vigorously resist Russian incursions in the former republics also meant that this issue could be handled without serious disruption of relations with the West.[45]

When other perceived threats turned out to be more ambiguous, however, as in the case of NATO's extension eastward or its policies toward the Bosnian Serbs, no such nationalist consensus emerged. Yeltsin's opponents accused him of "selling out" on Bosnia, and they vehemently criticized the decision to join the Partnership for Peace. In this respect, Russian politics became more fractious. Yet Yeltsin and his Atlanticist advisers weathered the criticism politically, precisely because neither the general public nor the Russian elite continued to perceive these issues as pivotal to state security. Thus, although an environment of low threat exacerbated foreign policy divisions in the Russian polity, as we would expect, it simultaneously strengthened the Atlanticist position, the whole logic of which was based on security through cooperation. If this interpretation is correct, it suggests that an environment of low threat is critical to the political strength of the Atlanticists in Russian politics. As long as such an environment prevails, it is unlikely that internal challenges to their dominance can succeed on the basis of foreign policy issues alone.

Conclusion: The Future of Russian Foreign Policy

The dramatic changes in Russia's security environment that have occurred since 1989 are both *outcomes* of that internal democratization and contributing *causes* of its success. The history of Russia and the course of its political development since the collapse of communism both suggest that an environment of low threat is an indispensable prerequisite to Russia's further liberalization and integration into the mainstream of Western life. If Russia can develop for ten or twenty years in a benign environment, the odds of the Westernizing line prevailing will increase substantially. In that case, the second path noted earlier could conceivably transform itself into a new, unprecedented third path for Russia, as shown in Figure 6.2.

If this path were followed, it would mean that the Russian state for the first time in history would acquire its security by means of international cooperation and internal legitimacy rather than raw military and police power alone. Over the long run, democratic development would tend to facilitate economic recovery, making possible a renaissance of national strength and prestige.

This is the path that the West must help Russia traverse. The above analysis suggests that it will be possible only in an environment of minimal threat. This means in turn that Russian politics can remain on a democratic course only by accepting a high degree of internal turbulence; it can alleviate that turbulence only through reversion to authoritarian rule. Although Russia's destiny is neither controlled nor

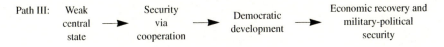

Path III: Weak   Security   Economic recovery and
            central   →   via   →   Democratic   →   military-political
            state   cooperation development   security

FIGURE 6.2   Potential Path for Russian Reform

determined by the capitals of the Western world, they can contribute to its passage through this stormy transition by means of sensitive diplomacy, a genuine spirit of cooperation, effective policies of reassurance, and awareness of Russia's historical proclivities. This must be done, of course, without compromising Western security or denying the possibility of Russia's resurgence as a threat.

The alternative is not encouraging. If Russia's external environment should again become more threatening, it may accelerate the coming to power of anti-Western Eurasianists or, worse, extreme nationalists. Such an eventuality could occur, for example, as the result of mismanaged Western efforts to extend NATO too rapidly or too aggressively to the East. If a "Russia First" line should at some future time prevail, an interesting question to ask is whether it will mean only the revival of an imperialist Russian elite or whether the appeal of Russian nationalism will extend downward and capture the enthusiasm of the Russian population at large. As noted earlier, there has traditionally been a huge gap between the Russian political elite and the Russian ethnic nation, and that gap has rarely been closed except during great wars of national survival. That gap remains today. The conditions may be ripe, however, given the new openness of media and speech in Russian life, for Russian nationalist thinkers to extend their influence deeper into society. If they can couple a broader appeal with the capture of the state, we may yet witness the fusion of nation and state that has for so long eluded the Russians. It is sobering to realize that this fusion in the case of both France and Germany resulted in violent explosions of nationalism and war in each of the past two centuries. This is another reason why the West should not interpret Russia's current travails as being to its strategic advantage or seek to take advantage of its weakness.

One caveat should be added, however, and it is a large one at that. A central tenet in the thinking of many Russian Eurasianists is that Russia should be looking eastward, toward Asia, in pursuit of its future destiny. There are numerous signs in the diplomacy, trade, arms sales, and statements of Yeltsin's government that this concept is being taken seriously. Given the new buffer zone between Russian and Europe, and the difficulty of reversing the post–Cold War arrangements put in place since 1989, it seems probable that the thrust of any resurgent Russian expansionism in the future—should there ever be such a thrust—will be in the direction of the Far East.[46] As we approach the end of the twentieth century, the cycle of great-power rivalry may be shifting to Asia. For once, perhaps, the whirlwind of change may bypass a peaceful Europe.

Notes

1. Otto Hintze, "The Formation of States and Constitutional Development: A Study in History and Politics," *Historische Zeitschrift* 88 (1902), reprinted in Felix Gilbert, ed., *The Historical Essays of Otto Hintze* (New York: Oxford University Press, 1975), p. 159.

2. Charles Tilly, ed., *The Formation of National States in Western Europe* (Princeton: Princeton University Press, 1975), pp. 3–83; Charles Tilly, ed., *Coercion, Capital, and European States,* A.D. *990–1990* (Oxford and Cambridge: Basil Blackwell, 1990); Max Weber, "Politics as a Vocation" and "The Meaning of Discipline," in *From Max Weber:*

Essays in Sociology, ed. H. H. Gerth and C. Wright Mills (New York: Oxford University Press, 1946), pp. 77–128, 253–264; Theda Skocpol, *States and Social Revolutions: A Comparative Analysis of France, Russia, and China* (Cambridge: Cambridge University Press, 1979); Bruce D. Porter, *War and the Rise of the State: The Military Foundations of Modern Politics* (New York: Free Press, 1994).

3. The bureaucratic politics approach was made popular by two works in the 1970s: Graham Allison, *Essence of Decision: Explaining the Cuban Missile Crisis* (Boston: Little, Brown, 1971), and Morton Halperin, *Bureaucratic Politics and Foreign Policy* (Washington, D.C.: Brookings Institution, 1974).

4. Adam Ulam observes regarding this period, "The evocation of Russia's past military weakness and defeats was one of the main rationalizations used by Stalin to justify the sufferings and privations of the forced industrialization and collectivization." Adam B. Ulam, "Nationalism, Panslavism, Communism," in *Russian Foreign Policy: Essays in Historical Perspective,* ed. Ivo J. Lederer (New Haven: Yale University Press, 1962), p. 53. See also my discussion of the impact of the external environment on the rise of Soviet totalitarianism in Bruce D. Porter, *War and the Rise of the State,* pp. 226–228.

5. For summaries of scholarly writing on the subject, see Arthur Stein, "Conflict and Cohesion: A Review of the Literature," *Journal of Conflict Resolution* 20 (March 1976): 143–144; Michael Stohl, "The Nexus of Civil and International Conflict," in *Handbook of Political Conflict: Theory and Research,* ed. Ted Robert Gurr (New York: Free Press, 1980), pp. 297–330.

6. Jean Bodin, *Six Books of the Commonwealth,* trans. M. J. Tooley (Oxford: Basil Blackwell, n.d.), book 5, chap. 5, p. 168.

7. William Shakespeare, *Henry IV, Part II,* act 4, sc. 5, lines 213–215. Recent research suggests that deliberate diversion is not a common phenomenon, though it does occur on occasion. See Jack Levy, "The Diversionary Theory of War: A Critique," in *Handbook of War Studies,* ed. Manus I. Midlarsky (Boston: Unwin Hyman, 1989), pp. 259–288. See also Leo A. Hazelwood, "Diversion Mechanisms and Encapsulation Processes: The Domestic Conflict–Foreign Conflict Hypothesis Reconsidered," in *Sage International Yearbook of Foreign Policy Studies,* vol. 3, ed. P. J. McGowan (Beverly Hills, Calif.: Sage, 1975), pp. 213–244.

8. Quincy Wright, *A Study of War,* vol. 2 (Chicago: University of Chicago Press, 1942), p. 1042; Michael C. Desch, "War and Strong States; Peace and Weak States?" *International Organization* (forthcoming).

9. The inspection effect is discussed in Alan Peacock and Jack Wiseman, *The Growth of Public Expenditure in the United Kingdom* (Princeton: Princeton University Press, 1971), pp. xxiv, 67–68. The term "audit of war" comes from Correlli Barnett, *The Audit of War: The Illusion and Reality of Britain as a Great Nation* (London: Macmillan, 1986), p. xi.

10. Bruce Bueno de Mesquita, Randolph M. Siverson, and Gary Woller, "War and the Fate of Regimes: A Comparative Analysis," *American Political Science Review* 86 (September 1992): 638–646, is a statistical study of 177 wars that demonstrates that violent regime changes occur far more frequently after wars than during periods of protracted peace.

11. Jerome Blum, *Lord and Peasant in Russia* (Princeton: Princeton University Press, 1961), pp. 250–259.

12. Geoffrey Alan Hosking, "Empire and Nation in Russian History," *The Fourteenth Charles Edmondson Historical Lectures, Baylor University* (Waco: Baylor University Press, 1993), p. 9. On the separation between the elite society and the peasantry, and its

consequences for Russian politics, see also Marc Raeff, *Understanding Imperial Russia: State and Society in the Old Regime* (New York: Columbia University Press, 1984), pp. 210–213.

13. On the role of the West in the origin of the modern Russian military, see Christopher Duffy, *Russia's Military Way to the West: Origins and Nature of Russian Military Power, 1700–1800* (London: Routledge and Kegan Paul, 1981).

14. Bruce D. Porter and Carol R. Saivetz, "The Once and Future Empire: Russia and the 'Near Abroad,'" *Washington Quarterly* 17 (Summer 1994): 75–90.

15. On Russia's proposal to renegotiate the CFE Treaty, see *Radio Free Europe/Radio Liberty (RFE/RL) Daily Report,* 7 October 1993; on the NATO response, see *RFE/RL Daily Report,* 5 April 1994. The details of the Russian proposal on CSCE are laid out in *RFE/RL Daily Report,* 15 July 1994; on the Russian charge that an extension of NATO would violate the CFE Treaty, see *RFE/RL Daily Report,* 22 July 1994.

16. Interview in *Segodnya,* 5 May 1994, cited in *RFE/RL Daily Report,* 6 May 1994.

17. Andrei Zagorsky, "Russia and Europe," *International Affairs* (January 1993): 47.

18. Sergei Stankevich, verbal presentation at Conference on Foreign Policy and Diplomacy at the Foreign Ministry of the Russian Federation (26–27 February 1992), cited in "A Transformed Russia in a New World," *International Affairs* (April-May 1992): 100.

19. On the deep-rooted Russian desire for national greatness and how it affects Russian thinking and politics today, see John W. R. Lepingwell, "The Soviet Legacy and Russian Foreign Policy," *RFE/RL Research Report* 3 (10 June 1994): 1–8.

20. Nikolai Ogarkov, *Vsegda v gotovnosti k zashchite Otechestva* [Always ready for defense of the fatherland] (Moscow: USSR Ministry of Defense, 1982), p. 59.

21. ITAR-TASS, 8 December 1993, cited in *RFE/RL Research Report* 2 (17 December 1993): 2.

22. Zyuganov announced the formation of a de facto bloc with the LDP on 13 May 1994; Moscow Ostankino Television, 13 May 1994, cited in *FBIS-SOV,* 13 May 1994, pp. 23–24. For historical background on the Red-Brown coalition, see Michael McFaul, *Post-Communist Politics: Democratic Prospects in Russia and Eastern Europe* (Washington, D.C.: Center for Strategic and International Studies, 1993), pp. 76–82; Richard Sakwa, *Russian Politics and Society* (London: Routledge, 1993), pp. 157–159.

23. *RFE/RL Daily Report,* 20 and 21 September 1993, and *RFE/RL Daily Report,* 25 July 1994.

24. Interview with Tokyo ASAHI Newstar Television network, 22 May 1994, cited in *FBIS-SOV,* 24 May 1994.

25. For example, on 4 April 1994, Zhirinovsky spoke out against Russia joining the Council of Europe; ITAR-TASS, 4 April 1994, cited in *FBIS-SOV,* 5 April 1994, p. 3. A few days later, he similarly spoke out against Russia joining the Partnership for Peace or having any contacts with NATO; Interfax, 8 April 1994, cited in *FBIS-SOV,* 11 April 1994, p. 7.

26. For a complete listing and summary of the various groups' platforms, see Vladimir Pribylovsky, "A Survey of Radical Right-Wing Groups in Russia," *RFE/RL Research Report* 3 (22 April 1994): 28–37.

27. See Wendy Slater, "Russia," *RFE/RL Research Report* 3 (22 April 1994): 23–27, in a special issue on extremist groups in the former Soviet bloc states.

28. Interfax, 22 May 1994, cited in *FBIS-SOV,* 23 May 1994, p. 27; *Segodnya,* 26 May 1994, cited in *FBIS-SOV,* 27 May 1994.

29. Elgiz Pozdnyakov, "Russia Is a Great Power," *International Affairs* (January 1993): 8.

30. Pozdnyakov, "Russia Is a Great Power."

31. His best-known work in the post-Soviet era is Elgiz Pozdnyakov, *Filosofiya politiki,* 2 vols. (Moscow: Paleya, 1994). Also of relevance are three volumes he edited and contributed to: *Geopolitika: teoria i praktika* (Moscow: Institut mirovoi ekonomiki i mezhdunarodnykh otnoshenii, 1993); *Natsionalizm: teoria i praktika* (Moscow: Institut mirovoi ekonomiki i mezhdunarodnykh otnoshenii, 1994); and *Balans sil v mirovoi politike: teoria i praktika* (Moscow: Institut mirovoi ekonomiki i mezhdunarodnykh otnoshenii, 1993).

32. *Moskovskiy komsomolets,* 15 May 1994, cited in *FBIS-SOV,* 18 May 1994, pp. 24–25. (The questionnaire was answered by 61.1 percent of Duma members. The question asked was, "As Russia develops, should it be trying to catch up with Western countries or should it follow its own road?")

33. Konstantin Pleshakov, "Russia's Mission: The Third Epoch," *International Affairs* (January 1993): 25.

34. See, for example, the report widely circulated in Russia by a private firm, the Russian-American University: RAU-Korporatsia, *Rossia: Problemy natsionalno-gosudarstvenoi politiki* (Moscow: Obozrevatel', 1993).

35. Stephen Sestanovich, "Andrei the Giant," *New Republic* 210 (11 April 1994): 24–27.

36. *RFE/RL Daily Report,* 9 and 10 February 1994; Stan Markotich, "Former Communist States Respond to NATO Ultimatum," *RFE/RL Research Report* 3 (25 February 1994): 10–11.

37. Cited in *RFE/RL Daily Report,* 11 April 1994.

38. ITAR-TASS and Interfax, 13 April 1994, both cited in *FBIS-SOV,* 14 April 1994, pp. 5–7.

39. On the emerging consensus in Russian foreign policy, see Suzanne Crow, "Russia Asserts Its Strategic Agenda," *RFE/RL Research Report* 2 (17 December 1993): 1–8.

40. Interview with Tokyo ASAHI Newstar Television, 22 May 1994, cited in *FBIS-SOV,* 24 May 1994, p. 24.

41. Moscow ITAR-TASS World Service, 28 April 1994, cited in *FBIS-SOV,* 29 April 1994, pp. 18–23.

42. Dmitri Simes, "The Return of Russian History," *Foreign Affairs* 73 (January-February 1994): 67–82; Zbigniew Brzezinski, "The Premature Partnership," *Foreign Affairs* 73 (March-April 1994): 67–82; Suzanne Crow, "Why Has Russian Foreign Policy Changed?" *RFE/RL Research Report* 3 (6 May 1994): 1–6.

43. *RFE/RL Daily Report,* 4 and 5 August 1994.

44. *RFE/RL Daily Report,* 29 July 1994.

45. According to Andranik Migranyan, a member of Yeltsin's Presidential Council, Russia was prepared to take a softer line on the Trans-Dniestr republic out of fear of Western reactions to its activities, but "after the Western countries refrained from serious protests to Russia, the Foreign Ministry's position began to change in the direction of unconditional defense of the Dniester republic." *Nezavisimaya gazeta,* 12 January 1994, cited in Crow, "Why Has Russian Foreign Policy Changed?" p. 6.

46. There are numerous reasons independent of Russian politics to think that East Asia is shaping up as a future locus of great-power rivalry. See Aaron Friedberg, "Ripe for Rivalry: Prospects for Peace in a Multipolar Asia," *International Security* 18 (Winter 1993/94): 3–33.

CHAPTER 7

Russian Identity and Foreign Policy in Estonia and Uzbekistan

Ted Hopf

There are, of course, a multitude of explanations for any state's foreign policy, and this is no less the case for Russia. In trying to explain or predict Russian foreign policy we could rely on international system structure; the international institutional environment; the nature of the state in Russia and its neighbors; domestic political, economic, institutional, and social arrangements; and the characteristics of foreign policy decisionmakers and reflectivist accounts of identity.[1]

I wish to suggest yet another potentially productive cut at the problem of assessing the sources of Russian foreign policy. I am not claiming that the alternatives I have already listed could not be gainfully employed for this task. However, given the nature of the foreign policy problem I have chosen to explore—Russian foreign policy toward the near abroad—a theoretical elaboration of the problem of identity construction is appropriate. Indeed, it could be argued that the issue of identity is uniquely implicated in this particular foreign policy problem for Russia. The story unfolds as follows.

Russian foreign policy makers in Moscow are aware of the 25 million Russians who are living in Central Asia, the Baltic States, the Transcaucasus, Ukraine, Moldova, and Belarus. The question is under what conditions Russia will consider the fate of these Russians to be an issue of national security necessitating a military response. I need not dwell on the horrific consequences for Russia, Russia's neighbors, and the West if a Russian leader opted for a military resolution of this question. Relations with the West would be severely tried, perhaps pushing the world back to the Cold War. Any trust accumulated between Russia and its neighbors since 1991 would evaporate without a trace, setting off a race for security guarantees from the West. In Russian domestic politics, such behavior would likely mean a dramatic turn toward a more forceful foreign policy.

What could cause such a fateful choice by Russian leaders? I hypothesize that the causal story lies in how Russians abroad adopt, and adapt to, their post-Soviet identities in their new homes. If Russians living in Uzbekistan see themselves as Russians, and not as Uzbek citizens, it is much more likely that these Russians will appeal to Moscow for help against their local government. I devote the bulk

147

of this chapter to an effort to answer how Russians come to see themselves as Russian rather than Uzbek.

Essentially, an identity is chosen by the individual, imposed by the state, and constructed by the community. If the state imposes an identity that is freely adopted and that the community socially reproduces through its practices, there is no basis for conflict. There is no disequilibrium among any of these three sources of identity. If, however, the state tries to impose an identity that the community rejects, it is very likely that the individual will opt for an alternative identity that will be socially reproduced, creating the conditions for conflict between the state on the one hand and the individual and the community on the other. Herein lie the seeds of a Russian foreign policy toward Russians living abroad that relies heavily on the use of military force.

In the pages that follow, I elaborate a pretheory of identity.[2] In this exercise, I explore the processes of choice, imposition, and construction and develop a set of testable assumptions about identity creation in the near abroad among Russians living there. These assumptions concern not only how identities are likely to develop in these regions but also the possible effects that different outcomes are likely to have on Russian domestic politics and foreign policy. I then assess these ideas in light of empirical evidence, albeit limited, from Uzbekistan and Estonia. I conclude by connecting identity construction in the near abroad to contemporary Russian foreign policy.

A Pretheory of Identity

Identity: A Working Definition

Before elaborating on the three avenues to identity acquisition, I should first clarify what I have in mind when using the word identity. It is easier to explicate what an identity does rather than what it is. An identity implies beliefs and behavior. Different identities produce different ideas and different actions. Different identities construct different realities. I am interested in effective identities: those that give rise to interpreted environments, particular discourses, and semiscripted behaviors. I am not interested in nominal identities that are only labels or names, only dormant or latent. My view of identity is relational. A person cannot have an identity independent of that person's community, or group. This means that one's identity is never purely personal; it always has external referents.[3] As Habermas put it, "no one can construct an identity independently of the identifications that others make of him."[4]

For example, members of the National Rifle Association may see themselves as defenders of a citizen's right to bear arms. Unless approached by a member of the Libertarian Party and engaged in a conversation about their beliefs on abortion rights and taxes, they might not have realized that they are libertarians as well. This identity as a libertarian was not completely absent prior to the conversation. They simply had not realized that their apparently unconnected beliefs added up to some more comprehensive ideological identity. Through conversation, the identity was actualized; this "new" identity could then become an effectuator of behavior in a larger political and social domain.[5] This is not to say that the NRA members' prior identity (as gun owners) was not meaningful or real, only that it gave rise to a more limited range of sociopolitical behaviors than the identity of libertarian.

Identity: Multiple Identities

An individual has more than a single identity. This implies that national or ethnic identities are not the only identities of political or social relevance. Instead, each individual has dozens of different identities, including nation, region, religion, language, ideology, profession, class, ethnicity, tribe, kinship group, clan, family, gender, and sexuality.[6] Any person can be many of these identities simultaneously or can be one or several in some situations and not in others. For example, Western scholars studying decolonizing Africa in the early 1960s expected to find modernizing effects from urbanization, industrialization, and marketization on class formation and ethnicity. They instead discovered that African identities were far more complicated and contextual than surmised. Robert Jackson wrote about an African peasantry that refused to think of itself as a "class-conscious and recognizable rural peasantry" because they still "remain conscious of themselves primarily as members of particular kin-groups, localities, lineage and ethnic communities."[7]

In sum, each of us holds many identities. Sometimes we hold them simultaneously; other times, in other contexts, one identity will predominate over others.

Sources of Identity: Individual Choice

Every day we choose an identity for instrumental purposes, hoping to gain something through that choice.[8] Almost as if I am maximizing some form of expected utility, I might choose to stress my Irish roots on St. Patrick's Day in bars in South Boston while hiding simultaneously that my Irish roots are as a Protestant Orangeman. Pierre Van den Berghe has called this "commuting" between identities.[9] An identity might be chosen if a community feels it is at risk of having its distinctive traits obliterated by another identity. For example, Bosnian Muslims declared themselves as such only in the early 1970s. Prior to that point, they were either Serb or Croat. But a renewed Serbian emphasis on their Orthodoxy and Croatian stress on their Catholicism impelled Bosnian Muslims to stress their religious affiliation to preserve their identity.[10] Similarly, Elie Kedourie recounts the story of a Hungarian statesman visiting a district whose status was disputed by Czechoslovakia and Poland. He asked how many Poles there were there and was told that the number varied between 40,000 and 100,000 depending on the villagers' economic interests.[11]

There are as many rational choices of identities as there are subjective preferences for identities. And these subjective preferences, as enumerated above, come in riotous variety. One may rationally choose an identity to avoid death, to avoid social discomfort, to gain material benefits or status, to advance economic interest, to be true to one's religious convictions, to reach psychological closure, to make a political statement, or to achieve immortality after death.

Sources of Identity: State Imposition

A second source of identity is any authority that imposes this meaning on an individual. An identity will be imposed when it suits the needs of this authority, most often the state. The state defines daily the identity of those living within its borders. Which identity a state may choose to impose varies widely according to historical context. The tsarist Russian state assigned people identities according to its Table of Rank, or *nomenklatura*. The modern Indian state has imposed, or at least strongly reinforced, identities according to caste. The United States and South Africa have imposed racial identities. The British state has imposed an official religious identity in the form of the Anglican church. The Estonian state has imposed a linguistic identity with its adoption of citizenship laws based, in part at least, on language competence.

By "the state" I have in mind the ruling elites at the state level. I assume that the primary interest of the state so defined is resource extraction, for whatever purpose, and that the state has an interest in gaining access to societal assets.[12] The importance of national identity in the modern era arises from the domestic logic of resource extraction and the structural desiderata of international politics.

States should prefer the propagation of a national identity, rather than an identity at some other level, because state authorities recognize the state's vulnerability as an unnatural social construct.[13] Giddens writes that "nationalism helps naturalize the recency and contingency of the nation-state through supplying its myths of origin." Moreover, its "discourse of national solidarity helps block off other possible discursive articulations of interest."[14] These other "possible discursive articulations of interest" are socially constructed identities (discussed below) that may compete with nationalism for the attention and adherence of the community's members.

An identity may also be imposed from outside the state itself: The international system, in some sense, imposes a national-state identity on actors in world politics.[15] By granting legitimate status only to states, the system of international politics imposes a national identity. You cannot play the game unless you are a player, defined by the rules of the game as a nation-state. So, a Nigerian foreign policy maker must adopt a Nigerian national identity when merely discussing some issue of concern, such as an IMF adjustment package. If Nigeria is to act effectively in the international arena, the same Nigerian foreign policy elite must maximize citizens' identities as Nigerians in order to extract resources from them to feed the national state.[16]

A combination of the two preceding lines of thought helps explain why the national identity, or nationalism, is so widespread. The state itself is unnatural, so its ruling elites resort to the imposition of a national identity to secure the state.[17]

Meanwhile, the arena of international politics demands that participation in the activities that constitute the world community be undertaken only by states. In sum, ruling elites are compelled by both international and domestic realities to construct national identities and impose them on their citizens.

That the state is very successful at imposing this national identity is due, in large part, to its monopolization, or at least domination, of the primary instruments of statewide identity creation, the most important of which is the public education system. Almost two hundred years ago, Napoleon said: "There will be no political stability so long as . . . children are not taught whether they must be republicans or monarchists, Catholics or free-thinkers, etc., the state will not constitute a nation but will rest on vague and shifting foundations, ever exposed to disorder and change."[18] As Rousseau advised the Polish monarch:

> It is education that must give souls a national formation, and direct their opinions and tastes in such a way that they will be patriotic by inclination, by passion, by necessity. When first he opens his eyes, an infant ought to see the fatherland, and up to the day of his death he ought never to see anything else. . . . At twenty, a Pole ought not to be a man of any other sort; he ought to be a Pole. . . . The law ought to regulate the content, the order and the form of their studies.[19]

Other identity constructing and propagating mechanisms include military conscription; boundary and institution demarcation; state religion; elite newspapers, radio, and television; information collection, storage, and distribution; and a statewide market.[20] The state has a near monopoly on all sources of mythmaking power.

Sources of Identity: Social Construction

Identities also are socially constructed by the community in which we live.[21] Identity is socially constructed as part of everyday life. Daily social interactions, through the repetition of language, ritual, culture, and discourse, reproduce the associated identity. The social reproduction of a socially constructed identity relies greatly on the creation and manipulation of history, culture, and myth. As Smith puts it, "the object of myth is not scientific objectivity, but emotional and aesthetic coherence to undergird social solidarity and social self-definition." Identities, which are a "matter of myths, memories, values and symbols, and not of material possessions or political power, are very robust and durable.[22]

In sum, the socially constructed identity is a product and a process, not a choice or a demand. Creating one's identity as a junior faculty member is the product of interaction with other nontenured faculty, where a repertoire of issues is discussed, behaviors are rehearsed, and vocabularies honed. Hundreds of small details, unnoticeable even to any of the community's members, are practiced, produced, and perfected so that the behavior and associated discourse become automatic. When two members of the junior faculty meet, their identities are constructed through a discussion of the tenure clock, teaching load, new course preparations, journal referees, and book manuscript turnaround. What you say and how you behave reproduces who you are, whether you know it or like it.

Sources of Identity: Choice, Imposition, Construction, and Imagination

Anderson's pathbreaking work on nations as imagined communities[23] is rich with suggestions for both why nationalism dominates state-imposed identities and why imposition by itself is insufficient to create a sustainable identity. Anderson's fundamental point is that one must imagine what one cannot experience. "Members of even the smallest nation will never know most of their fellow-members, meet them, or even hear of them, yet in the minds of each lives the image of their communion."[24] One possible implication here is that the smaller the community, the less imagination is required for its existence in the minds of its members. Whereas nations must be imagined, families, for instance, need not be.[25] As Weber writes about ethnic groups, "it does not matter whether or not an objective blood relationship exists. Ethnic membership . . . differs from the kinship group precisely by being a presumed identity."[26] So, whereas ethnic groups require imagination to make themselves real, kinship groups are made real through experience.[27]

The need for imagination also gives greater latitude to the state and other authorities to impose myths on a community's members. There should be far more imposition of identity at the national level than at lower levels of aggregation, such as the family or kinship group. We should see state authorities trying to propagate myths about the nation, the ethnos, and the class, and they should meet with some success. We should not see state mythmaking efforts associated with the family, kinship group, or tribe. If such efforts are made, they will fail because the members of the latter three groups do not rely on imagination to construct their identities; their identities are socially constructed, reinforced by real life experiences and conversations. This would make it hard for the state to penetrate the community with its own self-serving impositions.

That the state is confronted with obstacles at lower levels of social aggregation is apparent from the history of nationalist mythmaking. According to Smith, the most fundamental sentiments evoked by nationalism are those of the family. The metaphor of the family is indispensable to nationalism, so the mythmakers try to appropriate the family in its propagation of nationalist symbols.[28] The state, recognizing the elemental quality of the family, attempts to use its imagery to impose a nationalist identity.

In sum, the state can impose identities on its citizens and has an incentive to impose a national identity due to the artificiality of the state and its overriding interest in resource extraction. The national identity is further "privileged" by the fact that imagination is easiest at higher levels of social aggregation. Finally, the state enjoys great advantages over its competitors because it has superior resources for identity imposition in the form of an education system, media control, and information production.

Nationalism may be imposed by the state, but the maintenance and perpetuation of this identity may be the product of social construction. This process of acquiring identity by being compelled to adopt that identity has been described by Tajfel: "Social situations which force individuals to act in terms of their group membership also enhance group identifications which had previously not been very significant to them, or perhaps even create group memberships which were previously only dormant or potential."[29] The celebration of the nation, its rituals and myths, by the members of the nation is a form of reproduction of nationalism by those on whom it was previously imposed.[30] For example, when one attends a sporting event in the United States, everyone rises and faces the flag during the American national anthem. You may not want to, but you participate in the ritual anyway, either out of habit or out of mild apprehension, social stigmatization, or even genuine feelings of patriotism. But this act has social consequences for the robustness of national identity in the community.

The most effective state strategy would be for it to adopt an identity for imposition that would find ready acceptance as an identity for social reproduction. That is, the most effective state strategy is one that results in the coproduction of an identity, through a combination of state imposition and resources and social construction and reproduction.[31] This implies that the state cannot simply choose an identity that would most advance its interests against society but rather has to balance that choice with the characteristics of that society that will permit the state's identity choice to be socially reproduced. In effect, there are identities the state cannot impose, as they will never be reproduced by the society, such as the "new Communist man"—citizens who live and are the Marxist ideal—in the Soviet Union.

Pierre Bourdieu has described the interaction between impositions by the state and "actual social practices." He has argued that the imposed structures are often reconceptualized and reworked and that people always have "creative freedom" to "transform what they receive rather than simply repeat it."[32] There is a potentially interactive and mutually defining relationship between the exertions of the state to impose a preferred identity and the individual's self-definition mediated through social construction.

Implications for Russian Identity in the Near Abroad

Multiple Identities for Russians Living Abroad

A Russian is not only a Russian. Unfortunately, the shorthand used here to refer to those former citizens of the Soviet Union who speak Russian and now live outside the Russian Republic tends to reify the Russian national or ethnic identity at the expense of all others. Although this is clearly not my intention, it is very difficult to avoid such reinforcement in practice. Besides ethnic and national identities, there is a vast repertoire of identities available to Russians living in the near abroad. I will just catalog some of these possibilities below before discussing them in more detail.

A Russian might have a salient religious identity as a practicing member of the Russian Orthodox church. This person may also find gender to be a defining identity. Perhaps the fact that the individual can speak Latvian in Latvia will permit a linguistic identity. This Russian's commitment to the ideals of the former Communist Party of the Soviet Union might impart an ideological identity. A career as a playwright could imply a particular professional identity or an identity as a member of the intelligentsia. The critical point is that the Russian whose ethnic and national identity is consistently reinforced by the mere use of the label "Russian" in fact has many other identities, and the Russian's political and social behavior will often be determined by these alternatives.

Russian Identity Choices in the Near Abroad

To simplify matters mightily, I will only touch on two broad sets of Russian objectives in choosing an identity: either to gain some reward or to avoid some injury.

A Russian who speaks Estonian will choose an Estonian linguistic identity when this skill will lead to obtaining a job working for some government ministry in Tallinn. A Russian in Lviv will choose a liberal reformist identity when trying to win votes to gain a seat on a local governing board. A Russian in Tashkent will choose an identity as an entrepreneur to convince the Tashkent regional council that he should be allowed to take over the shoe factory of which he was the deputy director in the times of Soviet rule. A Russian in Tashkent will choose a Russian ethnic identity to convince the Tashkent regional council that he should be allowed to take over that same factory, the rationale being that he has connections in Moscow who can help save the plant. A member of the Russian peasantry may choose a peasant identity in Ukraine to qualify for a portion of the collective farm as it is privatized.

One can imagine a Russian's sense of Orthodoxy growing in order to defend the church from governmental attack. For example, if the Ukrainian government were to side with Uniate demands that some orthodox churches be returned, then more Russians will choose identities as Russian Orthodox Christians. If a conservative Islamic government were to come to power in Turkmenistan, enforcing strict dress and behavioral codes on Muslim women living there, Russian women in that country might choose a particular gendered identity calculated to avoid governmental scrutiny. Perhaps they would dress more discreetly, go out alone less frequently, stay at home after dark, and not enter public bars or restaurants unaccompanied. A Russian resident in the Donbass region of Ukraine may downplay this regional identity, with its fifth-column separatist connotations, instead choosing a Ukrainian civic national identity while visiting western Ukraine.

Russian Identities Imposed by Non-Russian States

As I have already suggested, the national identity is the one most likely to be selected by the state for imposition. The drive for resource extraction and the demands of the international system of states combine to push any state to propagate a national identity for its citizens. But this formulation leaves at least two important complications unexplored. First, there is more than one kind of national identity a state can choose to impose. Second, the state is not the only possible source of authority that can impose an identity.

To put matters starkly, the state could choose to impose either a civic national identity or an ethnic national identity on its citizens. The Ukrainian government, for example, could decide that all individuals within its boundaries should adopt identities as citizens of the Republic of Ukraine. Through its control over the public education system in Ukraine, the state could ensure that, at least until the university level, students would be exposed systematically to the state's preferred version of Ukrainian history, politics, geography, literature, and the arts. The curriculum would not stress acute differences among Russians and Ukrainians.

Other instruments of the state would be employed in imposing this identity. The training and education of military conscripts would be geared toward instilling loyalty to the Ukrainian republic. Geographic boundaries within Ukraine would not be drawn in such a way as to overlay already extant ethnic, religious, linguistic, or regional cleavages. State institutions would be arranged according to bureaucratic or functional structures, not according to ethnic, religious, or regional criteria. The state would refrain from making Ukrainian Catholicism the state religion. The state would ensure, whether through direct control or through the modes of deniable control familiar in liberal democracies, that the media assist in the propagation of this civic national identity. In sum, the Ukrainian state would use its formidable array of assets to propagate a new national identity while simultaneously trying to quash any sources of subnational or international identities that might interfere with that project.

The Republic of Estonia seems to have embarked on a completely different course of national identity imposition, choosing an ethnic, rather than a civic, identity to impose. The Estonian state has sought to impose an ethnic national Estonian identity based on ethnolinguistic criteria for citizenship. In other words, unlike in Ukraine, where Russians could become Ukrainian, in the Republic of Estonia no Russians would become Estonian. As in the case of Ukraine, the Estonian state would impose this identity through the many instruments at its disposal, beginning with the public education system. The curriculum would be aimed at advancing a view of Estonian history, politics, and culture that would advance an ethnic Estonian identity suitable only for Estonians.

Military training might, along with inculcating the need to defend the borders of Estonia, stress the need to defend ethnic Estonians from Russians. Geographic boundaries will be deliberately drawn to stress the difference between Estonians and Russians. For example, perhaps the Estonian state would designate Narva as a new province, hoping thereby to create a Russian settlement. Similarly, the Estonian state could bifurcate their state institutions into those serving Estonian ethnic nationals and those ministering to the dwindling needs of Russians. The Estonian state could make Estonian Lutheranism its state religion. Like Ukraine, the Estonian state would ensure that media help reinforce the state's message. The ethnic national identity propagated by the Republic of Estonia, in contrast to Ukraine's inclusiveness, would be exclusive. In actuality, because it is based on ethnolinguistic criteria of citizenship, the Estonian national identity is aimed not at including Russians as citizens of the republic but rather at excluding all Russians who cannot qualify as ethnic Estonians.

It is worth considering why one approach might be chosen over the other. Why would the Estonian state choose to exclude Russians from becoming citizens whereas the Ukrainian state would choose to include everyone living there as a Ukrainian citizen? Recall the dual domestic and international logics operating on states. The international desiderata are too vague here; they demand only a national state, not one distinguishing between a civic or a national version. Given these loose criteria, the Ukrainian state has performed as predicted, because its inclusive identity project maximizes revenues. A state, however, might have other values it considers to be far more important.

It turns out that a fair number of states in history, not just Estonia, have deliberately chosen not to maximize resource extraction from its citizenry in exchange for being able to adopt an exclusionary national identity. South Africa's state denied a South African national identity to its indigenous peoples for more than 300 years. The Israeli state has denied Palestinians an Israeli identity for over 25 years. States have noneconomic objectives, be they rooted in racism, domestic politics, or national security, that may override the imperative for an inclusive national identity. In the case of hypothetical Estonia, for instance, perhaps the domestic political costs of appearing accommodative to the oppressor nation make an exclusive national identity based on ethnicity and language the only logical outcome.

In sum, Russians living in the near abroad may have different national identities imposed upon them by their new states. They may find themselves as civic nationalists or they may find themselves as an identified national minority, barred from assuming a new ethnic national identity.

Nonstate Authorities and Identities

Russian identity may be imposed by the state, but it may also be imposed by other authorities competing with the state for this opportunity. The sociopolitical situation in the former Soviet Union is likely to give great ambit to the propagation of identities by nonstate authorities. The state, to varying degrees in each former republic, has been severely weakened. It is less able to raise revenues and has lost control over such key institutions as the media, the church, public education, and economic regulation; it has lost its capacity to articulate a coherent identity for its citizens. Given these conditions, we might expect other authorities to exercise influence over identity construction.

Four potential competitors for the state could be the Russian Orthodox church, the Russian mass media, a Russian political party, and private Russian schooling. If the Ukrainian state seeks to impose a Ukrainian civic national identity but does not restrict the operation of the alternative institutions, other authorities can have an effect. Russian attendance at Orthodox services permits the church to reinforce a Russian Orthodox identity for those who choose to worship. Russian radio shows, TV broadcasts, and newspapers advance a Russian viewpoint that underlines a Russian identity for the audience. The existence of a political party based on a Russian constituency provides yet another opportunity for a Russian identity to be inculcated. A private alternative to the state's single most potent weapon, public education, would be a significant source of Russian identity for any Russian community with such assets. This discussion ends precisely where the discussion of social construction begins. There is no wall between these two processes of identity creation. Although the alternative institutions sketched out above may indeed *impose* a Russian identity, they do so only if they have complicitous subjects. Russians in Ukraine have to go to church, buy Russian newspapers, support Russian candidates, and create alternative Russian private schools if these institutions are to have any effect on identity. These practices are the heart of social construction, which I take up below.

Social Constructions of Russian Identity Abroad

Russians in Estonia might seem to have little opportunity to retain their Russian ethnic identity. If the Estonian state is imposing an Estonian ethnic national identity on its citizens, Russians have to become Estonian to become citizens. And Russians, under such conditions, would have no incentives to choose a Russian identity, since no rewards are going to be set aside for Russians in the land of Estonia. Despite these obstacles to Russian identity, Russians have a most powerful asset: their social practices. Just by being ethnically Russian in their community settings, Russians can perpetuate a Russian identity in a land of Estonians. To the Estonian state's imagined national identity, the Russian community can respond by reproducing its experienced Russian identity as well as counter with mythmaking of its own.

Russian assets for this project come in two varieties. At an institutionalized, more formalized level, there are the nonstate structures described in the section above. Russians practicing the Russian Orthodox religion are both producing and reproducing their Russian identities for themselves and for the community as a whole. When they go home to their families, their practices in church may very well become part of the social practices at home. Organizing a Russian political party would have similar effects. The development of Russian private schools would provide an opportunity for the Russian community to construct its own identity and then reproduce it through its children. Through community banks, it can provide a source of capital, allowing Russians to avoid participation in, and hence reproduction of, the Estonian national market.[33]

At the level of uninstitutionalized daily social practices, any celebrations, rituals, parades, commemorations, feast days, holidays, and so on serve to reproduce a Russian identity in Estonia.[34] For example, if Russians in Estonia continued to observe June 22 as a day of solemn recognition of Russian losses during the war against Germany, they would be establishing a practice whose repetition reproduces a Russian identity for its participants and observers.[35] At the level of "bytovye" interaction, the use of the Russian language, preparation of conventional Russian cuisine, repetition of traditional ways of doing things,[36] and observance of manners and customs reproduce a Russian identity.

Russian Identity Abroad:
Chosen, Imposed, and Constructed

A Russian woman living outside the boundaries of Russia finds herself in a complex situation for constructing her identity. On the one hand, she has many choices open to her. She can choose to be a Russian, a Ukrainian citizen, a woman, a believer, and a daughter. On the other hand, the incentives in general point against her being a Russian, as foreign states surely will not be providing any special treatment for members of that group. Meanwhile, the state is trying to impose either of two new identities on her. One of these, the ethnic national identity, is impossible for her to adopt. The other, the civic national identity, allows her to adopt it without forsaking her Russian ethnic identity. At the same time, other authorities are competing to impose other identities, and many of these nonstate authorities could be interested in propagating a Russian ethnic identity. The Orthodox church, Russian newspapers and television, Russian political organizations, and Russian private education could all combine to create powerful sources of Russian identity for Russians living abroad. Finally, she daily reproduces her Russian identity through practices of social reproduction. Just by "being" Russian, she reproduces a Russian identity for herself and the community in which she is situated. In sum, the capacity for a Russian identity to survive abroad looks very good. At the very least, we should expect a stiff struggle before any state project aimed at erasing it.

Identity and Conflict

A Russian identity in the near abroad is unproblematic in itself. Only its conflict with the state or with other communities could make it Moscow's concern. If such a conflict occurs, it may set in motion a chain of events that could lead to Russian military intervention, a topic taken up in the next section. Below I discuss those conflicts most likely to be caused by Russian identity: conflicts between local Russians and the state and conflicts between that state and Moscow.

To put matters simply, conflict causes identity, not the reverse. Russians will not end up in conflict with Kazakhs because they are Russian and Kazakh; rather, conflict that is articulated along the identity lines of Russian and Kazakh will evoke these ethnic identities.

Much conflict has its origins in state policies. States may adopt policies that discriminate, either explicitly or implicitly. For example, governments at all levels make allocative decisions regarding taxation policy, public works contracts, and civil service requirements that confer advantages and disadvantages on different groups. When Estonia passes a law requiring knowledge of Estonian for a host of government jobs, the exclusion evokes an identity. State economic development plans may evoke a regional or ethnic identity, depending on how privileges are allocated.[37] Whenever the state allocates some benefit or sanction on a differential and systematic basis, the effect is to ascribe an identity to the favored and aggrieved communities.

Another source of conflict is differential access to economic resources.[38] If Chechens selling produce in a market in Simferopol appear to local Russians to be price gouging, this conflict will cause both Chechens and Russians, ceteris paribus, to see their conflict in ethnic terms. But there is nothing inevitable about an ethnic conflict per se. If class identity is more powerful than ethnic identity, then Russian and Ukrainian coal miners striking in the Donbass will see the owners of the mines as the other, not Ukrainians or Russians. A third source of conflict is a threat to a cultural community.[39] Russians who feel there is some possibility that their opportunity to choose or socially reproduce their Russian identity is being threatened by the actions of the state or some other authority will have their Russian identity evoked.

In sum, Russian identity can be evoked along three main avenues. The state can allocate resources in a discriminatory way. Russians may find themselves in difficult economic circumstances that can be explained according to ethnic affiliations. The Russian cultural community may find itself in danger of losing the social resources necessary to socially reproduce its Russian identity. In each of these three broad patterns, it is likely that conflict will cause a renewed sense of Russian identity. Whether this identity becomes a matter of Russian foreign policy made in Moscow is the subject of the next section.

Conflict, Identity, and Russian Foreign Policy

A complicated causal chain connects Russian identity in the near abroad with a decision by a Russian president in Moscow to use military, economic, or political means of coercion against some government of a former Soviet republic. (See Figure 7.1.)

The critical factors are Russian identity abroad, Russian domestic politics, state policies of former Soviet republics, and international politics. Russian identity is important but neither necessary nor sufficient to cause Moscow's interven-

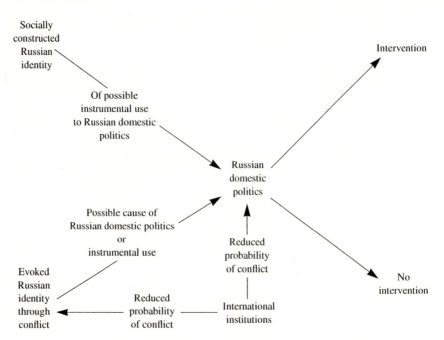

FIGURE 7.1   Russian Identity and Russian Foreign Policy in the Near Abroad

tion in the near abroad. Moscow might intervene for a host of reasons, not least being the behavior of these other states, but Russian identity abroad might be necessary to trigger the kinds of processes in Russian domestic politics that could lead to forceful Russian foreign and military policy. Intervention to save Russians abroad probably could not come about without Russians abroad having Russian identities.

Russian identity abroad is not sufficient to cause Moscow's intervention in the near abroad because in the absence of particular configurations in the domestic politics of Russia, it would not result in intervention. Given the social resources of Russians abroad, it is very likely there will always be a Russian identity being socially constructed and reproduced. But it will not, by itself, precipitate action from Moscow.

Similarly, conflict in the former Soviet republics over state policy, economic resources, and cultural integrity plays a contributory but not decisive role. Conflict is more important than merely the presence of identity. The process by which identity is evoked matters. Social construction is continuous and ordinary, but a Russian identity evoked due to conflict is both discontinuous and extraordinary. It is far more likely to spur movement in Russian domestic politics. It may even have a causal effect in Russian domestic politics, whereas "normal" Russian identity may be only an opportunity for actors in Russian domestic politics.

Therefore, the state of Russian domestic politics is a critical causal linchpin. If the constellation of political forces in Russia is already committed to vindicating the interests of Russians abroad, or merely recognizes the instrumental political value of advancing those interests in Moscow, or feels compelled by domestic political pressure and partisan politics to respond to these interests, then Russian identity abroad, especially if it is the product of conflict, will likely result in some kind of response from Moscow.

My aim in this chapter is not to elaborate a model of Russian domestic politics specifying the conditions under which we should expect a receptive political environment to the interests of the Russian diaspora; other authors in this volume have sketched out such conditions. Astrid Tuminez has indicated four such constellations of forces in this volume.[40] All four streams of post-Soviet nationalism contain a commitment to Russians living abroad. If she is right, then there is little to choose from among what she calls the liberal nativists, national patriots, centrist statists, and Westernizing democrats. Jack Snyder, at a more systemic level, claims that any democratizing regime will have a hard time resisting the path of forceful nationalism in its foreign policy.[41] This analysis would also seemingly imply a Russian predisposition to intervene in the near abroad. In sum, it would appear that Russian domestic politics is, at a minimum, not inhospitable terrain for political actors who are interested in the issue of Russians abroad. Indeed, it would appear that if cases of conflict evoked identities, Russians would find a ready response from politicians in Moscow.

This brings us to the last factor at work in shaping the role of identity in Russian foreign policy: international institutions. International politics pushes states to impose national identities on their citizens, but the current international system does not differentiate between civic or ethnonational identities. The international system, through a set of dedicated institutions and state practices, could select for one kind of national identity over another. If such institutions were to reward the civic national identity choice over the ethnonational version, then cases of Russian identity evoked by conflict would be less likely. It would be even less likely if international institutions went further to develop a code of conduct concerning acts of state discrimination that are political, economic, or cultural. Such an international system and state practices consonant with these norms do not exist, but they could fundamentally affect this causal model in two regards. First, they could influence the behavior of post-Soviet republics. Second, they could play a role in Russian domestic politics by offering an alternative to Russian military intervention to vindicate the rights of Russians in the diaspora.[42]

In sum, Russian identity in the near abroad will always be available for political forces in Moscow to protect and exploit. But this identity will not attract protection or acquiesce to exploitation if it remains only the product of social construction. If, however, this identity is evoked by conflict with post-Soviet states, by economic dislocation or by threat to the social resources necessary to its reproduction, then this Russian identity could spur political forces in Russia proper to come to its defense in the near abroad. Russian identity born of conflict is not inevitable. Russian domestic political incentives are not inevitably arrayed in favor of exploiting such an identity should it arise. Moreover, the practices and institutions of world politics could reduce the likelihood of a forceful Russian foreign policy by helping to construct a civic national identity in the near abroad.

Russian Identity in Uzbekistan and Estonia and the Consequences for Russian Foreign Policy

In this section I will use the cases of Uzbekistan and Estonia as rough contrasting illustrations of my arguments about Russian identity and Russian foreign policy. I must stress at the outset that the "findings" I present are heuristic and meant to generate questions. They are most definitely not intended to test theory. My information about developments in Uzbekistan comes from a research trip to Tashkent and Samarkand in October 1993, and my comments on Estonia are derived almost exclusively from written Western sources. That said, a comparative analysis of Russian identity in Uzbekistan and Estonia identifies promising avenues of future inquiry.

First, Uzbekistan's efforts to impose an Uzbek civic national identity have not evoked a Russian identity through conflict. This has made the Russian community in Uzbekistan less available to political entrepreneurs in Moscow who support a more forceful policy there and elsewhere in the former Soviet empire. Second, Estonia's contrary efforts to impose an Estonian ethnic national identity have evoked a Russian identity through conflict and have resonated in Russian domestic politics with the result that many voices in the Russian military, parliament, and government have called for armed intervention in Estonia. Third, different state policies in Tashkent and Tallinn have resulted in different opportunities for Russian social reproduction. The authoritarian nature of Islam Karimov's government has made it impossible for Russians there to build political institutions above the level of community, but Russian identity construction at or below that level is actively pursued. Estonia's much more liberal approach to civil and political liberties has resulted in Russian identity construction at both the community and the institutional level. Fourth, neither Estonia nor Uzbekistan has given members of the Russian community any incentive to choose a Russian identity for themselves. Fifth, international institutions have been important players in Estonia because of the conflict evoked by Russian identity there and its resonance in Moscow.

Uzbekistan

The Uzbek state under Islam Karimov has embarked on a comprehensive program of imposing some variety of Uzbek civic identity on all residents of that country. The state is advantaged in this undertaking by having complete control of the media. Anyone who wishes to start a newspaper, for example, need only apply to the Republic Press Fund for financing, but this fund is run by the Karimov government. As of January 1994, there were no independent newspapers in Uzbekistan. The five leading dailies were registered either under the Supreme Soviet or under the ruling party. Moreover, local governments have founded all the local papers.[43] The Uzbek state is further empowered through its control of political space. There are only two officially registered parties. The first is the successor to the Uzbek Communist Party, Karimov's Popular Democratic Party. The second is the party of Karimov's adviser, Usman Azimov, the Homeland's Progress Party. Through acts of intimidation, violence, and dirty tricks, no other parties have been permitted to register, including the two main opposition parties, Erkh and Birlik.

The state has been very careful to propagate an identity that is devoid of ethnonational content. On New Year's Day 1994, the official Karimov message was one of unity, based on "family, children, close friends and relatives, krai, and the land they live on, the land which unites us all."[44] Karimov even has gone so far as to defend his country's protracted use of the Russian ruble by claiming he did not want to behave insensitively to the Russian residents of Uzbekistan who would feel as if they "were being torn away from their homeland" by the introduction of the Uzbek sum.[45] The implementation of the language law is designed to allow for both a soft transition from Russian to Uzbek and a continued place for the Russian language in social reproduction. For example, even though Uzbek is the official state language, and it is to be used in judicial proceedings, one has the right to use one's own language in court or to have an interpreter. Moreover, new street signs in Tashkent are in Uzbek, but the Russian signs remain as well.

The official commemoration of World War II is also consistent with a strategy aimed at transcending any ethnonational identities while instilling a patriotic, civic Uzbek national one. So, for example, V-Day is celebrated on May 9, just as it was in the former Soviet Union and is in Russia today. A new medal has been created, "Zhasorat" (inscribed in Uzbek), which has been awarded to all 180,000 war veterans in the republic.[46] Even Uzbekistan's refusal to grant Moscow's demands for dual citizenship for Russians in Uzbek was explained in terms consistent with the construction of an Uzbek civic national identity. Karimov claimed that granting this right to Russians would only create an element of inequality between them and others in Uzbekistan. Instead, "Russians should believe that the Uzbek constitution provides them with equal rights alongside others living in the republic."[47] Moreover, it would "weaken their patriotic spirit" as Uzbeks.[48]

At least one other observer of developments in Uzbekistan has been struck by the state's efforts at civic identity construction. Vladimir Berezovskiy, writing in *Rossiskaya Gazeta,* noted that Karimov is groping for a new ideology, one based on patriotism. Historical symbols are being resurrected and appropriated by the state for use as civic totems. For example, the Basmachis are now esteemed as "champions of faith and freedom." Nationalist writers and poets repressed under Stalin are being rehabilitated, and streets are being renamed in their honor. The author remarks that one aim of this new ideology/identity is to overcome "regionalism, the separation of Uzbeks into Fergana, Khorezm, Bukhara, and Tashkent Uzbeks." Finally, he notes that a very clever generational game is being played. By replacing the Cyrillic alphabet with Latin in school, the younger generation is being effectively cut off from all Soviet and Russian literature. But the old are not forgotten, as statues of Pushkin and Gorky remain.[49]

But the strong state of Karimov has a double-edged effect. By propagating a civic Uzbek identity, it does not threaten the Russian ethnic identity. But the state's imposition of this inclusive identity has come at the cost of denying any political or social space to any alternative organizational forms. Consequently, the Russian community cannot develop parties, associations, or other organizations on any scale. Social reproduction must remain a local community endeavor. The Uzbek state's commitment to a civic identity that does not entail discriminatory government policies has avoided a conflict-evoked Russian identity. This circumstance has favored the predicted outcome. Russian politicians in Moscow have not identified Russians in Uzbek as Russians abroad in need of rescue by the Russian state. Instead, as Foreign Minister Kozyrev told journalists after his November 1993 visit to Central Asia, it is wrong to compare the "state level discrimination in Latvia and Estonia" to the avowed policies of Uzbekistan, Kazakhstan, and Tadzhikistan.[50] Finally, the Uzbek state choice of a civic identity has obviated the need for international involvement in the construction of Russian identity in Uzbekistan.

In sum, Uzbekistan's selection of an inclusive civic identity that transcends Uzbek ethnonationalism has meant minimal conflict with local Russians, which has in turn resulted in minimal effects on Russian domestic politics and minimal response from the international community. Virtually none of this is true in the case of Estonia.

Estonia

The issue of identity in Estonia is the virtual opposite of that in Uzbekistan. The Estonian state has chosen to impose an exclusive ethnonational Estonian identity. It has provided plenty of political and civil space for Russians to construct a Russian identity at both the community and institutional level. The Estonian state's discriminatory policies with respect to Russians living there have evoked a conflictual identity that has resonated in Russian domestic politics. Finally, international institutions have played a significant role in constructing identity in Estonia.

The Estonian state has significant resources to accomplish its aim of imposing an exclusive ethnonational Estonian identity on those living within its borders. All the radio stations in Estonia, though private, are dependent on government subsidies. Moreover, although Russian radio stations and newspapers exist, they receive no such aid from the state. The government has stopped rebroadcasting Radio Moscow and has suspended all Ostankino broadcasts from Russia, and it produces its own Russian-language radio program.[51] The content of the Estonian message differs dramatically from the Uzbek message. For example, Estonian president Lennart Meri, on the seventy-sixth anniversary of the Republic of Estonia, mentioned nothing but Estonian ethnonational symbols. The presence of 500,000 Russians in Estonia went unremarked.

The Estonian state's understanding of identity and legislation based on that understanding have shaped different kinds of identities for Russians living in Estonia. Citizenship laws have affected the status of these individuals; therefore, Russians living in Estonia have adopted different Russian identities based on these laws. For example, an Estonian Legal Citizens' Association was formed in August 1993 because of the 70,000 Russians who had applied for identity cards by 1991. This was essentially one group of Russians whose identity was defined by their status under Estonia's citizenship law. A second, quite different Russian identity was associated with the League of Russian Citizens and the Russian Community of Estonia. These were citizens of Russia living in Estonia who had no hope or desire of becoming Estonian citizens.[52] Again, Estonian state law structured the choice of Russian identity for this particular group of residents.

The Estonian state's commitment to democracy has allowed Russians to create a number of organizations whose practices serve to socially construct and reproduce a Russian identity. These bodies include the Estonian Ethnic Minorities Association, the Russian Representative Assembly, the Union of Russian Citizens, the Council of the Russian Community, and the Russian Citizens' Union.

The Estonian state's adoption of discriminatory legislation has provoked a conflictual Russian ethnic identity within Estonia. This, in turn, has influenced Russian domestic politics in the direction of interventionism in Estonian domestic affairs. For example, Russian president Yeltsin responded to Estonia's June 1993 citizenship law by accusing Riga of "ethnic cleansing" and "apartheid." He suggested that the Estonian government had forgotten "certain geopolitical and demographic realities . . . [and] Russia has the means to remind it of them."[53] Yurii Baturin, Yeltsin's security adviser, told *Der Spiegel* that it was "the duty of Russia as a great power to protect ethnic Russians in former Soviet republics, if their rights were violated, as in the Baltic states."[54] Defense Minister Grachev, accusing Estonia of apartheid, threatened to increase the Russian military presence there, rather than withdraw by the August 31, 1994, deadline, if abuse of Russians did not stop.[55] Yeltsin has also linked the treatment of Russians in Estonia and Latvia to Russian troop withdrawals by the deadline. In a phone conversation with President Clinton, Yeltsin reportedly said he would be willing to sign a schedule on troop withdrawals if the Baltic states would nullify their "discriminatory legislation" against Russians.[56] Finally, at the extreme, Petr Rozhok, a member of Zhirinovsky's Liberal Democratic Party, its representative in Estonia, and a resident of Narva, urged retired Russian officers and soldiers in Estonia to form military units, asserting that they should be "aware of the protection and support of great Russia."[57]

In sum, the Estonian state's policies on Russians within its borders exerted significant influence on politics in Moscow, but this result was not matched in the case of Uzbekistan, whose government has not adopted similar policies. The role of international institutions mirrors this difference. Whereas the Uzbek identity project was more or less ignored by organizations such as the OSCE and the UN, the Estonian state's efforts to create an ethnonational Estonian identity received continuous attention from international, especially European, institutions.

Estonian officials appealed to the OSCE and the Council of Europe (CE) for approval of their citizenship laws in order to counter criticism emanating from local Russians, Moscow, Europeans, and Washington. Moscow appealed to the OSCE and the CE to evaluate Estonia's citizenship laws and to press Tallinn to make changes in these laws that would help the Russian community gain Estonian citizenship. One member of the Russian parliament suggested that they should be consulting with the European Union, Nordic Council, and the United States "so they can tell us what they think our attitude toward Estonia should be,"[58] implying that Russian politicians wish to craft their positions on Russian rights in Estonia according to the normative consensus in the West on this issue. The international community, or at least its most powerful members, participate in the production of identity for Russians in Estonia.

Russian foreign minister Kozyrev pointed out an extremely important function of international institutions: They may persuade another country to adopt a position it would never adopt if it had to do so at the hands of a great power like Russia. In an interview, Kozyrev asserted that the issues separating Estonia and Russia "will be settled only with the opinions of the CE and CSCE being taken into account. My hope is that if Estonian leaders consider this criticism calmly— not as some dictatorial instruction from Moscow—then they can start to put the situation to rights with the help of international experts."[59]

Meanwhile, Russians in Estonia who felt aggrieved by Estonian laws on citizenship appealed for help to the UN, the OSCE, the CE, and other organizations,[60] and these appeals got results. In July 1993, after the Estonian parliament passed a "Law on Foreigners" that more or less made every non-Estonian a noncitizen, the OSCE High Commissioner on Ethnic Minorities, Max Van Der Stael, met with Estonian prime minister Mart Laar. They ultimately agreed that the law was causing apprehension among Russians and that the Russian community had not been adequately consulted. Several days later, the Estonian president, Lennart Meri, refused to sign the law because OSCE and CE legal experts agreed that it did not conform with the "European legal system."[61]

Estonia's state choice of an exclusive ethnonational Estonian identity, though giving free rein to the social construction of Russian identity at both the institutional and the community level, provoked a conflict over Russian identity in Estonia. This in turn played into Russian domestic politics, resulting in threats and pressure from Moscow. The presence of international institutions whose normative foundations are biased somewhat against any ethnonational identity project helped ameliorate the conflict between the Estonian state and Russians, both at home and abroad.

Conclusion: Russian Foreign Policy and Russian Identity in the Near Abroad

It would be difficult to explain Russian foreign policy in the non-Russian countries of the former Soviet Union without reference to the 25 million Russians still living there. Although Moscow could adopt a forceful policy toward the former republics independently of the Russian presence, it is no doubt also true that the presence of Russians increases the probability that policymakers in Russia and the interested public and electorate in Russia will pay more attention to developments in these fourteen new states than they otherwise would. Moreover, the importance accorded internal events in these states is also magnified because of the Russian presence. Finally, the potential for events in the near abroad to echo through Russian domestic politics is greatly enhanced, if not created, by the presence of Russians abroad.

Given the influence of these communities in Russian foreign policy making, we need to understand how these people might play a role in determining Moscow's policy toward them and toward the countries in which they reside. In this chapter I have sketched out a general argument about how at least one scenario could work. I have argued that a Russian identity can be created by three different processes: A Russian can choose such an identity for instrumental reasons; the identity can be imposed by the state; and the community can socially construct an identity that the Russian then reproduces through either discursive or institutionalized interactions. Each process has different implications for Russian foreign policy, as mediated through Russian domestic politics.

Any of the three processes may be exploited by Russian political entrepreneurs, either in Russia or in the new state. Since all three produce a Russian identity, a Russian nationalist politician can use the presence of Russians abroad to begin the call for their defense. The three different processes vary, however, in their effects on Russian domestic politics. Russians abroad choosing their own Russian identities are less likely to inspire Russian politicians to demand protection for Russians living in former republics. Indeed, the fact that some gain is to be had from being Russian implies that Russians are likely to feel unthreatened in that republic. The social construction of Russian identity is also unlikely to cause a hostile reaction in Moscow. In fact, precisely the opposite is most probable. The demonstrated ability of Russians abroad to reproduce their Russian identities locally, and even more so institutionally, will reassure Russians in Russia that their diaspora is not at risk.

It is the state imposition of identity that promises to cause the most alarm in Russia. If a state chooses to impose a civic national identity, as in Uzbekistan, then no political reaction is likely. If, however, a state chooses to impose an ethnonational identity that excludes Russians from adopting that identity, then Russia is likely to respond, as it did in Estonia. Of course, the state need not impose an identity quite so bluntly. It could indirectly evoke a Russian identity through conflict, most likely through the discriminatory distribution of governmental largesse or by depriving the Russian community of the ability to socially reproduce itself.

Finally, events in Russia and the fourteen former Soviet republics do not occur in a political vacuum. The existence of international institutions that promulgate and protect norms of citizenship and treatment of ethnic minorities promises to reward states that choose civic national identities and that avoid the measures that would discriminate unduly against ethnic minorities. These same institutions can also help inform Russians in Russia about the condition of Russians abroad while evaluating the concerns expressed by the Russian diaspora.

The danger of a forceful Russian foreign policy in the near abroad is most acute if a new state adopts an exclusive national identity and discriminatory legislation against its Russian minority, if it suppresses Russian identity construction, and if no international institutions enforce norms of acceptable conduct. Russian foreign policy is less likely to be forceful if a state adopts both an inclusive civic national identity and neutral allocative policies, if it permits Russian identity construction, and if international institutions are available to provide trusted information to Russians and non-Russians alike.

Notes

I would like to thank Jackie Stevens, Bob Axelrod, Doug Blum, Matt Evangelista, Lowell Barrington, Bear Braumoeller, Bob Pahre, Zvi Gitelman, Joe Underhill-Cady, Dave Rousseau, Karl Mueller, Maria Fanis, and Mike Desch for very helpful comments on previous drafts. Kelly McMann, Denise DeGarmo, Karen Blumenthal, and Kevin Clarke provided both indispensable research assistance and comments on earlier drafts. I also benefited greatly from opportunities to present various versions of this chapter to meetings at Wolfson College, Oxford; the Center for Russian and East European Studies, the Program in the Comparative Study of Social Transformations, and the Department of Political Science, all at the University of Michigan; the Watson Institute Seminar Series at the Watson Institute for International Studies, Brown University; the Olin Critical Issue Series at the Russian Research Center, Harvard University; and the 1994 meeting of the International Studies Association.

1. Examples are, respectively, Ken Waltz, *Theory of International Politics* (Reading, Mass.: Addison-Wesley, 1979); Stephen Krasner, ed., *International Regimes* (Ithaca: Cornell University Press, 1983); Michael W. Doyle, "Kant, Liberal Legacies and Foreign Affairs, Parts 1 and 2," *Philosophy and Public Affairs* 12 (Summer and Autumn 1983): 205–235, 323–353; Susan Peterson, *The Politics of Crisis: Domestic Institutions and International Bargaining* (Ann Arbor: University of Michigan Press, forthcoming); George W. Breslauer and Philip E. Tetlock, eds., *Learning in U.S. and Soviet Foreign Policy* (Boulder: Westview Press, 1991); Alexander Wendt, "Collective Identity Formation and the International State," *American Political Science Review* 88 (June 1994): 384–398.

2. Although it is a pretheory in the sense that it is not complete, it has sufficient logical coherence and prima facie empirical validity that it merits serious evaluation. See James Rosenau, "Pre-Theories and Theories of Foreign Policy," in *Approaches to Comparative and International Politics,* ed. R. Barry Farrell (Evanston, Ill.: Northwestern University Press, 1966), pp. 29–92.

3. My position is captured in part by the following definition: "identity [is] the way(s) in which a person is, or wishes to be, known by certain others." Anthony P. Cohen, "Culture as Identity: An Anthropologist's View," *New Literary History* 24 (Winter 1993): 195.

4. Jurgen Habermas, *Communication and the Evolution of Society* (Boston: Beacon Press, 1979), p. 107.

5. For a similar conceptualization, see Joseph Rothschild, *Ethnopolitics: A Conceptual Framework* (New York: Columbia University Press, 1981), pp. 1–2.

6. Paul Brass, *Ethnicity and Nationalism: Theory and Comparison* (New Delhi: Sage Publications, 1991), p. 267; Cynthia H. Enloe, *Ethnic Conflict and Political Development* (Boston: Little, Brown, 1973), pp. 15–16; Erving Goffman, *The Presentation of Self in Everyday Life* (Garden City, N.Y.: Doubleday, 1959); Donald L. Horowitz, "Ethnic Identity," in *Ethnicity: Theory and Experience,* ed. Nathan Glazer and Daniel P. Moynihan (Cambridge: Harvard University Press, 1975), p. 118; Rasma Karklins, *Ethnic Relations in the USSR: The Perspective from Below* (Boston: Allen and Unwin, 1986), p. 4; Rothschild, *Ethnopolitics,* pp. 2, 130–135; Anthony D. Smith, *National Identity* (Reno: University of Nevada Press, 1991), pp. 4–24; Howard F. Stein and Robert F. Hill, *The Ethnic Imperative: Examining the New White Ethnic Movement* (University Park: Pennsylvania State University Press, 1977), pp. 19–23; and Ronald Grigor Suny, *The Revenge of the Past: Nationalism, Revolution, and the Collapse of the Soviet Union* (Stanford: Stanford University Press, 1993), pp. 9–11.

7. Robert H. Jackson, "Political Stratification in Tropical Africa," *Canadian Journal of African Studies* 7 (Fall 1973): 381–400.

8. See, for example, Karklins, *Ethnic Relations in the USSR,* p. 41; and Sandra Wallman, "Ethnicity and Boundary Process in Context," in *Theories of Race and Ethnic Relations,* ed. John Rex and David Mason (Cambridge: Cambridge University Press, 1986), p. 230.

9. Pierre L. Van den Berghe, *The Ethnic Phenomenon* (New York: Elsevier Publications, 1981), p. 254. See also Rothschild, *Ethnopolitics,* p. 7.

10. Horowitz, "Ethnic Identity," p. 116.

11. Elie Kedourie, *Nationalism* (New York: Praeger, 1960), p. 124.

12. I fully acknowledge that such a set of assumptions could provoke charges of gross anthropomorphism. I consider these early efforts to develop a usable theory of identity construction to justify grand simplifying assumptions at the outset, and I intend to disassemble the state in future work.

13. As Connor has shown, when states "nation-build," that is, create and impose a stateside identity, they simultaneously must destroy, or at least transcend and supersede, ethnonational identities. Walter Connor, "Nation-Building or Nation-Destroying," *World Politics* 24 (July 1972): 319–355.

14. Anthony Giddens, *The Nation-State and Violence* (Cambridge: Polity Press, 1985), p. 221.

15. For a fascinating account of how the Greek national identity was begat by the expectations of European great powers, see Michael Herzfeld, *Ours Once More: Folklore,*

Ideology, and the Making of Modern Greece (Austin: University of Texas Press, 1982), pp. 7–12.

16. The argument here parallels nicely Robert Gilpin's contention that the U.S. state risked losing power if it continued to allow U.S.-based multinational corporations to move their capital, and hence U.S. jobs and industrial base, abroad at will. See Robert Gilpin, *U.S. Power and the Multinational Corporation* (New York: Basic Books, 1975).

17. Just how unnatural it was has been suggested by Connor, who found that of a total of 132 states in 1971, only 12 were ethnically homogenous. Connor, "Nation-Building," p. 320.

18. Quote is from J. C. Herold, ed., *The Mind of Napoleon* (New York: Columbia University Press, 1955), p. 118. For a most powerful explication of the unique power of the state, see Pierre Bourdieu, *The Logic of Practice* (Stanford: Stanford University Press, 1990), pp. 4–66; Pierre Bourdieu, *Outline of a Theory of Practice* (Cambridge: Cambridge University Press, 1977), p. 190; and Pierre Bourdieu and Jean-Claude Passeron, *Reproduction in Education, Society and Culture* (London: Sage, 1990), pp. 108–125. See also David Gross, "Temporality and the Modern State," *Theory and Society* 14 (January 1985): 68–70.

19. Jean-Jacques Rousseau, *Considerations on the Present of Poland* (London: Nelson, 1953), pp. 176–177, as quoted in Zygmunt Bauman, "Modernity and Ambivalence," *Theory, Culture, and Society* 7 (June 1990): 155.

20. On how the state's creation of "artificial" boundaries leads to communities adopting particular identities, see Horowitz, "Ethnic Identity," pp. 132–137. Also see Peter Sahlins, *Boundaries: The Making of France and Spain in the Pyrenees* (Berkeley: University of California Press, 1989), pp. 112–124. David Gross describes how the modernizing state "gradually removed from the field all of its principal competitor institutions," with the result that the state gained unchallenged authority to interpret the historical past. See Gross, "Temporality and the Modern State," p. 74, and the sources he cites in note 41. North and Thomas make a similar argument about the rise of the state in early modern Western Europe. Only after the state established itself as the dominant or monopolistic protector of property rights did national and international markets develop. See Douglass C. North and Robert P. Thomas, *The Rise of the Western World* (Cambridge: Cambridge University Press, 1973).

21. For an early effort to develop a theory of socially constructed identity, see Peter L. Berger and Thomas Luckmann, *The Social Construction of Reality* (Garden City, N.Y.: Doubleday, 1966), pp. 159–168.

22. Anthony D. Smith, *The Ethnic Origins of Nations* (New York: Basil Blackwell, 1987), pp. 25, 28.

23. Benedict Anderson, *Imagined Communities: Reflections on the Origin and Spread of Nationalism* (London: Verso, 1983).

24. Anderson, *Imagined Communities,* p. 15.

25. This may explain why the last ethnic marker to disappear is cuisine. Van den Berghe, *The Ethnic Phenomenon,* p. 260.

26. Max Weber, *Economy and Society. An Outline of Interpretive Sociology.* Fuenther Roth and Claus Wittich, eds. (Berkeley: University of California Press, 1978), 389. My emphasis.

27. This observation fits well with the 100-year-old discussion begun by Tonnies on the difference between gemeinschaft and gesellschaft. Gemeinschaft could refer to those com-

munities that need little imagining, "a state of intense and comprehensive solidarity in a relatively small group in which there is opportunity for direct interaction." Edward Shils, "Primordial, Personal, Sacred and Civil Ties," *British Journal of Sociology* 8 (1957): 132.

28. Smith, *The Ethnic Origins of Nations,* p. 79.

29. Henri Tajfel, *Human Groups and Social Categories: Studies in Social Psychology* (Cambridge: Cambridge University Press, 1981), p. 239.

30. For instance, see Smith, *The Ethnic Origins of Nations,* pp. 3–14.

31. For a discussion of the state-society nexus in identity production, see Brass, *Ethnicity and Nationalism,* pp. 43–77.

32. Quoted in Gross, "Temporality and the Modern State," pp. 78–79.

33. Banton argues that precisely these two elements, alternative education and community capital, allow communities to maintain identities, even when situated in a hostile sea. See Michael P. Banton, *Racial and Ethnic Competition* (Cambridge: Cambridge University Press, 1983), pp. 155–163.

34. For the effects of the annual Notting Hill carnival on the reproduction of West Indian identity in London, see Anthony P. Cohen, *The Symbolic Construction of Community* (Chichester: Ellis Horwood, 1985), pp. 54–56.

35. For a discussion of the role of ritual in constructing and reproducing identity, see Paul Connerton, *How Societies Remember* (Cambridge: Cambridge University Press, 1989), pp. 44–54.

36. Giddens, *The Nation-State and Violence,* p. 200.

37. For manifestations of identity evocation through differential allocative policies in Africa, see P. H. Gulliver, *Tradition and Transition in East Africa* (Berkeley: University of California Press, 1969), p. 24; and Nelson Kasfir, *The Shrinking Political Arena* (Berkeley: University of California Press, 1976), pp. 50–51. Cynthia Enloe describes an interesting and important counterexample. When the Malaysian government passed laws favoring Islam, the Chinese community's Chinese identity was not evoked because Chinese have only the very weakest of religious identities. Enloe, *Ethnic Conflict and Political Development,* p. 20.

38. See, for example, James G. Kellas, *The Politics of Nationalism and Ethnicity* (London: Macmillan, 1991), p. 40; Anderson, *Imagined Communities,* p. 64; and Rothschild, *Ethnopolitics,* pp. 39–40, 52–57.

39. On threats to cultural identity, see Smith, *National Identity,* pp. 55–56; Peter Weinreich, "The Operationalisation of Identity Theory in Racial and Ethnic Relations," in *Theories of Race and Ethnic Relations,* ed. John Rex and David Mason (Cambridge: Cambridge University Press, 1986), pp. 301–302; William Bloom, *Personal Identity, National Identity, and International Relations* (Cambridge: Cambridge University Press, 1990), p. 143; and Brass, *Ethnicity and Nationalism,* p. 284.

40. Astrid S. Tuminez, "Russian Nationalism and the National Interest in Russian Foreign Policy," Chapter 3 of this volume.

41. Jack Snyder, "Democratization, War, and Nationalism in the Post-Communist States," Chapter 2 of this volume. See also Jack Snyder, *Myths of Empire: Domestic Politics and International Ambition* (Ithaca: Cornell University Press, 1991); and idem, "Averting Anarchy in the New Europe," *International Security* 14 (Spring 1990): 5–41.

42. For a further articulation of ideas on how institutions could affect state behavior in this area, see Ted Hopf, "Managing Soviet Disintegration: A Demand for Behavioral Regimes," *International Security* 17 (Summer 1992): 44–75; Ted Hopf, "Managing the

Post-Soviet Security Space: A Continuing Demand for Behavioral Regimes," *Security Studies* 4, no. 2 (Winter 1994/95): 242–280; and Stephen Van Evera, "Hypotheses on Nationalism and War," *International Security* 18 (Spring 1994): 5–39.

43. *FBIS-SOV*-94-006, 10 January 1994, p. 75.

44. *FBIS-SOV*-94-001, 3 January 1994, p. 61.

45. In a September 1993 Moscow TV interview, recorded in *FBIS-SOV*-93-172, 8 September 1993, pp. 87–88.

46. *FBIS-SOV*-94-088, 6 May 1994, p. 49.

47. *FBIS-SOV*-94-008, 12 January 1994, p. 78.

48. *FBIS-SOV*-93-249, 30 January 1993, p. 69.

49. *FBIS-SOV*-94-109, 7 July 1994, pp. 63–64.

50. *FBIS-SOV*-93-222, 19 November 1993, p. 6.

51. Uzbekistan also has suspended Ostankino broadcasts, for the same reason offered by Estonian authorities: Ostankino owes them money. Saulius Girnius, "Media in Countries of the Former Soviet Union," *Radio Free Europe/Radio Liberty (RFE/RL) Research Report* 2 (2 July 1993): 11–12.

52. There are 42,000 Russian citizens in Estonia. *FBIS-SOV*-94-007, 21 April 1994, p. 86.

53. Quoted in the *Economist,* 10 July 1993, p. 39. Foreign Minister Andrei Kozyrev has repeated the ethnic cleansing charge. Stephen Foye, "Kozyrev Again Accuses Baltic States of Abuses," *RFE/RL Daily Report,* 8 February 1994.

54. Alexander Rahr, "Yeltsin's Security Advisor Takes Harsh Position," *RFE/RL Daily Report,* 8 February 1994.

55. Stephen Foye, "Grachev Threatens Estonia with Reinforcements," *RFE/RL Daily Report,* 9 May 1994. On 26 July 1994, Russia agreed to abide by the deadline in exchange for Estonian assurances on treatment of retired Russian military personnel living in Estonia.

56. Dzintra Bungs, "Yeltsin Links Troop Pullouts to Russian Minorities," *RFE/RL Daily Report,* 6 July 1994. Yeltsin reiterated this linkage at his press conference following the G-7/8 meeting in Naples on 10 July 1994.

57. Dzintra Bungs, "Svirin, Rozhok, Duma on Russians in Estonia," *RFE/RL Daily Report,* 4 February 1994.

58. The quote is from Nikolai Medvedev, a member of the Russian Supreme Soviet and the chair of its department for federal and interethnic relations. *FBIS-SOV*-93-127, 6 July 1993, p. 17.

59. *FBIS-SOV*-93-127, 6 July 1993, p. 18.

60. *FBIS-SOV*-94-026, 30 January 1994, p. 57.

61. *FBIS-SOV*-93-126, 2 July 1993, p. 85; and *FBIS-SOV*-93-128, 7 July 1993, p. 63.

CHAPTER 8

From Each According to Its Abilities: Competing Theoretical Approaches to the Post-Soviet Energy Sector

Matthew Evangelista

Of the sources of Soviet conduct during the Cold War, the international economy is rarely paid much attention. Indeed the "administrative-command" economy that so characterized the Soviet system was established, among other reasons, deliberately to insulate the USSR from the vagaries of the international market. Only in the 1970s did the Soviet Union increase its participation in the world economy, mainly through the sale of raw materials, primarily energy products, and the import of grain and machinery. Thus, the questions that interested political scientists working on economic matters in other countries—the determinants of free trade or protectionist trade policies, for example, or the impact of the world economy on domestic political coalitions and cleavages—seemed irrelevant to the Soviet case.[1]

Even if this were true for the Soviet period—and there is reason to doubt that such questions were entirely irrelevant—one would expect that the international economy would play an increasingly important role in the post-Soviet period, as the former republics of the USSR open their borders to foreign trade and investment and move away from Soviet-style central planning and state ownership. Under those circumstances we might also expect that theoretical approaches to studying the relationship between the international economy and domestic politics in the rest of the world would become more useful for understanding the sources of Russian conduct as well.

This chapter examines the Russian energy sector—the part of the economy that has the greatest contact with the international economy. The Russian Federation is the second-largest energy producer and the largest energy exporter in the world. It exports about 40 percent of its total energy production, despite that in its own domestic use it is one of the world's most energy-intensive economies. Energy products constituted 43 percent of all Russian exports to non-Soviet areas in 1989. They continued to dominate Russian exports in the years following the breakup of the USSR.[2]

173

The first part of this chapter summarizes two contending approaches to understanding the impact of the international economy on domestic politics—economistic and institutionalist—and evaluates their applicability to the post-Soviet case. The second part provides a brief discussion of the Soviet institutions that structured economic life and sought to insulate the Soviet economy from the world market; it considers the extent to which their legacy still affects energy policy in the former Soviet republics. The third part of the chapter examines the regional politics of energy policy in the Soviet and post-Soviet periods. The fourth section presents a case study of the coal industry from 1989 to 1994, a period marked by unprecedented levels of worker activism and discontent that produced cleavages along class, sectoral, and regional lines of the sort that theories of political economy seek to explain.

The International Economy and Domestic Politics

Bringing theories of international and comparative political economy to bear on the post-Soviet case is complicated by a number of factors. First, the economies of Russia and the other former Soviet republics are still at the early stages of transition from state ownership and central planning and it is not clear how soon, if ever, they will develop the market institutions and infrastructure that the theories assume. Second, the questions that the theories seek to answer—their dependent variables—differ among themselves and in their degree of applicability to the post-Soviet cases. In the following sections I summarize the various theories and the relationships they posit between the international economy and domestic politics and I suggest how one might use the theories to answer questions of interest about the post-Soviet political economy.

Economistic Accounts

The theories I term "economistic" are based on neoclassical economics and share the assumptions of that body of theory: that individuals possess a stable set of preferences—a "utility function"—and that they behave "to maximize their utility as rational actors who calculate the costs and benefits of every option."[3] Analysts in this tradition tend to neglect the influence of institutions, either by defining institutions as the product of individual and group interests or by putting them far down on a list of more important influences on behavior.[4] The various economistic accounts differ primarily in their unit of analysis—the level at which they aggregate individual economic actors—and in the political phenomena they seek to explain.

Factors of Production.   The highest level of aggregation focuses on factors of production and is represented most prominently by Ronald Rogowski's study *Commerce and Coalitions.*[5] Rogowski seeks to explain the formation of broad political coalitions and cleavages in response to the expansion or contraction of

international trade by drawing on the Stolper-Samuelson theorem. His explanation makes predictions about the locus of conflict within society on the basis of
relative endowments of three factors: land, labor, and capital. An expansion of
trade benefits the owners of factors in relative abundance and hurts owners of
those in relative scarcity and vice versa. Thus, the relative endowment of factors
in a given country suggests the nature of the political alignments that will form
during periods of expanding or declining trade: urban-rural conflict, class conflict
(labor versus capital), or a Red-Green coalition (labor and agriculture against
capital).

Although Rogowski's theory was developed to explain political alignments in
countries with open economies as responses to expanding or contracting trade in
the international economy as a whole, an autarkic economy opening up to the
world market should be expected to conform to the theory's predictions as well.
As Rogowski and Frieden argue elsewhere, "even under Communist regimes
people became aware of, and responded to, export and import opportunities."[6] A
few specific problems arise, however, in considering the post-Soviet case. First,
Rogowski considers the USSR during the interwar period and the depression to
have been rich in land and labor but poor in capital. However, he describes the
Soviet Union during the postwar expansion of trade as still rich in land, relatively
rich in capital, but poor in labor.[7] Relative factor endowments—especially labor
scarcity—in the Soviet case, however, owed more to policy and inefficiency.[8]

Furthermore, Rogowski's assumptions about factor mobility—perfect mobility
of factors within national borders but immobility between countries—may not be
met in the Russian case. Capital is transnationally mobile, but the fact that much
of domestic capital is invested in obsolete technology and plants makes the assumption of its mobility dubious.[9] This is compounded by the possibility that the
traditional three-factor model may have become anachronistic. A more useful
threefold categorization might focus on factors such as skilled labor, unskilled
labor, and capital or labor, human capital, and physical capital.[10] These categories
may well prove more appropriate for analyzing the post-Soviet cases. They are
consistent with the way most scholars and journalists in the former Soviet Union
write about the politics of economic policy.[11]

If we do, however, accept Rogowski's basic three-factor model and its theoretical implications, we would expect to find conflict in the Russian energy sector
pitting labor (the relatively scarce factor) against capital and land (the relatively
abundant factors) as trade in energy products expands. In these economic models,
natural resources such as oil and coal fall under the definition of land. So the expansion of trade in energy products should lead, for example, to conflict between
oil workers and coal miners (labor), on the one hand, and the owners of oil fields
and collieries (land) and oil refineries and coal extraction equipment (capital), on
the other. The difficulty in identifying who these "owners" in fact are in the post-
Soviet economic context does, however, render Rogowski's approach problematic.[12]

Sectors, Classes, and Firms.   Many analysts have sought to disaggregate socioeconomic interests into categories that, they argue, would provide more precise explanatory and predictive power than the three-factor approach.[13] Jeffry Frieden and others put most of their emphasis on sectors, whereas Helen Milner focuses on firms.[14] What they seek to explain varies.

Frieden seeks to explain why some sectors choose to lobby the government for favorable policies whereas others try to overthrow the existing order. The key variable for Frieden is "asset specificity"—the degree to which owners of particular assets (including their own labor) are able to be put them to alternative uses. The cost of transforming the asset to make it available for another use is, according to Frieden, what determines the propensity of owners of assets to lobby their government: "Owners of assets in an industry will expend resources to influence government policy toward their industry up to the point where it would make more sense for them to find another use for their resources."[15] Frieden expects that most political cleavages will fall along sectoral lines. In cases where the degree of asset specificity varies greatly between factors—for example, if skilled labor is tied to production of a particular product while capital is much more mobile—one could expect class conflict within sectors instead.

Frieden's model has the potential to provide insights into the conditions under which economic actors in Russia and elsewhere will expend resources to lobby or oppose their government. As with Rogowski's approach, however, some of the assumptions underlying Frieden's work may be problematic for the post-Soviet cases. His assumption that economic actors behave as self-interested utility maximizers may not be troublesome, even for the prereform Soviet Union. His definition of utility as *income* and his use of *relative prices* to characterize the economic environment could, however, be misleading.[16] The popular mot of the Russian worker during the Soviet era—"We pretend to work, and they pretend to pay us"—raises some doubts about income maximization as a primary goal under conditions where prices and wages did not reflect the actual value of products or labor and where shortages, forced savings, and "hidden" inflation made it difficult to measure changes in workers' standards of living or firms' profits.[17] Presumably one could come up with ways to evaluate the price of labor in terms other than wages that would be more germane to the post-Soviet circumstances (e.g., access to food and consumer goods at shops where one works). The measurement problems entailed in such an endeavor would, however, be daunting.

Helen Milner's work focuses on a level of analysis below both the factor and the sector: the firm. She seeks to explain states' trade policies (protection versus free trade) as a function of the degree to which their firms are integrated into the international economy. Firms that produce mainly for export naturally favor free trade. Firms that depend on inputs from abroad also prefer their country to maintain low tariffs on those goods to keep their prices down. The more a firm is "internationalized"—linked in a multinational network of suppliers and customers—the more it favors free trade. These generalizations should help to understand the preferences of Russian and other former Soviet firms for government trade policy, although the translation of firm preferences into government policy in a period of political uncertainty may be difficult to understand.

Institutionalist Accounts

Institutionalist approaches to political economy are not, strictly speaking, comprehensive alternatives to economistic ones. Whereas economistic accounts are grounded in neoclassical economics, for example, institutionalists do not deliberately seek to violate tenets of economic theory. Nor are institutionalist accounts necessarily "nonrational."[18] On the question of rationality and the source of actors' preferences, there is, however, a divide within the school of thought characterized as institutionalist. One recent review of the literature has distinguished "rational-choice institutionalism" from "historical institutionalism."[19] As with any dichotomy, this one is not entirely satisfactory, but it serves adequately to distinguish the different types of behavior that we could observe in the post-Soviet cases, all of which would otherwise fall under a general category of institutionalist explanation.

According to Steinmo and Thelen, rational-choice theorists view institutions as "features of a *strategic context,* imposing constraints on self-interested behavior" of rational actors. Historical institutionalists, by contrast, "find strict rationality assumptions overly confining." Some assume "bounded rationality" instead; others prefer to conceive of actors as rule-following "satisficers" (that is, as seeking satisfactory rather than best outcomes) rather than utility maximizers. Perhaps the key difference is that unlike rational-choice institutionalists, historical institutionalists are wary of assuming the preferences of economic actors as given. In their view, not only actors' strategies and behavior but also their very goals are influenced by the institutional context.[20] In some historical institutionalist accounts, institutions serve as sources of *internalized* goals or norms, whereas for rational-choice institutionalists they serve only as external constraints.[21] As with economistic approaches, institutionalist approaches to political economy seek to explain a range of phenomena, from a government's adoption of new economic ideas (such as Keynesianism or developmentalism) to the relative performance of states faced with a common external economic shock (such as oil price increases) or the constant pressure of international competition.[22] For the purposes of this chapter I evaluate the extent to which the institutional context helps to account for the observed behavior of actors in the post-Soviet energy sector in ways that noninstitutional, economistic approaches fail to explain. I start out with consideration of the obvious institutions associated with links between the international economy and post-Soviet domestic politics but consider, in discussion of the empirical material, some of the less apparent normative influences as well.[23]

The main insight from the institutional literature that we should expect to apply to the post-Soviet cases is the notion of "path-dependent" change. As David Stark explains, "Actors who seek to move in new directions find that their choices are constrained by the existing set of institutional resources. Institutions limit the field of action, they preclude some directions, they constrain certain courses. But institutions also favor the perception and selection of some strategies over others."[24] According to notions of path dependence, then, we might find the behavior of post-Soviet actors to diverge from economistic expectations in ways that reflect the constraints of the Soviet institutional legacy.

Institutions of Soviet and Post-Soviet Economic Policy

The Institutional Basis for "Socialism in One Country"

The two main institutions that sought to insulate the Soviet economy from the international economic environment were the state monopoly on foreign trade and the "administrative-command system" of central planning.[25] The foreign trade monopoly was deliberately designed to separate Soviet producers of exported goods and consumers of imported goods from their foreign customers and suppliers. Soviet enterprises were subordinate to the central planning organizations and ministries and were constrained to follow directives from the center rather than market signals from abroad.[26] In the command economy prices were centrally determined and used as accounting devices rather than as signals for allocation of resources. Thus, the USSR was able to insulate its development process from major international disturbances, such as the Great Depression. It certainly helped that, as the world's largest country and enormously rich in natural resources, the USSR was in an especially favorable position to attempt a policy of economic autarky, in pursuit of Stalin's goal of "socialism in one country."

Even when the USSR began to move away from autarky by expanding its international trade after Stalin's death, it was still able to blunt the effect of world economic changes. Unlike the case for open, market economies, changes in the international economy did not affect the Soviet economy directly through the medium of prices. The central planning system was deliberately designed to cushion and delay, if not nullify, the impact of world prices, and in many respects it succeeded. The so-called price equalization system kept domestic and foreign prices separate by offsetting changes in the foreign currency price of exports or imports through taxes and subsidies. Consequently, changes in external prices affected the Soviet state budget but had "no impact on domestic prices, production or consumption," as a major international study recently concluded.[27] Contrary to its role in market economies, the exchange rate in the USSR before 1987 was used, like domestic prices, as an accounting unit and played no part in the allocation of resources.[28]

Under the old system, prices played no role as signals for enterprises to alter their production. If a particular enterprise produced a product for export whose international price was increasing, the enterprise would see no change in its own receipts. The additional profits would be transferred to the state budget.

As a consequence of the price equalization system, Soviet enterprises had no incentive to export. Material incentives—in the form, for example, of worker and management bonuses—were tied to plan fulfillment, and standards for domestic goods were typically lower than those for exports. As Shmelev and Popov point out, "export deliveries were paid for in the same rubles and at the same prices as deliveries for the domestic market, but they were far more bothersome than products earmarked for a local consumer who was not very demanding."[29] Thus, Soviet enterprises preferred to fulfill the plan in products for the domestic market.[30]

Soviet economic institutions such as central planning and the foreign trade monopoly clearly shaped the economic incentives facing enterprises and workers dealing with international markets. Soviet groups and individuals were further constrained by a key political institution—democratic centralism—according to which the Communist Party leadership enforced discipline through the *nomenklatura* system of appointments at all levels of the economic and political administration.[31] Thus, even if groups and individuals could clearly recognize their interests vis-à-vis the international economy, they could not always act upon them.

Institutions of the Post-Soviet Energy Sector

The end of the Soviet Union and the advent in Russia and the other former republics of leaders who espouse pro-market economic policies have changed little in the energy sector. Many of the Soviet-era institutions no longer exist, but their legacy lives on in successor institutions and practices that influence the behavior of economic actors in much the same way.

In Russia, as elsewhere, the legacy of Soviet economic institutions remained strong, despite the Yeltsin government's avowed commitment to a market system. In many sectors of the economy the mechanism of central planning was replaced by a system of "state orders" (*goszakazy*) that amounted to much the same thing. For more than a year after the demise of the USSR, the "free market" for coal, for example, was hardly in evidence. In a typical case, the Vorkuta coal conglomerate (Vorkuta Ugol'), which consisted of fifty enterprises, including a dozen mines, received *goszakazy* requiring each mine to provide 83 percent of its output to the government. Only the remaining 17 percent could be sold through market mechanisms, such as they were. Coal required to fulfill *goszakazy* had to be sold at artificially low prices that did not cover the mines' costs. The difference was made up by government subsidies.[32] The same situation prevailed in the Donetsk coal-mining region of Ukraine.[33]

Well into 1993, the Russian oil and gas sectors were still run as government monopolies. When Russian and foreign press reports indicated in mid-May of that year that the industry might be broken up and privatized to spur competition and increase output, the minister of fuel and energy objected with the argument that "there is no more efficient industry in Russia than the fuel and energy complex."[34] He particularly opposed plans to divide up the industry on regional lines.

Plans for privatization of Gazprom, the state natural gas monopoly, were announced only in April 1993. The government proposed to retain 40 percent of the shares. Half of the shares would go to workers in the industry and to residents of gas-producing regions. Only 10 percent would be available to the general public.[35] The first privatization in the Russian oil industry came only at the end of 1993, when 12 percent of the stocks of the giant Iuganskneftegaz Production Association were sold at auction.[36]

Democratic centralism ended when the Communist Party lost its official monopoly on power during the last years of the Gorbachev period. Yet members of the old *nomenklatura* still maintain positions of economic and political power throughout the former USSR. Alumni and representatives of the energy sector are particularly prominent in the Russian government, starting with Viktor Chernomyrdin. Before his appointment as prime minister in December 1992, he served as deputy prime minister responsible for energy policy, and before that he was minister of the Soviet gas industry under Gorbachev. The new State Duma, elected in December 1993, contains many leading industrialists from the energy sector, including Vladimir Medvedev, head of the Union of Oil Producers and leader of one of the largest parliamentary factions, "New Regional Policy."[37] The potential for collaboration between the Chernomyrdin government and Soviet-era bureaucrats in the Duma alarmed some reformists. Ella Pamfilova, the ally of Yegor Gaidar, who resigned as minister of social protection after the election, criticized what she viewed as the dominance of the old energy sector *nomenklatura* in Russian politics. She claimed that the government was now in the hands of people who sought only to "grab Russia's petrodollars for themselves."[38]

Thus, much of the centralized, bureaucratic management of the Soviet era, with its attendant inefficiencies and corruption, remains. An institutionalist analysis of the post-Soviet energy sector would expect the behavior of relevant economic actors to continue to be shaped by that institutional environment.

Institutional Constraints and Regional Politics

A striking feature of the old Soviet Union was the vast disparity of resource endowments—particularly in the energy sector—and levels of economic development among the fifteen constituent republics.[39] Economistic theories would expect the disparity in energy endowments to yield tangible political consequences during a period of expanding international trade in the 1970s and 1980s. For example, those regions that had the most to gain from direct access to world markets would, according to this logic, be the first to seek economic autonomy from the central planning system. Institutionalist approaches, by contrast, would stress the power of Soviet institutional structures to distort the impact of the international environment, preventing actors from pursuing, and perhaps even recognizing, their interests vis-à-vis the world economy.

The central Soviet economic and political institutions succeeded in obscuring the influence of the international economy on Soviet domestic actors and hindering efforts at reform. More important, however, as theories of path dependence would predict, the central planning system in effect set the agenda and terms of debate about economic reform by its inefficient management of the domestic economy. The first item on the agenda of any reformer—including regional economic authorities—was weakening the power of the central planners, reducing hypercentralization and bureaucratic arbitrariness. In short, those whose interests might have been affected by changes in the international economic environment had first to fight against the institutions of the administrative-command economy that prevented them from clearly perceiving their interests let alone acting upon them.

Soviet Regional Politics and the Energy Sector

The energy sector is where we would most expect to see the influence of the international economy on Soviet regional politics. Energy accounted for 57 percent of Soviet exports to nonsocialist countries in 1985 (arms exports accounted for a further 16 percent). Oil alone represented 44 percent.[40] The institutions of "socialist federalism" and the administrative-command economy constrained the pursuit of local interests but did not eliminate all manifestations of them. Nevertheless, it is difficult to argue that the behavior of regional actors in energy-rich areas came in response to external economic trends (changes in the world market prices for oil, for example) rather than as a function of the shortcomings of Soviet economic and political institutions. On the contrary, as Bahry argues, "energy, fuels, and natural resources were a major regional preoccupation long before the energy crisis of the 1970s pushed them higher on the national government's agenda."[41] Scholars have found evidence of competition between coal-producing territories and gas- and oil-producing territories for priority in the allocation of central investment funds, but such competition would exist in a centrally planned, shortage economy regardless of the international situation.[42]

The Soviet authorities deliberately sought to limit the domestic impact of internationalization in the energy sector by relying on manipulation of relative prices. Whereas the world price for oil rose manyfold in the 1970s, for example, the domestic price remained almost constant for the Soviet oil-producing enterprises from 1971 to 1982 (see Table 8.1).

Although the artificial domestic price stability probably reduced the potential for regional conflict in the short to medium term, it had economic consequences that weakened the system in the long run. As Hewett, Gustafson, and others describe, attempts at insulation from foreign market pressures undermined important regime goals in the energy sector and in the economy at large. Maintaining constant domestic oil prices gave no incentives to enterprises to conserve energy, for example, and eliminated the potential payoffs to oil exploration teams for finding new oil.[43]

TABLE 8.1   World Oil Prices Versus Soviet Producer and Export Prices, 1971–1982
(in dollars per barrel)

	Soviet Prices			
	Paid to Oil Producers[a]	Export to West	Export to CMEA	World Prices[b]
1971	3.33	2.42	2.28	1.75
1972	3.63	2.42	2.73	1.90
1973	4.05	4.58	2.96	3.39
1974	3.96	11.23	3.29	11.29
1975	4.17	11.45	6.40	11.02
1976	3.99	12.31	6.68	11.77
1977	4.02	13.88	8.61	12.88
1978	4.38	13.41	11.15	12.93
1979	4.56	25.52	13.01	18.67
1980	4.62	34.76	14.59	30.87
1981	4.17	35.81	17.20	34.50
1982	4.14	33.00	N.A.	33.63

NOTE: All prices are best approximations, intended only to demonstrate trends.
[a]The prices paid to Soviet energy producers (as opposed to the prices Soviet industrial firms had to pay for oil) converted from rubles at the official exchange rate for the given year.
[b]Mideast Light Crude.
SOURCES: Ed A. Hewett, *Energy, Economics, and Foreign Policy in the Soviet Union* (Washington, D.C.: Brookings Institution, 1984), pp. 135, 155, 163; U.S. Central Intelligence Agency, "Economic and Energy Indicators," Report no. DI EEI 86-002, Washington, D.C., 17 January 1986.

From a political standpoint, the institutional constraints represented by the price equalization system, government censorship, and other limitations on information about world energy prices combined to prevent potentially affected groups from pursuing their interests vis-à-vis the international economy in ways that comparable groups in an open economy would do. Only when the institution of the administrative-command economy came under attack did regional interests even have the opportunity to express themselves in ways that economistic approaches would expect.

It is significant, however, that economic autonomy was not sought first by the natural resource-rich regions of Siberia and Kazakhstan but by the Baltic republics, which seemingly benefited the most in the energy field from their relationship with the center, namely, through receipt of subsidized energy.[44] Indeed, as Table 8.2 indicates, there is little correlation between the timing of a given republic's declaration of economic autonomy or independence and its relative endowment of the former USSR's main earner of hard currency—energy resources. Thus, concern to limit the international economic opportunity costs of membership in the "socialist federation" does not seem to have been the driving force behind the declarations of sovereignty.

It seems only reasonable to conclude that there were other reasons behind the various republics' demands for sovereignty besides the desire to limit the eco-

TABLE 8.2   Energy Export Shares and Timing of Sovereignty Declarations by the Soviet Republic

	Oil and Gas as Percentage of Republic's Exports, 1988	Timing of Sovereignty[a]	Resource Rank	Sovereignty Rank
Armenia	0.0	29	15	12
Azerbaijan	16.7	18	2	4
Belorussia	7.5	28	6	10
Estonia	0.3	8	12	1
Georgia	1.7	20	8	5
Kazakhstan	9.7	31	4	14
Kirghizia[b]	0.4	33	11	15
Latvia	0.1	16	13	3
Lithuania	8.2	14	5	2
Moldavia	0.0	27	14	8
RSFSR	16.5	27	3	6
Tadzhikistan	0.7	29	10	13
Turkmenistan	28.5	29	1	11
Ukraine	1.6	28	9	9
Uzbekistan	6.1	27	7	7

NOTE: Spearman correlation coefficient = .04, p-value = .90.

[a]Time elapsed, in months, between March 1988 and declaration of republican sovereignty or the equivalent (e.g., in Georgia, constitutional amendments gave the republic legislative sovereignty and the right to its natural resources; in Armenia, parliament passed a declaration of independence).

[b]Parliament failed to pass formal declaration of sovereignty after having approved first reading of draft; declared independence instead.

SOURCES: Misha V. Belkindas and Matthew J. Sagers, "A Preliminary Analysis of Economic Relations Among Union Republics of the USSR: 1970–1988," *Soviet Geography* 31 (November 1990): 629–654; Ann Sheehy, "Fact sheet on Declarations of Sovereignty," *Report on the USSR,* 9 November 1990, pp. 23–25.

nomic opportunity costs of relative isolation from the world economy. The most plausible explanations do, however, contain economic components. Roeder, for example, seeks to explain the counterintuitive finding that the most "successful" ethnic groups in the USSR—in terms of level of education and occupation—experienced the earliest and most intense expressions of unrest and dissatisfaction with the existing federal structure. He argues that the declining growth rates of the 1970s and 1980s forced ethnic leaders to press Moscow harder for investments and simultaneously brought questions of regional redistribution to the fore: "The cadres in the more developed union republics have been particularly quick to raise the banners of autonomy and sovereignty in order to blunt the redistributive consequences of all-union policies."[45]

In some cases the policies pursued by the independence-minded republics reflected efforts at international integration free of Moscow's interference. The Baltic republics' claims for control over their seaports are a case in point. More telling, though, were the measures intended to isolate their economies from those of the rest of the Union.[46] It is hard to argue that the policies of the republics in trying to break away from Moscow were driven strictly by pursuit of economic utility. Virtually all of them stood to lose. Half a year after the dissolution of the USSR, a U.S. intelligence report described the situation as follows:

> The non-Russian states are likely to suffer more damage than Russia from the disruption of trade among the former republics. All have smaller, less diversified economies—some with particularly narrow specialties—and almost all are considerably more dependent on trade, often in energy and food. Moreover, all but Azerbaijan and Turkmenistan will lose from the move toward world market prices because their export earnings will not rise nearly enough to cover the increases in the import bills.[47]

For some republics—most notably Latvia, Lithuania, and Estonia—it is doubtful that the goal of full independence was decided after careful benefit-cost analysis of the other alternatives. For most republics, the disintegration of the Soviet Union, and consequent independence, were the inadvertent results of their attempts to reform institutions (primarily the administrative-command economy) that were highly resistant to reform.[48]

Energy in Post-Soviet Economic and Foreign Policy

With the breakdown of most of the institutions of Soviet economic integration, economistic theories of political economy would anticipate an increasing tendency toward behavior driven by market forces and world prices. Institutionalist approaches would expect the legacy of Soviet integration to continue to influence behavior. The reality is more complicated than either theory would predict. Economic goals have come into conflict with broader foreign policy goals (not to mention domestic political imperatives) and, in considerable measure, have become subordinated to them. Wars and ethnic conflict have disrupted energy production, supplies, and trade relations in ways that would confound any theory, particularly those that incorporate only economic considerations.

Even after the breakup of the USSR, the former republics have failed to pursue policies consistent with simple economic rationality, as economistic theories might anticipate.[49] The same states whose resource endowments (as depicted, for example, in Table 8.2) could afford them a considerable measure of independence from Russia—Kazakhstan and Turkmenistan, for example—have been most favorably disposed toward economic integration within the framework of the Commonwealth of Independent States. By contrast, some of the states with the most to lose—the Baltic republics, Ukraine, and Georgia, for example—have resisted integration.

In one respect, the disintegration of the USSR should have favored "marketization" as the centrally planned system of interrepublic trade broke down. We might have expected an attenuation of the institutional arrangements that would create a market environment and favor noninstitutional, economistic explanations for behavior. Such an outcome is still possible, but for now the old structures have been replaced by a mixed market/barter system of interrepublic trade, with Russia playing a dominant role in negotiating prices.[50]

Generally the energy-exporting republics, led by Russia, have sought to impose world prices on their ex-Soviet trading partners.[51] That attempt has created a crisis of nonpayment, a buildup of arrears, a series of mutual recriminations, and Russian threats to cut off energy. Probably not by coincidence most of the conflicts have come between Russia and the republics with which it has other serious disputes—for example, with Ukraine over its nuclear arsenal, the Black Fleet, and Crimea, and with the Baltic republics over their treatment of Russian-speaking citizens and units of the Russian military remaining on their territory.[52] It is hard not to suspect that Russia is using energy resources as an instrument of broader foreign policy goals.[53] The government managed to use Belarus's desperate energy situation to persuade it to join with Russia in a monetary union—a step back toward Soviet-era integration that many Russian politicians favor.[54] Sometimes in the absence of other causes for dispute, energy policy has strained relations, as with Russia's otherwise reliable ally, Kazakhstan.[55]

Struggles over energy resources, especially oil, have contributed to conflict in various regions of the former USSR, particularly in the dispute between Armenia and Azerbaijan.[56] Oil is also a factor in many regional disputes within Russia and could contribute to instability and possibly disintegration of the federation.[57]

As a guide to future developments in regional policy related to the energy sector, the economistic and institutionalist approaches to political economy shed light on some of the relevant actors' motives and some of the constraints on their behavior. But in the post-Soviet period, questions of energy policy have become so enmeshed in broader issues of foreign policy, ethnic conflict, and war that even the best theories of political economy will fall short. A more modest and appropriate goal would be to use the theories to examine a particular sector of the energy industry and the behavior of economic actors within that sector. Accordingly, the following section looks at the coal industry. Although we cannot expect to study that sector in isolation from all noneconomic events—the dramatic transformation of the Soviet Union left nobody unaffected—we can provide a more reasonable testing ground for the competing theories.

The Coal Industry: Path Dependence and Ideology

The coal industry in the former Soviet Union provides a useful case study for exploring the relative merits of economistic versus institutionalist approaches. In its position vis-à-vis the international economy, coal mining resembles the oil industry: During the 1970s, prices for coal increased on world markets while remaining stagnant on domestic ones (see Table 8.3).

Although demand for coal from the former USSR is not as high on international markets as for oil, coal as a "substitutive good" should be affected by changes in the world energy market, even if they are driven mainly by supply and demand for oil.[58] Prices for coal should track those of oil and gas. In the countries of the former USSR, coal still accounts for 24 percent of energy production. More than a quarter of all the coal produced is consumed by iron and steel pro-

TABLE 8.3   Soviet and U.S. Coal Prices, 1970–1989 (in dollars per metric ton)

	Soviet Prices[a]	U.S. Prices[b]
1970	13.24	6.90
1971	13.24	7.79
1972	14.43	8.44
1973	16.11	9.40
1974	15.75	17.36
1975	16.58	21.19
1976	15.87	21.41
1977	15.99	21.84
1978	17.42	24.00
1979	18.13	26.06
1980	16.05	27.02
1981	14.29	28.97
1982	13.50	29.91
1983	18.64	28.49
1984	16.95	28.11
1985	17.02	27.66
1986	26.34	26.12
1987	22.34	25.35
1988	23.40	24.24
1989	22.25	23.99

NOTE: All prices are best approximations, intended only to demonstrate trends.
[a]Steam coal.
[b]Bituminous coal and lignite; free on board, mines.
SOURCES: Organization for Economic Cooperation and Development and International Energy Agency, "Russian Energy Prices and Taxes," 11 June 1992; Energy Information Administration, *Coal Data: A Reference* (Washington, D.C.: U.S. Government Printing Office, 1993).

ducers alone. Moreover, there is an extensive interrepublic trade in coal.[59] In these respects, then, the coal industry should serve as a good test of theories of political economy.

The case of the Soviet coal miners offers an opportunity to illustrate in some detail the interplay between the external economic environment and internal institutional legacies. The case provides evidence of sectoral, regional, and class conflict, some of which conforms to expectations of the economistic approach to political economy. Other evidence suggests the importance of path dependence and institutional legacies as well as normative and ideological influences that go beyond the standard institutionalist accounts but are favored by some historical institutionalists.

The coal industry in the former Soviet Union came to national and international attention thanks to an unprecedented level of strike activity by coal miners. The first wave occurred in July 1989 when over 400,000 miners carried out the largest strikes in Soviet history.[60] The miners struck again in spring 1991 when it became clear that the Soviet state was incapable of fulfilling the agreement that ended the earlier strikes. At this point, the miners contributed to the disintegration of the USSR by successfully agitating for the republics to take control of the mines and for demanding the resignation of Gorbachev, his cabinet, and the USSR Supreme Soviet. In Russia, following the breakup of the Soviet Union, the situation in the mining regions remained tense, as the miners' economic situation became increasingly desperate, despite (or because of) halfhearted attempts by the government to implement reforms. Throughout 1993, warning strikes and threats of mass strikes were frequent. Regional strikes occurred in late 1993 and early 1994; an industrywide strike on 1 March 1994 involved some 75 to 80 percent of the miners.[61]

We can test the utility of economistic and institutionalist explanations for the miners' behavior by organizing our discussion according to the three main periods of strike activity—summer 1989, spring 1991, and 1993–1994—and trying to account for peculiarities and anomalies within and between them.

The First Wave: Summer 1989

The main questions of interest here are Why did the coal miners strike? What accounts for regional differences in the miners' demands? What determined the pattern of coalitions and cleavages that emerged on sectoral, regional, or class lines?

Regional Differences.   Regional variation makes the coal industry of particular theoretical interest.[62] Three of the major coal-producing areas—the Kuznetsk basin (Kuzbass) in western Siberia, the Donetsk Basin (Donbass) in eastern Ukraine, and Karaganda in Kazakhstan—accounted for more than half of total Soviet coal production.[63] They differ in several respects. The Kuzbass has generally high-quality coal in relatively accessible deposits. Worker productivity was high by Soviet standards, owing in part to substantial bonuses for working in Siberia. The Kuzbass miners initially seemed confident that their mines could be run profitably. They demanded self-management of their mines and within a year of the strike had succeeded in signing export contracts with Japan.[64] The Donbass miners were more pessimistic—with good reason. Their mines are "old and near exhaustion, marked by deep shafts (in excess of one kilometer), high temperatures, narrow seams (less than one meter on average), high accident rates, and low pay."[65] The profitability of the Karaganda mines was also open to question. Moreover, the quality of its coal—its caloric content—is too low for world market standards.[66] A fourth area—the Vorkuta and Inta mines of the Pechora Basin—is unusual in several respects. Located north of the Arctic Circle in the Komi Autonomous Republic (part of Russia), Vorkuta's climate is harsh and work conditions are severe. As a former "island" in the Gulag archipelago of prison work camps, it has long borne the heavy institutional legacy of Stalinism.[67]

The economic policies promoted by the strike committees in the four regions appeared to correspond to their situations, with the Kuzbass workers most enthusiastic about economic autonomy and regional self-management, the Donbass and Karaganda regional committees less willing to risk loss of central government subsidies, and the Vorkuta workers exhibiting the most militant and hostile attitudes toward Moscow and its local representatives.

Against the System.   Perhaps most revealing, though, is that all of the miners expressed the same criticisms and frustrations about the hypercentralized planning system and the inefficiencies and irrationalities it introduced into their work. Thus, in all cases demands for regional economic autonomy and control over local resources seemed overshadowed by, or at least conflated with, demands for less interference from the planners of the Party bureaucracy or apparat. At least at first, the miners seemed less concerned about earning world market prices for their coal than about making their work situation tolerable by doing away with the absurdities of Soviet central planning. A 1989 survey of striking Donbass miners, for example, revealed that their main grievance—ahead of low wages, high prices, and poor working conditions—was the shortage of basic goods, particularly soap.[68]

As theories of path dependence would suggest, the miners' actions were constrained by the existing institutional structures. In the hypercentralized Soviet system the only way to get their demands met was to appeal to the "Center"—to the Coal Ministry and to the Soviet government in Moscow. Mine managers and local authorities were usually able to deflect pressure from themselves to Moscow and even to incorporate their own concerns into the miners' list of grievances.[69]

Many activists believed that dramatic measures were necessary to break the power of the central apparatus. An adviser to the Kuzbass strike committee suggested, for example, that although many manifestations of regional separatism were extreme, they were necessary for transforming the hypercentralized economic system into something more efficient: "We are compelled to seek to split off in order to break that rigid centralization, to break with that *stupid* phenomenon existing in our country. And only after we have broken that rigid centralization, when we have local budgets, local financing—only if local governments have their own funds—will they possess real power, because money is power."[70]

Not only were the perceptions and behavior of the miners conditioned by the existing institutional structures, but—again, as the notion of path dependence implies—so were the outcomes. Only in the Soviet system, characterized by what Crowley describes as the "mutual dependence" between the Soviet worker, the enterprise, and the ministry,[71] could one find such a peculiar and internally contradictory document as the agreement that ended the miners' strike in the Donbass in July 1989. The first item of agreement was "to grant complete economic and legal independence to mines, enterprises, and organizations of the coal-mining industry in Donbass." The remaining forty-six items were appeals to the Ministry of Coal for such specific measures as permission to declare Sunday a common day off in the mines, wage and pension increases, full payment for the time needed to travel from the mine shaft entrance to the coal face and back, and agreement "to establish a supply quota for toilet soap for workers in the Donbass coal-mining industry at 800 grams a month, starting from August 1989."[72]

Up until the end of Gorbachev's experiment in perestroika, the uneasy relationship persisted between the miners' demands for more economic autonomy and the institutional legacy of the centralized system that was responsible for providing for everyone's needs. It is aptly illustrated by a couple of anecdotes. In December 1989, the radical miners of Vorkuta in Siberia ended the longest strike in recent Soviet history (thirty-eight days) after a promise from the minister of the coal industry guaranteeing complete economic independence for the Vorgashorskaia mine. The next day, as if in reward for ending the strike, 120 Panasonic television sets arrived in the nearby town of Sykyvkar—causing a riot that the police broke up with tear gas.[73] Following the successful wave of strikes during 1989, many workers' committees sought to pursue their economic and political goals through participating in the electoral campaigns for local and republic Soviets in early 1990. Political mobilization reached its height in February in Donetsk, where a nonstop, seven-day meeting was held in the main square. Ironically, the citizens had originally assembled there in response to a rumor that a shipment of imported shoes had arrived—they wanted to find out where it had gone.[74]

Sectoral and Regional Conflict and Collaboration.   During the strikes of 1989, many of the miners recognized the potential for sectoral conflict and deliberately sought to foster good relations with workers from other branches of the economy. At the same time, they accused the central authorities of pursuing a strategy of divide and conquer by portraying the miners as selfishly seeking advantages over other socioeconomic groups, telling "everybody that we were demanding specific consumer goods of which there are shortages."[75]

A natural reaction to conflict with the Party apparat and the central authorities was to pursue solidarity with other workers on a regional basis. Thus, in the Kuzbass the Regional Council of Workers' Committees that emerged from the July 1989 strikes eventually came to include not only miners "but chemical industry workers, railwaymen, steel workers, power generation workers, agricultural workers—the whole economy."[76] A similar situation developed in the Donbass: "The workers of other branches of the economy did not support us [at first], neither did the rest of the country. But after a while the coke-chemical workers, the steel workers, realized that the miners had, after all, taken the right path. So they decided to join with us and present a united front."[77] In Kazakhstan, the miners pursued creation of a broad front encompassing "all progressive organizations, from the greens, the ecology movement at one end, to the Communist

Party on the other."[78] The miners of Kazakhstan had close links to the region's large grass-roots antinuclear movement and threatened a general strike if the government did not abide by its demands to close the nuclear test site at Semipalatinsk.[79]

Sometimes cooperating with other sectors required the miners to sacrifice some of their own objectives. In October 1989, the miners of Vorkuta planned a major work stoppage to protest the government's recent limitations on workers' right to strike. They came under pressure, however, from steelworkers at a nearby combine who argued that its furnaces would be damaged if coal supplies were not resumed.[80] Perhaps more important, the workers would have lost their bonuses if they failed to produce their quota of steel. In any case, the coal miners compromised and limited their action to a two-hour stoppage.

Despite the efforts at intersectoral solidarity, some of the interests of workers in related sectors were clearly at odds and probably irreconcilable under the Soviet system. Higher wholesale prices for energy products would benefit workers in the coal and oil industries, for example, but would hurt workers in energy-intensive industries because profitability would decline under the new system of cost accounting (*khozraschet*) and workers' wages would suffer. In early 1990, threats of strikes from workers in steel mills and pulp plants forced the Soviet government to retreat after it had proposed to increase fuel costs to enterprises as part of a supposed move to a market economy. At the same time, oil and mine workers were demanding higher prices for their commodities.[81]

In some instances, competition with other sectors mitigated class conflict within the mining communities. Sometimes the new independent miners' unions cooperated with their supposed nemesis, the Ministry of the Coal Industry, as when they allowed the ministry to finance the second Congress of Miners in autumn 1990.[82] Cooperation with local officials was not uncommon either. In one town in the Kuzbass, the chief of the regional police provided the striking miners with daily reports ("as you instructed") on the situation in town.[83] In another town, a delegation from the strike committee went to inspect the apartments of local officials and found, to their surprise, that "the contents of their refrigerators were the same as everyone else's."[84] Such occurrences undoubtedly made it easier for the miners to downplay class conflict in favor of regional solidarity.

One should not, however, understate the degree of worker-management conflict in the mining industry. In some particular areas it was quite intense, even before the strike wave of 1989. The Vorkuta workers in the far north were particularly noted for their hostility to local officials and management—very likely the legacy of the region's history as a prison labor camp.[85]

The Second Wave: Spring 1991

The strike wave of spring 1991 was precipitated by immediate economic concerns—namely, the Soviet government's failure to abide by the terms of

Resolution 608, the agreement that ended the strike of 1989. But the strike soon became politicized, with the miners demanding the transfer of coal and other industries to republican control; the resignation of Gorbachev and his cabinet; and the dissolution of the USSR Supreme Soviet and Congress of People's Deputies.[86] Why did the miners' grievances shift from bread-and-butter issues to political demands for regional autonomy and a market economy? Why did some mines choose not to strike at all?

Who's the Boss?   The strikes of 1989 gave rise to an independent coal miners' movement and new leaders who saw their role as representatives of a work force in an essentially adversarial relationship with its employer—something very different from the traditional role of Soviet trade unions.[87] But in the Soviet case, the employer was not simply the management of the factory or mine, as one activist argued in a speech to his comrades: "Go ahead, conclude a contract. But remember one thing—where is the money you need? You can remove the director, but you won't find the money. . . . I see a different answer: The contract should be with the owner, and we have only one owner—the state."[88] The implications of that reality became clearer in the period between 1989 and 1991. As a leader of the Independent Miners' Union described:

> For many years we were told that we, the workers and peasants, were the masters of our country, and that property in the USSR belongs to the entire people. However, in 1990 the USSR Supreme Soviet adopted the Law on Property, and it turned out that it no longer belongs to the people: [the majority of it] belongs to the state. . . . Therefore, this law confirmed that a certain opposition exists in our country between the state . . . and hired labor. This opposition is part of an objective reality, and that is why trade unions should reckon with it.

Thus the miners concluded that "the main task of our trade union is to oppose the employer, that is the state."[89]

The opposition of workers to the state seems consistent with Rogowski's expectation that in Russia—a relatively labor-poor, but capital- and land-abundant economy—conflict should pit the workers against capital and land. In the early 1990s, the state was still the main provider of capital and the main owner of land and natural resources. In Rogowski's theory, the expansion of international trade in energy products should put pressure on workers and drive their wages down while providing benefits to the owners of capital and land—in this case, the state.[90] The situation appears compatible with Frieden's focus on asset specificity as well. Many mines are located in isolated villages that function, in effect, as "company towns." The miners, by their skills, are very much tied to their profession (consequently their demands to the government usually include appeals for job retraining). The state-as-capitalist, by contrast, has considerable flexibility in deciding where to invest its resources—in this case, subsidies from the state budget. Frieden would under these circumstances predict more class conflict, between the miners and the state, than sectoral conflict between the coal industry and other industries.

The first realization for the miners then was that the main conflict was between them and the state. The next realization was that the Soviet state, unlike conventional employers, was unable, or unwilling, to carry out agreements to which it had committed itself. As a leader of the Kuzbass miners put it, "When the strike commenced, the miners' demands were limited to economic concerns—the doubling of wages. But then we realized that this government is not capable of fulfilling this demand. We then made the realization that under this government, under this system, none of our economic demands can be fulfilled."[91] Consequently the miners decided, in effect, to fire their boss—the Soviet government—and seek a new owner and negotiating partner in the republican governments.

Republican leaders, most notably Russia's Boris Yeltsin, recognized the benefits to their personal political fortunes of securing the backing of the miners. The strikes ended when Gorbachev, Yeltsin, and eight other republic leaders signed the so-called Nine Plus One Agreement, which transferred jurisdiction over the mines to the republics.[92]

What's a Market?   The failure of the Soviet government to fulfill the miners' demands, combined with a keen understanding on the miners' part of the adverse consequences of Soviet overcentralization, goes far in explaining the miners' quest for regional autonomy. But why did they agitate for transition to a market economy? An economistic approach, such as Frieden's, that focuses on the impact of relative price changes on economic actors' behavior would call attention to the discrepancy between world market and internal producers' prices for coal. The miners' action, in this explanation, would be a straightforward effort to eliminate the opportunity costs of selling coal on the domestic market to capture the additional revenues from the world market price. Although some evidence suggests that internal and world prices for coal had already come into alignment by the late 1980s (see Table 8.3), many miners still perceived that they were not receiving the prices that coal commanded on world markets.[93]

Other analysts have suggested that the miners pursued a rather narrow notion of economic self-interest—one that could not abide a market economy—but that they were essentially duped by neoliberal politicians into supporting the capitalist project.[94] This account, however, underestimates the extent to which the miners genuinely advocated what they considered a "market" system.

The key to resolving this puzzle lies in figuring out what the miners understood by "market."[95] They essentially appear to have meant a mechanism that would ensure them a more equitable, just wage than what they received through the administrative-command system. Frieden's insight is right that the miners noted a discrepancy between the value of their product and its price in the Soviet economy. But in their view, the product they sold was labor, not coal. Both absolutely and relatively speaking, they thought the price was too low. A Kuzbass miner, explaining his union's goals in advocating a new strike in 1991, said: "Now we sell ourselves for 10 percent of what we earn and live like slaves." After concluding an agreement on wages and on monthly wage indexation, "then we will sell our labor power every month" for a fair price.[96] Miners at both the rank-and-file and leadership levels were quick to compare their wages to those of U.S. miners, in the same terms. A key negotiator for the miners pointed out in an interview, for example, that "if a worker in the USA gets 70 percent of his labor's worth or even more, in the USSR we get only 5–10 percent."[97] A miner from Rostov argued, along the same lines: "For every dollar you earn you get 60–75 cents, while we get only 13 kopeks from every ruble. And from that 13 kopeks they still take out taxes. With the remaining 87 kopeks, 'they' buy whatever they want."[98]

Soviet miners clearly felt that they were being exploited by "the system," that unproductive bureaucrats and officials were siphoning off money that rightfully belonged to them, and that a shift to "the market" would end the exploitation and bring about social justice. As one miner colorfully explained to Steve Crowley:

> For what is all this wealth lumped together from above, and then handed out, to whoever needs it? Like some great uncle sitting on a sack: to you Vanya, I'll give you this, but to you Fedya, nothing. This is no market. A market is this: I earn my own, I buy my own, having sold my labor power. But we don't have this. Here they say to you, Vanya, you'll receive this much. Receive, and not earn. There's a big difference in this—each should get according to his labor.[99]

It may be apparent by now that what the miners describe as a market is founded on Marx's labor theory of value. The slogan "From each according to his ability, to each according to his labor" does not depict modern capitalism. It was Lenin's definition of socialism.

So those who argue that the miners did not genuinely support the neoliberal project of market reform are probably right. But they did support their own notion of reform, to which they gave the name "market." This terminological confusion would appear to be an important part of the explanation for how the coalition of militant workers and free-market reformers who helped break apart the Soviet Union found common cause. The explanation is not captured at all by economistic approaches to political economy. Institutionalist approaches work only if we assume that the ideological and normative influences that shaped the miners' conception of social justice were the product of Soviet institutions—a plausible, but not necessary, assumption.[100] Unions in the United States and elsewhere often negotiate with reference to how much their company earned in a given period and whether the workers were receiving a "fair share" of the profits—a similar notion of social justice as the one espoused by Russian coal miners.[101]

Why Some Mines Did Not Strike.   The economistic accounts, despite their failure to explain key aspects of the miners' behavior, are still of some use. They direct us to the underlying economic forces that often motivate actors in the absence of strong institutions. In this case an economistic approach might explain why some mines failed to join the strike wave in 1991. In his important study, Crowley compares enterprises in the steel industry to coal mines to understand why the latter struck while the former for the most part did not. He also compared mines that struck to those that did not. In his analysis, mines and firms that remained open "all shared a common characteristic: the enterprises were all linked to a trading partner in such a way that a strike would cut off the provision of vital goods or services to the work force."[102] So economic self-interest underlay workers' decisions about whether to strike. But only certain enterprises afforded their workers the opportunity to improve their welfare by staying on the job. They were the ones that had, in effect, evaded the institutional constraints of the hierarchically organized Soviet economy in favor of regional, horizontal links with other enterprises; these ranged from local collective farms to joint ventures with foreign trading partners.[103] The logic of this explanation resembles somewhat Milner's argument that firms that benefit from a network of international suppliers and customers do not seek protectionist trade policies.[104]

The Third Wave: 1993–1994

The third wave of strike activity, threatened throughout 1993, erupted in the late autumn and continued into the following year. It saw a curious reversal of many of the miners' previous demands. Instead of economic autonomy and increases to world market prices for their coal, the miners came to demand more subsidies from the central government and, on the surface at least, the return to a more paternalistic relationship with the state.

Throughout 1993 pressure had been building in the mining communities in Russia based on a straightforward economic grievance: The miners were not being paid. Already in 1992 shortages of cash had prevented some miners in Vorkuta from sending their children to summer camps in the south.[105] In February 1993, some mines in the Kuzbass reported that they had received no wage allocations since November 1992.[106] A year later the Vorkuta Ugol' association reported that none of its mines had received money for wages since the previous August. Some Vorkuta miners went on a two-week hunger strike to convince the Russian government to come up with the funds.[107] By all appearances the government was delaying the wage payments as a cheap way to contain the budget deficit. With high rates of inflation, the miners' money lost much of its value over a several-month delay.

The miners threatened to strike and issued demands including regular payment of wages, wage indexation, and in some cases privatization of the coal industry.[108] During the period preceding Yeltsin's April 1993 referendum, the coal miners of Kuzbass and Vorkuta announced an impending strike but agreed to postpone it until after the vote. Yeltsin responded by making a play for their support—by lowering the taxes on coal exports and implying that there would be future wage increases.[109]

In July the Russian government raised coal prices—something that would appear to have been in the miners' interests and was included among their demands during previous strikes. The government simultaneously sought to eliminate state subsidies and get plans under way to close the least productive mines.[110] At the same time it continued its practice of delaying wages. The miners protested the increase in coal prices and the threatened mine closures by engaging in warning strikes.[111] Mine builders in Vorkuta went on strike in February 1994 and a mass strike, in which 75 to 80 percent of the miners participated, took place on 1 March.[112]

Explaining the high level of strike activity under conditions of chronic nonpayment of wages poses little problem. Strikes were endemic in the Russian economy during 1993–1994 in many industries besides mining: teachers, radio and television workers, ambulance drivers, lumber workers, nuclear re-searchers.[113] What at first glance seems more puzzling is why the coal miners reversed their position on coal prices—opposing the government decision to free them—and sought a return to state subsidies. At a general level the finding that the government wanted to free coal prices while the miners wanted to maintain subsidies is consistent with Rogowski's expectation. In his terminology, the state, as the owner of abundant factors, land and capital, would prefer free trade, therefore allowing prices to reach their world market levels. The miners, as the owners of the scarce factor, labor, would demand protection in the form of subsidies.

But how does the miners' demand for subsidies square with proposals issued by some mines for full privatization?[114] Understanding the miners' behavior requires taking into account their conceptions of privatization, relations between the state and the mines, and the impact of Soviet-era price distortions on the welfare of the Russian mining communities. To take the last point first: The miners came to see price increases in the energy sector as ultimately damaging to their interests. The higher prices caused inflation throughout the economy and specifically contributed to higher costs for metal and mining equipment, for heat and electricity in the coal industry complex, and, perhaps most significant, to higher rail transport costs, which threatened the competitiveness of Russian coal prices on world markets.[115] Higher energy prices also contributed to a recession in the iron and steel industry—one of the main consumers of Russian coal.[116] The hard-won wage increases—the result of the earlier strike waves—only contributed to resentment among nonminers in the coal communities, who were forced to pay the higher prices (sometimes 50 percent more than in surrounding regions) triggered by the miners' wage increases, but often on one-tenth the salary.[117]

The miners' attitude toward subsidies, as with their conception of "the market," seems to have been based on the labor theory of value. Social justice, in their view, demanded that they be paid a fair wage as compensation for their difficult and dangerous work. The state, as the main customer for their product, was required to pay a price high enough to secure a fair wage or, instead, to provide subsidies to make up the difference between the market price and the amount that would provide the workers appropriate remuneration for their labor. In fact, this understanding was reflected in the price system itself within the coal conglomerates—making the price system, in effect, the institutional manifestation of a norm ("social justice," as defined by the labor theory of value). The *short price* represented the cost to the mine of extracting the coal; the *long price* consisted of the short price plus the additional cost of social infrastructure (daycare centers, the sewage and water department, the collective farms) and the administrative apparatus of the conglomerate itself. State subsidies typically made up the difference between the short and long prices. The administrative apparatus of the conglomerate controls the distribution of the subsidies, although, according to one account, some portion of the funds "goes back upstairs" to the association, Rossiia Ugol', "a political interest group in Moscow that bargains on behalf of the mines with the Ministry of Fuel and Energy."[118]

The appeal to some miners of privatization can be best understood again within the context of the labor theory of value and their sense of exploitation under the old system. First of all, privatization for the miners meant a transfer of ownership and day-to-day management to the workers. They did not by and large expect outside corporations to take over control of their mines. In Crowley's words, "They had no intention of replacing the exploitation of the state with that of a private owner."[119] Worker self-management gave the miners the opportunity to eliminate the bloated staff of administrators, who, in the miners' view, were essentially unproductive and certainly undeserving of their relatively high wages. Miners who sought privatization were especially keen to take control of the subsidies (the difference between the short and long prices) out of the hands of the conglomerate's administrators. They believed that they could organize the work and provide social services more efficiently than the bureaucracy. In fact, in those mines "privatized" to the workers' collective, labor productivity has increased, whereas elsewhere in the industry it has continued to fall.[120] There appears to have been some economic basis to the miners' sense of exploitation.

Thus with the labor theory of value informing their notion of what a market system means, the miners would see no contradiction between subsidies, privatization, and the market. Nor would the miners need to have read Marx to come to those conclusions.[121] Consistent with a historical institutionalist explanation, one might argue that Soviet institutions indoctrinated Soviet workers to believe in Marxist notions of social justice (although the reality of the "workers' state" might have caused some cognitive dissonance). One should also entertain the possibility, however, that the perceptions of the Russian coal miners reflect more universal notions of social justice, in which case an institutional explanation would be superfluous. Finally, Russian coal miners understand that their demands—however internally contradictory they might seem by the lights of economic theory—are not peculiar to their situation. They are well aware, for example, that all modern market economies subsidize their coal mining industries in one way or another, even if the industries operate mainly in the private sector.[122]

Some prominent U.S. politicians and economists have argued that successful Russian economic reform requires the government to remove subsidies to the coal industry and shut down inefficient mines. They have implied that further economic aid is contingent on following Western prescriptions.[123] Meanwhile, analysts in Russia and abroad give conflicting accounts of the prospects for the coal industry, even if it overcomes its current crisis. Some studies predict a "substantial contraction in the total market for coal," whereas others anticipate stability or moderate growth.[124] Undoubtedly, pressure from Western countries and international financial institutions that provide aid to the former Soviet economies will play some role in the fate of coal industries there, as will international market conditions. The discussion here suggests, however, that other factors, such as the normative perceptions of the miners themselves and the institutional legacy of the Soviet economic structure, must be considered as well.

Contributions and Limitations
of Political-Economy Approaches

Both economistic and institutionalist theories of political economy have something to contribute to understanding the impact of the international economy on Soviet and post-Soviet domestic politics. Institutionalist accounts performed best in explaining why changes in the international environment—especially the increase in energy prices after 1973—failed to translate into demands for regional autonomy on the part of energy-rich republics, as economistic approaches might have expected. Economistic theories did better in accounting for some of the behavior of economic actors within specific sectors, such as the coal industry. For example, Rogowski's theory, based on a three-factor model of international trade, seemed to account in broad terms for the main locus of conflict—between workers and the state. Frieden's work contributed to our understanding of some of the motives of the miners, but many of his assumptions—for example, about the role of wages and prices—seemed difficult to apply to the Soviet and post-Soviet cases.

Institutionalist approaches captured well the structural constraints on miners' perceptions and actions and the path-dependent nature of their efforts at effecting change. Particularly important for explaining the nature of the miners' demands was the understanding that much of their thinking about the market was based on the labor theory of value. Only some historical-institutionalist approaches would include such ideological and normative considerations within their purview.

This discussion has highlighted not only the contributions but also the limitations of the political-economy approaches. Moreover, it appears to call into question the initial assumption of this chapter—that the international economy would exert a greater influence on post-Soviet domestic politics of energy in the future than in the past. The role of the international economy contributes comparatively little to making sense of the politics of the energy trade among the former Soviet republics. The sources of Russian conduct are tied up so much more with broader issues of foreign policy, ethnic conflict, and outright war than international economics.[125] Even understanding the narrower subject of the coal industry requires more than consideration of the effect of the international economy or the use of theories that link international economics and domestic politics. The ideological, normative, and institutional legacy of the Soviet Union exerts a powerful influence on economic actors in the former USSR. Studying the sources of Russian conduct, therefore, requires combining broad theoretical generalizations with attention to the specific historical context. In doing so, we preserve an important methodological tradition of Soviet studies—one of the more valuable legacies of the Soviet experience.

Notes

I am grateful to Sharon Werning for research assistance. I have benefited from the comments of Celeste Wallander, Rob Darst, and the other participants of the Olin series as well as those of Dale Copeland and Peter Katzenstein.

1. This chapter draws on my discussion of the impact of the international economy on the demise of the USSR: Matthew Evangelista, "Stalin's Revenge: Institutional Barriers to Internationalization in the Soviet Union," in *Internationalization and Domestic Politics,* ed. Robert Keohane and Helen Milner (Cambridge: Cambridge University Press, forthcoming). It includes an extended discussion of the institutional basis of the Soviet political economy, summarized in this chapter, and a discussion of the coal industry up to 1990, some of which appears here as well. I thank the editors of that volume for stimulating my interest in this subject.

2. World Bank, *Russian Economic Reform: Crossing the Threshold of Structural Change* (Washington, D.C.: World Bank, 1992), p. 175; Jeffrey W. Schneider, "Republic Energy Sectors and Inter-state Dependencies of the Commonwealth of Independent States and Georgia," in *The Former Soviet Union in Transition,* papers prepared for the U.S. Congress Joint Economic Committee, ed. Richard F. Kaufman and John P. Hardt (Armonk, N.Y.: M. E. Sharpe, 1993), pp. 475–489.

3. For a summary and critique of the neoclassical model, see Gary R. Orren, "Beyond Self-Interest," in *The Power of Public Ideas,* ed. Robert B. Reich (Cambridge: Harvard University Press, 1988), pp. 13–29.

4. Describing institutions as "congealed tastes" or as mechanisms that "serve to aggregate interests in ways that make it unnecessary to recalculate continually the balance of political forces" tends to accord them little explanatory power. See Jeffry A. Frieden and Ronald Rogowski, "The Impact of the International Economy on National Policies: An Analytical Overview," in *Internationalization and Domestic Politics,* ed. Keohane and Milner. Rogowski does, however, consider the role of institutions in mediating the impact of economic forces in his article "Trade and the Variety of Democratic Institutions," *International Organization* 41 (Spring 1987): 203–223. For an argument that institutions

matter less than "the nature of domestic interest groups, the goals of political elites, and the constraints of the international system," see Helen Milner, "Maintaining International Commitments in Trade Policy," in *Do Institutions Matter? Government Capabilities in the United States and Abroad,* ed. R. Kent Weaver and Bert A. Rockman (Washington, D.C.: Brookings Institution, 1993), pp. 345–369, at p. 369.

5. Ronald Rogowski, *Commerce and Coalitions: How Trade Affects Domestic Political Alignments* (Princeton: Princeton University Press, 1989).

6. Frieden and Rogowski, "The Impact of the International Economy."

7. Rogowski, *Commerce and Coalitions,* pp. 69, 119–122.

8. A useful analysis of the labor situation in the 1950s and 1960s is found in Jutta Tiedtke, *Abrüstung in der Sowjetunion: Wirtschaftliche Bedingungen und soziale Folgen der Truppenreduzierung von 1960* (Frankfurt am Main: Campus, 1985). She links the shortages to Soviet disarmament policy at the time (particularly the unilateral reduction of troops).

9. Rogowski, *Commerce and Coalitions,* p. 178. Kimberly Marten Zisk makes a similar point regarding the Russian military industry in *The Foreign Policy Preferences of Russian Defense Industrialists: Integration or Isolation?* Olin Critical Issues Series (Cambridge: Russian Research Center, Harvard University, February 1994), pp. 5–6.

10. Rogowski, *Commerce and Coalitions,* pp. 177–178.

11. For example, Tatyana Zaslavskaya, *The Second Socialist Revolution: An Alternative Soviet Strategy* (Bloomington: Indiana University Press, 1990).

12. On this point, see also Zisk, *Foreign Policy Preferences.*

13. Frieden argues that the threefold categorization of factors (land, labor, capital) is equivalent to a class analysis that focuses on capitalists, the peasantry, the proletariat, the petite bourgeoisie, and so on. See Jeffry A. Frieden, *Debt, Development, and Democracy: Modern Political Economy and Latin America, 1965–1985* (Princeton: Princeton University Press, 1991), pp. 29–30; also Stephan Haggard, *Pathways from the Periphery: The Politics of Growth in the Newly Industrializing Countries* (Ithaca: Cornell University Press, 1990), pp. 34–35. I will discuss the works that focus on classes separately from the discussion of Rogowski's three-factor theory, however, because they often combine their treatment of classes with elements of sectoral analysis.

14. Jeffry A. Frieden, "Winners and Losers in the Latin American Debt Crisis: The Political Implications," in *Debt and Democracy in Latin America,* ed. Barbara Stallings and Robert Kaufman (Boulder: Westview Press, 1989); Jeffry A. Frieden, "Invested Interests: The Politics of National Economic Policies in a World of Global Finance," *International Organization* 45 (Autumn 1991): 425–451; idem, *Debt, Development, and Democracy;* Helen V. Milner, *Resisting Protectionism: Global Industries and the Politics of International Trade* (Princeton: Princeton University Press, 1988). Haggard, *Pathways from the Periphery,* offers a more eclectic approach, discussing sectors and classes as well as the role of ideas and of the state itself.

15. Frieden, *Debt, Development, and Democracy,* p. 21.

16. Ibid., pp. 17–19, 28–29.

17. Igor Birman, "The Budget Gap, Excess Money and Reform," *Communist Economies* 2, no. 1 (1990): 25–46; Ed A. Hewett, *Reforming the Soviet Economy: Equality Versus Efficiency* (Washington, D.C.: Brookings Institution, 1988).

18. For a review of some rational institutionalist work, see Ronald Rogowski, "Structure, Growth, and Power: Three Rationalist Accounts," *International Organization* 37 (Autumn 1983): 713–738.

19. Kathleen Thelen and Sven Steinmo, "Historical Institutionalism in Comparative Politics," in *Structuring Politics: Historical Institutionalism in Comparative Analysis,* ed. Sven Steinmo, Kathleen Thelen, and Frank Longstreth (Cambridge: Cambridge University Press, 1992), pp. 1–32.

20. Ibid., pp. 7–11.

21. I owe this formulation to Celeste Wallander.

22. See, for example, Peter A. Hall, ed., *The Political Power of Economic Ideas* (Princeton: Princeton University Press, 1989), esp. the editor's introduction and conclusion and the chapter by Margaret Weir, "Ideas and Politics: The Acceptance of Keynesianism in Britain and the United States," pp. 53–86; Kathryn Sikkink, *Ideas and Institutions: Developmentalism in Brazil and Argentina* (Ithaca: Cornell University Press, 1991); Peter Katzenstein, ed., *Between Power and Plenty: The Foreign Economic Policies of Advanced Industrial States* (Madison: University of Wisconsin Press, 1978); Peter Katzenstein, *Small States in World Markets: Industrial Policy in Europe* (Ithaca: Cornell University Press, 1985); Jeffrey A. Hart, *Rival Capitalists: International Competitiveness in the United States, Japan, and Western Europe* (Ithaca: Cornell University Press, 1992).

23. For definitions of institutions, see Thelen and Steinmo, "Historical Institutionalism," p. 2. Similarly, Douglass C. North, *Institutions, Institutional Change and Economic Performance* (Cambridge: Cambridge University Press, 1990), p. 3: "Institutions are the rules of the game in a society or, more formally, are the humanly devised constraints that shape human experience."

24. David Stark, "Path Dependence and Privatization Strategies in East Central Europe," *East European Politics and Societies* 6 (Winter 1992): 17–53, at p. 21. For a discussion of the origins of path-dependence analysis in the study of technological change, see North, *Institutions, Institutional Change and Economic Performance,* pp. 93–94.

25. This summary draws heavily on the more extensive discussion in Evangelista, "Stalin's Revenge." See also Jerry F. Hough, *Opening Up the Soviet Economy* (Washington, D.C.: Brookings Institution, 1988), pp. 11–12.

26. Ed A. Hewett, *Energy, Economics, and Foreign Policy in the Soviet Union* (Washington, D.C.: Brookings Institution, 1984), p. 13. Also, Nikolai Shmelev and Vladimir Popov, *The Turning Point: Revitalizing the Soviet Economy,* trans. Michele A. Berdy (New York: Doubleday, 1989), p. 221.

27. International Monetary Fund, the World Bank, Organisation for Economic Co-operation and Development, European Bank for Reconstruction and Development, *A Study of the Soviet Economy,* 3 vols. (Paris: IMF, World Bank, OECD, 1991), vol. 1, p. 363.

28. Ibid. For a good summary of these points and an account of the period after 1987, see Simon Clarke, "The Crisis of the Soviet System," chap. 2 in Simon Clarke, Peter Fairbrother, Michael Burawoy, and Pavel Krotov, *What About the Workers? Workers and the Transition to Capitalism in Russia* (London: Verso, 1993).

29. Shmelev and Popov, *Turning Point,* p. 221.

30. Aleksandr Bykov, "Ne neft'iu edinoi," *Literaturnaia gazeta,* 10 February 1988, p. 14.

31. The classic discussion is found in Merle Fainsod, *How Russia Is Ruled,* rev. ed. (Cambridge: Harvard University Press, 1963), pp. 209–210.

32. Michael Burawoy and Pavel Krotov, "The Rise of Merchant Capital: Monopoly, Barter, and Enterprise Politics in the Vorkuta Coal Industry," *Harriman Institute Forum* 6 (December 1992): 5–6.

33. Stephen Crowley, "From Coal to Steel: The Formation of an Independent Workers' Movement in the Soviet Union, 1989–1991" (Ph.D. diss., University of Michigan, 1993), pp. 172–173.

34. Eric Whitlock, "Oil Sector Slated for Competition?" *RFE/RL Daily Report,* No. 94, 18 May 1993. (This and all subsequent references to *RFE/RL Daily Report* cited here are the electronic versions.)

35. Keith Bush, "Gas Industry to Be Privatized," *RFE/RL Daily Report,* No. 66, 6 April 1993. Who initially controls the shares would not be an issue if there were no restrictions on their resale. As of the first half of 1994, however, there were many such restrictions, including the fact that foreigners were not allowed to purchase shares in "the defense and mining sectors, in the fuel and energy complex, and in certain extractive industries," and that permission of the Finance Ministry was required for sales to foreigners even in less strategically important industries. See Keith Bush, "Privatization and Foreign Investment," *RFE/RL Daily Report,* No. 38, 24 February 1994. I thank Celeste Wallander for discussion of this point.

36. Sergei Dukhanov, "The First Privatized Oil Company," *Moscow News,* no. 45, 5 November 1993, p. 9.

37. Wendy Slater, "Factions Determined in State Duma," *RFE/RL Daily Report,* No. 9, 14 January 1994.

38. Elizabeth Teague, "Why Pamfilova Resigned," *RFE/RL Daily Report,* No. 26, 8 February 1994.

39. Gertrude E. Schroeder, "Regional Economic Disparities, Gorbachev's Policies, and the Disintegration of the Soviet Union," in *The Former Soviet Union in Transition,* ed. Kaufman and Hardt, pp. 121–145; Schneider, "Republic Energy Sectors and Inter-state Dependencies," in ibid.

40. Ed A. Hewett with Clifford G. Gaddy, *Open for Business: Russia's Return to the Global Economy* (Washington, D.C.: Brookings Institution, 1992), p. 11.

41. Donna Bahry, *Outside Moscow: Power, Politics, and Budgetary Policy in the Soviet Republics* (New York: Columbia University Press, 1987), pp. 87–88.

42. Howard Biddulph, "Local Interest Articulation at CPSU Congresses," *World Politics* 36 (October 1983): 28–52, at p. 41.

43. Ed A. Hewett, *Energy, Economics, and Foreign Policy in the Soviet Union* (Washington, D.C.: Brookings Institution, 1984), p. 14; Thane Gustafson, *Crisis amid Plenty: The Politics of Soviet Energy Under Brezhnev and Gorbachev* (Princeton: Princeton University Press, 1989).

44. John Tedstrom, "Baltic Independence: The Economic Dimension," *Report on the USSR,* 8 February 1991, pp. 22–28; Gail W. Lapidus, "Gorbachev and the 'National Question': Restructuring the Soviet Federation," *Soviet Economy* 5 (July–September 1989): 201–250.

45. Philip Roeder, "Soviet Federalism and Ethnic Mobilization," *World Politics* 43 (January 1991): 196–232, at p. 219. See also Donna Bahry, "*Perestroika* and the Debate over Territorial Decentralization," *Harriman Institute Forum* 2 (May 1989).

46. Roeder, "Soviet Federalism," pp. 219–220.

47. Central Intelligence Agency and Defense Intelligence Agency, "The New Russian Revolution: The Transition to Markets in Russia and the Other Commonwealth States," a paper presented by the Central Intelligence Agency and the Defense Intelligence Agency

to the Joint Economic Committee's Subcommittee on Technology and National Security, Washington, D.C., 8 June 1992, p. 28. Other analyses suggest that the only republics that would benefit from a shift to world market prices are Russia, Ukraine, and Turkmenistan. See Misha V. Belkindas and Matthew J. Sagers, "A Preliminary Analysis of Economic Relations Among Union Republics of the USSR: 1970–1988," *Soviet Geography* 31 (November 1990): 629–654, at p. 651.

48. Stuart S. Brown and Misha V. Belkindas, "Who's Feeding Whom? An Analysis of Soviet Interrepublic Trade," in *The Former Soviet Union in Transition,* ed. Kaufman and Hardt, pp. 163–183.

49. The following discussion was stimulated by some of Celeste Wallander's comments.

50. In this respect, Russia's behavior may be better explained by traditional realist, power-politics explanations rather than by institutionalist or economistic ones. See Fiona Hill and Pamela Jewett, "Back in the USSR: Russia's Intervention in the Internal Affairs of the Former Soviet Republics and the Implications for United States Policy Toward Russia," report of the Ethnic Conflict Project of the Strengthening Democratic Institutions Project, John F. Kennedy School of Government (Cambridge: Harvard University, January 1994).

51. Boris Kuzmenko, "Former Soviet Republics Prefer Dollars," *Moscow News,* no. 33, 13 August 1993, p. 8; Jozef M. van Brabant, "The New East and Its Preferred Trade Regime—The Impact of Soviet Disintegration," in *The Former Soviet Union in Transition,* ed. Kaufman and Hardt, pp. 146–162.

52. Sheila Marnie, "Russian-Ukrainian Gas Dispute Still Unresolved," *RFE/RL Daily Report,* No. 66, 6 April 1993; Ustina Markus, "Russia Cuts Oil to Ukraine," *RFE/RL Daily Report,* No. 105, 4 June 1993; Ustina Markus, "Russia Switches Ukraine Off Power Grid," *RFE/RL Daily Report,* No. 226, 26 November 1993; Ustina Markus, "Gazprom Cuts Gas to Ukraine," *RFE/RL Daily Report,* No. 25, 7 February 1994; Sergei Ikk, "Estonia Prefers Trade with the West," *Moscow News,* no. 33, 13 August 1993, p. 8; Dzintra Bungs, "Russia Revokes Gas Supply Contract with Baltics," *RFE/RL Daily Report,* No. 30, 14 February 1994; Keith Bush, "Further Cuts in Gas Supplies," *RFE/RL Daily Report,* No. 45, 7 March 1994; Dzintra Bungs, "Russia's Gazprom to Supply Gas to the Baltics," *RFE/RL Daily Report,* No. 45, 7 March 1994; "Russia Presses 2 Baltic Lands on Minorities," *New York Times,* 7 March 1994.

53. This is the main argument of Hill and Jewett, "Back in the USSR." Acknowledging the tactic, Russia's neighbors have sometimes responded in kind. In an article entitled "Ukrainian Hints Deal on Warheads Is in Danger," the *New York Times,* 7 March 1994, reported: "As Russia's natural-gas company announced a further deep cut in supplies to Ukraine over the weekend, President Leonid M. Kravchuk suggested that the move could derail the deal to give up his country's large arsenal."

54. Ustina Markus, "Belarusian Fuel Reserves Almost Used Up," *RFE/RL Daily Report,* No. 225, 24 November 1993; Ustina Markus, "Russia-Belarus Monetary Union," *RFE/RL Daily Report,* No. 31, 15 February 1994.

55. John Helmer, "Russia-Kazakhstan Ties Slip on Oil," *Moscow Times,* 10 July 1992, p. 14.

56. "Armenia-Azerbaijan War: Manoeuvres Around Oil," *Moscow News,* no. 38, 17 September 1993, pp. 1, 8.

57. Andrei Neshchadin, "Russian Regions Oppose the Government on Economic Reforms," *Moscow News,* no. 26, 28 June 1992, p. 9.; Ann Sheehy, "Chukotka's Separation from Magadan Oblast Legal," *RFE/RL Daily Report,* No. 91, 13 May 1993.

58. Frieden and Rogowski, "The Impact of the International Economy."

59. Schneider, "Republic Energy Sectors and Inter-state Dependencies."

60. David Mandel, "The Rebirth of the Soviet Labor Movement: The Coalminers' Strike of July 1989," *Politics and Society* 18 (September 1990): 381–404.

61. Elizabeth Teague, "Russia Hit by Strike Wave," *RFE/RL Daily Report,* No. 33, 17 February 1994; idem, "Strike Update," *RFE/RL Daily Report,* No. 42, 2 March 1994.

62. This discussion draws on Crowley, "From Coal to Steel"; Theodore Friedgut and Lewis Siegelbaum, "Perestroika from Below: The Soviet Miners' Strike and Its Aftermath," *New Left Review,* no. 181 (1990): 5–32; Peter Rutland, "Labor Unrest Movements in 1989 and 1990," *Soviet Economy* 6 (October–December 1990), reprinted in Ed A. Hewett and Victor H. Winston, eds., *Milestones in Glasnost and Perestroyka: Politics and People* (Washington, D.C.: Brookings Institution, 1991), pp. 287–325; David Mandel, "The Struggle for Power in the Soviet Economy," in "Communist Regimes: The Aftermath," *Socialist Register 1991,* ed. Ralph Miliband and Leo Panitch (London: Merlin, 1991), pp. 95–127; Mandel, "Rebirth of the Soviet Labor Movement"; Michael Burawoy and Pavel Krotov, "The Rise of Merchant Capital: Monopoly, Barter, and Enterprise Politics in the Vorkuta Coal Industry," *Harriman Institute Forum* 6 (December 1992); Gustafson, *Crisis amid Plenty*; and Ed A. Hewett, *Energy, Economics, and Foreign Policy in the Soviet Union* (Washington, D.C.: Brookings Institution, 1984).

63. Hewett, *Energy, Economics, and Foreign Policy,* p. 86.

64. Mandel, "The Struggle for Power in the Soviet Economy," p. 111. For more background on the Kuzbass, see Crowley, "From Coal to Steel," pp. 166–172.

65. Rutland, "Labor Unrest," p. 293; Friedgut and Siegelbaum, "Perestroika from Below," pp. 6–8; Hewett, *Energy, Economics, and Foreign Policy,* pp. 88–89; Mandel, "The Struggle for Power," pp. 112–113.

66. "Soviet Miners Speak," interviews conducted by Willliam Mandel, *Station Relay* 5, nos. 1–5 (1989–1991): 26.

67. Burawoy and Krotov, "Rise of Merchant Capital."

68. Simon Clarke and Peter Fairbrother, "The Origins of the Independent Workers' Movement and the 1989 Miners' Strike," in Clarke et al., *What About the Workers?* p. 129.

69. Ibid., p. 131.

70. Adviser to Kuzbass Coal Miners Strike Committee, February 1990, in Mandel, "Soviet Miners Speak," p. 7.

71. Crowley, "From Coal to Steel."

72. "Protocol on agreed measures between the miners' strike committee of the city of Donetsk and the Commission of the USSR Council of Ministers and the All-union Central Council of Trade Unions," in Michael McFaul and Sergei Markov, *The Troubled Birth of Russian Democracy: Parties, Personalities, and Programs* (Stanford: Hoover Institution Press, 1993), pp. 189–192.

73. Rutland, "Labor Unrest," pp. 306–307.

74. Ibid., p. 312.

75. Kuzbass miner, February 1990, in Mandel, "Soviet Miners Speak," p. 8.

76. Chair of the Kuzbass Coal Miners Strike Committee, February 1990, in Mandel, "Soviet Miners Speak," p. 8.

77. Donbass miner in Mandel, "Soviet Miners Speak," p. 18.

78. Miner interviewed by Mandel at Karaganda, September 1990, in ibid., p. 33.

79. Rutland, "Labor Unrest," p. 315; Mandel, "Soviet Miners Speak," p. 28.

80. Rutland, "Labor Unrest," pp. 305–306.

81. Ibid., pp. 314–315.

82. Mandel, "The Struggle for Power," p. 110.

83. Rutland, "Labor Unrest," p. 295.

84. Ibid., p. 295.

85. Ibid., p. 294.

86. "Statement by plenipotentiary representatives of striking enterprises that took part in talks with the USSR Cabinet of Ministers and president on April 2–3, 1991 (April 4, 1991, Moscow)," in Michael McFaul and Sergei Markov, *The Troubled Birth of Russian Democracy: Parties, Personalities, and Programs* (Stanford: Hoover Institution Press, 1993), p. 198.

87. Simon Clarke and Peter Fairbrother, "Trade Unions and the Working Class," chap. 4 in Clarke et al., *What About the Workers?*

88. Crowley quotes from his transcript of a meeting of miners' representatives, the Independent Miners' Union, and the Confederation of Labor, in Moscow, February 1991, in Crowley, "From Coal to Steel," p. 218.

89. Quoted in Crowley, "From Coal to Steel," p. 218.

90. Rogowski, *Commerce and Coalitions*, p. 121.

91. "Interview with Anatoly Malykhin (May 1991)," in Michael McFaul and Sergei Markov, *The Troubled Birth of Russian Democracy: Parties, Personalities, and Programs* (Stanford: Hoover Institution Press, 1993), p. 175.

92. Simon Clarke and Peter Fairbrother, "The Strikes of 1991 and the Collapse of the Soviet System," chap. 7 in Clarke et al., *What About the Workers?* esp. pp. 166–167. McFaul and Markov, *The Troubled Birth of Russian Democracy*, p. 171.

93. Electronic mail message from Steve Crowley, 21 March 1994.

94. This characterization neglects the nuances but captures the essence of the argument in Clarke et al., *What About the Workers?* esp. chaps. 5 and 7.

95. Credit for resolving this puzzle belongs to Crowley, "From Coal to Steel," esp. pp. 219–223, 233–235. See also Lewis H. Siegelbaum, "Labor Pains in the Soviet Union," *The Nation,* 27 May 1991, p. 693.

96. Representative of the Kuzbass miners in Crowley's transcript from the Moscow meeting in February 1991, quoted in Crowley, "From Coal to Steel," p. 220.

97. "Interview with Anatoly Malykhin (May 1991)," in McFaul and Markov, *The Troubled Birth of Russian Democracy,* p. 176.

98. Crowley, "From Coal to Steel," p. 220. Crowley heard remarks of this sort from miners from several regions.

99. Ibid., p. 223. I have slightly revised Crowley's translation of "kazhdyi dolzhen poluchat' po trudu," with his permission.

100. In addition to his discussion of miners' conceptions of the market, Crowley argues that part of the explanation for the shift from economic to political demands in 1991 was also normative in origin: "Political demands were seen as better normatively and as less selfish than economic demands." Crowley, "From Coal to Steel," p. 219; see also p. 227.

101. I owe this point to Dale Copeland and to participants in the Olin seminar.

102. Crowley, "From Coal to Steel," p. 153.

103. For some examples, see ibid., pp. 153–157.

104. Milner, *Resisting Protectionism.*

105. Burawoy and Krotov, "Rise of Merchant Capital," pp. 9–10.

106. Crowley, "From Coal to Steel," p. 230. Sheila Marnie, "Kuzbass Miners Vote for Strike," *RFE/RL Daily Report,* No. 37, 24 February 1993.

107. Svetlana Babayeva, "Miners' Distrust of Government Grows," *Moscow News,* no. 48, 26 November 1993, p. 3.

108. Sheila Marnie, "Strike in Russia's Northern Pits," *RFE/RL Daily Report,* No. 3, 7 January 1993; idem, "Miners' Protest in Vorkuta," *RFE/RL Daily Report,* No. 31, 16 February 1993; idem, "Kuzbass Miners Vote for Strike."

109. Sheila Marnie, "Miners Postpone Strike Action," *RFE/RL Daily Report,* No. 63, 1 April 1993; Keith Bush, "Pre-Referendum Handouts," *RFE/RL Daily Report,* No. 70, 14 April 1993.

110. Erik Whitlock, "Coal Prices to Be Freed," *RFE/RL Daily Report,* No. 116, 22 June 1993.

111. Sheila Marnie, "Miners Protest Government Decision to Free Coal Prices," *RFE/RL Daily Report,* No. 117, 23 June 1993; idem, "Miners' Strike," *RFE/RL Daily Report,* No. 136, 22 July 1993; Ann Sheehy, "Vorkuta Miners Threaten Action over Proposed Pit Closures," *RFE/RL Daily Report,* No. 143, 29 July 1993.

112. Vera Tolz, "Vorkuta Mine Builders Strike Spreads," *RFE/RL Daily Report,* No. 29, 11 February 1994; Elizabeth Teague, "Miners Strike," *RFE/RL Daily Report,* No. 41, 1 March 1994.

113. Elizabeth Teague, "Russia Hit by Strike Wave," *RFE/RL Daily Report,* No. 33, 17 February 1994.

114. Miners at the Severniaia and Vorgashorskaia mines, for example, sought privatization. See Sheila Marnie, "Russian Miners' Strike Action," *RFE/RL Daily Report,* No. 22, 3 February 1993.

115. Andrei Baranovsky, "Coal Price Rises 4–5 Times," *Moscow News,* no. 29, 16 July 1993, p. 10; Mikhail Klasson, "Drop in the Coal Industry Continues," *Moscow News,* no. 46, 12 November 1993, p. 8.

116. "Recession in Iron and Steel Industry Goes On," *Moscow News,* no. 28, 9 July 1993, p. 10. World Bank, *Russian Economic Reform,* p. 168.

117. Simon Clarke and Peter Fairbrother, "After the Coup: The Workers' Movement in the Transition to a Market Economy," chap. 8 in Clarke et al., *What About the Workers?* esp. pp. 186–187.

118. Burawoy and Krotov, "Rise of Merchant Capital," p. 6.

119. Crowley, "From Coal to Steel," p. 235. Also see Siegelbaum, "Labor Pains," p. 694.

120. Clarke and Fairbrother, "After the Coup," p. 175.

121. This point came up in our Olin seminar discussion.

122. Burawoy and Krotov, "Rise of Merchant Capital," p. 6; World Bank, *Russian Economic Reform,* p. 179. Consider, for example, the case of Belgium in the postwar period, discussed in Alan S. Milward, *The European Rescue of the Nation-State* (Berkeley: University of California Press, 1992), chap. 3.

123. Thomas L. Friedman, "Clinton to Press Russia to Use Aid to Assist Jobless," *New York Times,* 6 January 1994; idem, "U.S. Slightly Eases Conditions for Aid to Moscow," *New York Times,* 13 January 1994.

124. Compare World Bank, *Russian Economic Reform,* p. 179, from which the quote is taken, to Vladimir Merkulov, "Consumption of Coal Will Grow the World Over," *Moscow News,* no. 36, 3 September 1993, p. 7, citing an International Energy Agency study.

125. Hill and Jewett, "Back in the USSR." Traditional realpolitik explanations might fare better in explaining some of Russia's current behavior.

CHAPTER 9

Ideas, Interests, and Institutions in Russian Foreign Policy

Celeste A. Wallander

Although the authors contributing to this volume view their subjects from different theoretical perspectives, they arrive at a striking common focus in their attempts to explain Russian foreign policy: the relationship between a weak and unstable domestic institutional context, ideas as a source of legitimacy in competition for political power, and the weight of the international environment in activating interests and influencing policy choice. This common focus suggests that the linkages between ideas, institutions, and interests, and the linkages between domestic political power and the international environment, are important themes to explore further in this chapter as well as in future research.

For all of the authors, the partially changed and *democratizing* character of Russian domestic political institutions is crucial for understanding Russian foreign policy interests and the policymaking processes. As the chapter authors demonstrate, however, it is more accurate to characterize this as the removal of centralized, closed political processes and institutions than the creation of new democratic institutions and processes.

Yet although this points to the impact of a vacuum in democratic institutions, the evidence also suggests that Russian foreign policy does not begin from an entirely clean slate. Significant political institutions exist, usually in the form of holdovers or reincarnations of Soviet institutions. In a context where new processes and legally based lines of authority are weak or absent, old institutions with established resources—finances, infrastructure, or even information—can have disproportionate impact. For example, as Zisk explains, the managers of Soviet defense industries were able because of their position, knowledge, and access to firm resources to become "owners" of the capital of their enterprises, either by literally acquiring the enterprises through legal or other means or by being so crucial to the successful operation of these enterprises that they could not be removed and thus were able to enjoy the financial benefits of "ownership."

So even though there has rarely been such a complete change of political institutions as in the transition from the Soviet Union to Russia, there is more continuity in Russian institutions than meets the eye—for two reasons. First, nearly all the institutions of the Soviet state existed for some time after 1991. Most have been modified, but few disappeared entirely. For example, the Russian Foreign Ministry simply absorbed the buildings and personnel of the Soviet Foreign Ministry, despite that the latter was some thirty times the size of the former.

Second, to the extent that old institutions have disappeared in the Soviet system, by and large they have not been replaced by new institutions. For example, although many of the laws and practices of the Communist economy have been abandoned, institutions of a market economy have been implemented gradually and to a limited degree. Similarly, most of the political institutions of the repressive state were disbanded, and Russia took on many standard features of democratic political systems, such as an elected president and legislature. Yet it lacks other institutions—including a rule of law, independent judicial system, and free and articulate media—which, though not part of formal definitions of democracy, contribute to democratic processes.[1] Under these circumstances, old institutions often continue to exert effects. This is clear in the chapters by Zisk and Evangelista, which show that the centralized and state-owned economy has been only partially replaced by market institutions and practices. As a result, even firms and workers with clear and overwhelming material interest in international economic market competition sometimes oppose privatization and support state subsidization of industry.

In addition to the continuing existence of some ministries and bureaucracies, elements of the Soviet political and economic institutional context persist as well. We need to keep in mind that political institutions include not only ministries and bureaucracies—which might be more properly called organizations—but also rules and norms that regulate their actions and structure relationships between state and society. State industrial subsidies, a weak banking system, the Soviet (non)distribution system, state pensions, subsidized energy prices, media subsidies, and the system of higher education and research all contribute to Russia's unstable foreign policy processes, discussed by the authors. The legacy of the Soviet media and educational system and the scarcity of Russian resources to maintain and upgrade them have crippled the role of "evaluative units" and the "marketplace of ideas." Tuminez and Snyder see this trend as conducive to the rise of statist and exclusionary nationalism in political discourse and even in official policy. Continued reliance on subsidies at every level of the Russian economy contributes to the public backlash against reformist Western-oriented policies, as Russian citizens choose to hold on to what little security they have rather than to trust further unknown reforms. The persistence of this economic and legal infrastructure has in turn eroded the government's ability to make a strong case for early and substantial infusions of Western economic assistance and financial investment.

In the absence of a strong and coherent constitutional order designed to create both the institutions and processes of democracy, and with a sharp break in the Soviet traditional and informal processes in the making of foreign policy, three factors have increasing significance for the making of Russian foreign policy since 1992: elite coalitions and leadership politics, authority and legitimacy, and ideas. Elite coalition building and leadership politics are crucial to the making of

Russian foreign policy. Without systematic mechanisms to ensure accountability and to place constraints on elite ambitions and personalistic relations, foreign policy priorities derive from shifting ties and alliances within and among elites. This political competition is not entirely unconstrained, but the constraints that matter are authority and legitimacy. Since Russia's domestic problems are almost entirely the result of its internal failures, foreign policy "successes" by and large do not produce substantial societal benefits, and "failures" are not all that costly. Consequently, Russians as individuals and potential interest groups have not focused on foreign policy.

One area of foreign policy where most Russians do experience material and moral costs is in relations with the countries of the former Soviet Union, where economic ties and security issues directly influence Russian domestic well-being. To the extent that public opinion has played some role in Russian foreign policy, it has been focused on the "near abroad." Therefore, policy toward the near abroad has become crucial to the legitimacy and authority of all Russian elites or leaders competing for power, especially in terms of Russian nationalism.

As Richter argues, ideas play an important role in elite competition for authority because of the shifting definitions of Russian identity. In one sense, policy success and failure are "objective": It is better to have a successful economy than economic decline, and it is better for Russia to be more secure. But the defining terms of success and failure in Russian domestic and foreign policies are open to interpretation and debate. It may be better to have a higher living standard, but is it better to have an unconstrained opportunity to compete for a better life or to have secure employment, social services, and a guaranteed minimum? It may be better to have greater national security, but is it better to be secure because you threaten no one and have no enemies or because you are powerful and cannot be threatened? In Western political orders, we tend to take these answers for granted for many reasons, especially the stability of economic and political institutions and processes. They arise in times of crisis, such as the Persian Gulf War and debate over the North American Free Trade Agreement. But Russia has been in economic and political crisis for more than four years—longer if we count the Gorbachev era—and the answers to these questions are central political issues. With the terms of success and failure undefined and contested, authority and legitimacy become more important in political and policy competitions. As I will argue in the next section, under these circumstances ideas play a greater role in politics and consequently in Russian foreign policy making.

As all but one of the authors of this volume conclude, in this uncertain and constantly shifting domestic political environment, the international system and the policies of foreign states have had a more significant effect on Russian foreign policy than we might have expected. Although the sources of Russia's democratization were internal, they were reinforced by a benign (or at worst ambiguous) external security environment that provided few incentives to create a centralizing or unifying political force in Moscow, as Porter argues. In the one issue area where a relatively unambiguous threat to national interests exists (the near abroad), Russian politics and foreign policy have become very united and coherent. Hopf's analysis reinforces this model of external influence on domestic political processes and shows further that variation in the degree of threat to Russian interests is clearly linked to variation in the degree to which elites are mobilized and united in support of assertive policies. Furthermore, both Porter and Hopf show how Western efforts to go beyond nonthreatening policies to cooperative solutions to Russia's perceived security threats not only prevent consolidation of a centralized strong state but also reinforce the authority and legitimacy of liberal Russian foreign policy elites.

Ironically, Evangelista, who sets out to assess the effect of the international economic environment on the newly opened economies of the former Soviet Union, finds little evidence of systematic effects. He concludes that the international economic environment has not had a liberalizing impact on the development of economic relations among the post-Soviet states because traditional and security-oriented foreign policy concerns have predominated. What might look like an obvious economic logic prompting energy-rich states such as Kazakhstan to seek their own fortune in the international system has not exerted much influence over foreign relations. The same logic that should encourage dependent states such as the Baltics to favor accommodation to or integration with Russia has not determined relations among the former republics. Nor has increased international openness created a strong domestic constituency in the Russian energy sector favoring foreign investment, increased marketization, and entry into international competition. In an area where we would most expect material benefits to be strongly and directly related to activated political interests, Evangelista finds instead that the weight of preexisting domestic political and economic institutions and the influence of historical path dependence exert a stronger pull on domestic interests and politics and therefore on Russian's foreign policy tendencies.

In summary, the questions we posed at the outset, which took their cue from models of Soviet foreign policy, have led to promising research and some unexpected answers. The standard building blocks for an explanatory model of Russian foreign policy—political institutions, ideology, leadership competition, interests and groups, and the external security and economic environments—suggest appropriate research questions and a broader research agenda. But the relative influence of these factors is somewhat surprising, especially the lack of a systematic relationship between political institutions and powerful political and economic interests, as compared to the salience of elite competition of a very traditional cast and the central role of ideas, authority, and legitimacy.

Ideas, Legitimacy, and Uncertainty in Russian Foreign Policy

It is all too easy to observe contemporary Russian politics and see instability, especially when tanks are sent into the streets of Moscow to settle a constitutional and political dispute. However, we should distinguish between two distinct meanings of the word "instability." Perhaps the more commonsense meaning is that of chaos or unpredictability. Although it may appear sometimes that this kind of instability is precisely that which plagues Russian politics, I would argue that it is more useful to think of instability in game theoretic terms: Instability means that political players can always get a better deal with different partners or coalitions by changing their choice of policy, and they will do so unless constrained in some way by rules of the game or other factors that make constant shifting for even slight advantage more costly than staying with acceptable outcomes.[2]

The politics of Russian foreign policy making is unstable in this sense because many of the important institutional structures and "rules of the game" have been removed but not yet replaced with new ones. Institutions affect politics by establishing norms to serve as consensual rules, by creating power resources, by structuring the aggregation of interests, or by establishing a pattern of outcomes or historical "path."[3] Institutions constrain political strategies and reduce uncertainty for political actors by stabilizing their expectations about the rules of the game. Furthermore, institutions can provide information about the interests and strategies of other political actors, either directly by serving as forums for exchange of information (such as parliamentary debates and committee meetings) or indirectly by creating a context in which past behavior can be observed and interests and strategies inferred.[4] Finally, institutions can provide political actors with information about the relationship between policy and outcomes in a technical sense.[5]

In this regard, Soviet foreign policy institutions encompassed not only state bureaucracies and party organs but also the norms and rules of the game that ordered the policy process and terms of political competition. The demise of the Soviet Union entailed the loss of the integrated political and economic institutional context that had tended to produce stability—one might even say ossification—in Soviet foreign policy. In particular, the apparatus of the Communist Party had been the main locus of information gathering, analysis, option formulation and assessment, and political competition until the Gorbachev reforms of 1987. Gorbachev also changed the norm of secrecy in political affairs in implementing the policy of glasnost. When the Party apparatus and key norms were swept away in late 1991, the Russian state only incompletely replaced them, which is the fundamental cause of the ensuing instability and cycling in Russian foreign policy.[6]

Russia lacks (though it is beginning to develop) political parties, legal structures, economic structures, and civic norms. Although Yeltsin came to power via democratic elections, he has ruled at times through emergency powers and by presidential decree. Furthermore, the threat that he could declare a national emergency and rule by decree has at times constrained political debate, and his disbanding of the Supreme Soviet in October 1993 was unconstitutional. Russia's Security Council, which though technically constitutional and answerable to democratic processes, appears to operate without constraint[7] and has come to dominate the making of Russian foreign and security policy. As a consequence, coalitions are unstable and shifting and the Security Council serves as an increasingly important locus of decisionmaking. This is why elite bargaining and coalition building have grown in importance in the Russian foreign policy process. Snyder cautions us to distinguish between democracies and democratizing states because foreign policy making in the latter lacks the types of institutions that tend to produce pacific behavior; thus such states appear to be especially prone to nationalistic and hostile foreign policies.

Where we observe stability in Russian foreign policy, it tends to be the result of one of three influences: persistent Soviet-era institutions, mobilizing ideas, and significant international constraints. Greater coherence, continuity, and unity of purpose have characterized Russian military policy because the CIS command preserved the structure of the Soviet military in large measure and because the Russian military forces have in turn inherited the CIS command. The continued presence of Russian military forces in near abroad countries produced a more deliberate, and perhaps even strategic, foreign policy than overall Russian policy.[8]

Foreign policy studies commonly focus on national interests and those of domestic political and economic groups as a guide to understanding the country's foreign policy. Interests in this regard play such a modest role in the analyses in this volume because of the absence of a strong sense of stable interests in Russian domestic politics that are related systematically to foreign policy. Recall that both Zisk and Evangelista find that the potential for links to the international economy was not realized or fully developed because of unclear political and economic rules of the game that could tell Russians what kinds of domestic and foreign policies would serve or threaten their interests. It would be wrong to conclude, however, that Russian domestic issues are not affected by its foreign policy. Instead, there are lots of interests floating around in the domestic context, but whether and how they become activated and enter the political and policy process is usually a result of the institutional context. With the uncertain and contradictory context in Russia, the process by which interests are articulated and fought for depends far more on other factors, especially ideas and the international environment.

Ideas encompass worldviews, principled beliefs, and causal beliefs.[9] They define an understanding of how the world works, how it should work, and specific cause-and-effect relationships that tell people how they can pursue their objectives. In this respect, they are similar to ideology but can also include knowledge. In a recent influential study of the role of ideas in foreign policy, the editors conclude that ideas are most likely to have a significant effect on policy when they serve as road maps, as focal points for aiding people in agreeing to a joint course of action when multiple agreements are possible and when embedded in institutions.[10]

That is, ideas are likely to affect policy most when there is a great deal of uncertainty about the world and about the policies that best enable political actors (whether they be leaders, bureaucracies, groups, or individuals) to secure their objectives. Ideas are also likely to affect policies most insofar as they serve as stable focal points in an environment of unstable political competition.

This helps explain why ideas—especially Russian nationalism and economic beliefs held over from the Soviet era—play such an important part in all the chapters in this volume. Russian leaders and the Russian public are faced with an almost paralyzing degree of uncertainty about the policies that will produce economic reform, a better standard of living, and greater national security. Beginning in 1992 they found it very difficult to define Russian economic and security interests as well. Furthermore, it was not clear what kinds of policies would be successful or even how to define the terms of a successful Russian foreign policy. This uncertain environment was compounded, as I have argued, by a strange institutional context that was a combination of some old Soviet institutions, some new democratizing and marketizing institutions, and failure to create other political and economic institutions.

Uncertainty combined with instability enhanced the importance of ideas in determining political and policy outcomes. Since a coherent institutional context, knowledge about the relationship of policies and outcomes, and a clear understanding of political and economic interests were missing, ideas helped political elites and publics grasp potentially beneficial foreign policies. Since institutions did not provide a source of stability for organizing and channeling political competition, that competition and stable coalitions organized instead around attractive worldviews and principled beliefs. Ideas matter in part because the only policies that contribute to political power are successful policies. But since policies are not yet implemented in a period of contending political power, publics and/or elites need some sort of measure by which to judge whether policies *will* be successful. Ideas can serve as that guide.

Soviet-era ideas about economics remained influential—despite their clear failure and the extent to which they contributed to the Soviet demise—because they were embedded in many institutions serving many interests that survived the collapse of communism. Nationalism became a central focus in foreign policy because ideas about nationalism answer basic questions about how the world works, how it should work, and what Russia is. Without answers to these questions, it is difficult to imagine how Russia's elites and public could begin to define what Russian interests are and how they may be pursued in Russian foreign policy.

Legitimacy, authority, and elite coalition building centered on issues of nationalism because those ideas served as focal points for political competition and provided information that both the elites and the public need in order to stake out political positions and to offer policies that would serve their interests. If my explanation is correct, then as the rules of the game crystallize and as a new political economic institutional context develops, ideas such as nationalism should begin to play a less weighty role in the making of Russian foreign policy, unless they become embedded in the new institutions. That means, however, that the current period of institution building in Russian domestic politics is crucial to the form of its foreign policy in the future. It will determine which ideas generated in this period of uncertainty, insecurity, and instability will be more influential in the process of evaluating Russian objectives and means to pursue them, and it will determine the rules of the game for that political process. This is the reason, I believe, why all of the authors in this volume express concern—and hope—about the effects of Western policy on Russian politics and policy during this crucial period.

Yet the general importance of ideas in Russian foreign policy under conditions of uncertainty and instability provides few clues as to which of the multiple competing ideas will "win" in the end. It may be the case that when there are multiple potential policy outcomes in political competition, ideas serve as focal points that permit political actors to coordinate and choose a policy.[11] The problem is that, as Tuminez demonstrates and as Porter and Richter explore, there are multiple plausible ideas embodied by Russian nationalism—ideas that offer different worldviews, principled beliefs, and causal beliefs. In such an environment, it is difficult to see how any given idea could serve as a focal point for coordination.

Furthermore, work on the role of ideas in international relations has a deficiency pointed to by the chapters in this volume. Although researchers recognize that "ideas do not float freely"[12] and that they are embedded in institutional contexts, the studies fail to specify the constraints that act on ideas and to explain why ideas should matter to competitive politicians at all. That is, they lack an explicit treatment of the international system as a constraint on which ideas are adopted, which ideas are successful, and the relationship of ideas, policies, and success in domestic contests over power and policy. In this regard, studies of Soviet learning and the studies in this volume contribute analytical power to theories of the role of ideas in foreign policy because they suggest the political purposes for which political actors choose or champion ideas and the consequences of success and failure for domestic foreign policy coalitions.

Why and When the International Environment Matters in Russian Foreign Policy

Hopes that Western policies will influence Russian politics in a liberalizing and cooperative direction are based on an assumption that the international environment has some systematic relationship to domestic politics and policymaking. Research on the interaction of comparative and international politics has already begun to negate the assumption that national interests and preferences for foreign policy are first formed at the domestic level and then pursued at the international level. Instead, the interaction of bargaining at the two levels can shape both the definition of national interests and foreign policies and the potential for international agreement and conflict.[13] In particular, this work suggests that potential agreements or outcomes at the international level can cause new coalitions to form at the domestic level, either in support or in opposition. Therefore, the international environment can change national foreign policies by changing the domestic politics and coalition building that underlie them.[14]

Given this potential, under what conditions is the international environment more likely to have a substantial impact on the political process and foreign policy making? At least one likely condition mirrors the current Russian political context, in which ideas are disproportionately influential in coalition formation and policy advocacy, and for the same reasons. In a situation where domestic institutional structures are weak, clear criteria for success or failure of foreign policies are lacking, and multiple ideas permeate Russian foreign policy debates, the international environment plays a larger role in Russian foreign policy. It serves as a mix of opportunities, constraints, and feedback on successful and failed policies for Russian political elites and publics as well as a source of financial and technical resources. As long as uncertainty and instability are high in Russian foreign policy, the nature of the external environment is a major factor in determining legitimacy, authority, and the plausibility of competing ideas and claims.

Thus, a benign and supportive international environment appears to bolster the claims of liberal reformers that international threat is low and opportunity high. It would provide information in the short term that the fundamental long-term policies of marketization and integration are sound, thus bolstering the legitimacy and authority of leaders and coalitions that advocate them. The key to this argument—advanced in different forms by Snyder, Tuminez, Richter, Zisk, Porter, and Hopf—is that support for policies must be evaluated in the short term, before their long-term success and costs can be evaluated. Therefore, foreign policies in this uncertain and unstable Russian domestic context tend to be supported based upon claims to legitimacy and authority, which are in turn derived from ideas about Russia's place in the world and information about how the world views and deals with Russia.

In this regard, although the authors emphasize the influence of ideas and identity in contemporary Russian politics and foreign policy, international structure and material reality are part of the equation as well. Russian preoccupation with the near abroad is a product of Russia's geopolitical reality and historical legacy as well as of nationalist ideas. Although the idea of Russian hegemony in the former Soviet empire is a major force in Russian foreign policy today, that idea gained predominance over time with the emergence of significant problems in security, economic, and political relations with these new countries. Recognition of these problems was not only a function of ideas: It was also a function of practice, as Russia suddenly had to deal with concrete problems created by the legacy of the Soviet Union, such as the division of the Black Sea Fleet, the status and rights of Russian minorities abroad, and economic relations of substantial interdependency. The problems in the near abroad may have been exploited by nationalist extremists, but they were not entirely concocted by them.

Nor are other issues in which Russian foreign policy clashes with Western preferences the result solely of nationalist manipulations and competition among elites for authority and political power. For example, NATO expansion under some circumstances and in some forms could threaten legitimate Russian security interests, although as of mid-1995 it appears likely that NATO will expand only if that event is accompanied by measures to reassure Russia and limit the threat. Russian interests in arms sales are based not on the type of political interests that Soviet programs were but on the kinds of economic interests that Western arms manufacturers commonly pursue. When Western countries try to control arms sales in a way that asymmetrically places limits on Russian customers, the perception of a hostile international environment is based on something more than ideology.

That is, although legitimacy and authority are crucial political resources in competition over Russian foreign policy and whereas ideas have been an especially important influence in that competition, the constraints and opportunities of the international environment independently and strongly influence the plausibility of ideas and the tendencies in Russian foreign policy. As Hopf shows, the degree to which Russia adopts a cooperative or coercive foreign policy—even in the near abroad, where Russian power could easily, if not costlessly, determine outcomes—is strongly related to real threats to Russian interests. The international environment and policies of foreign countries can serve as focal points for elite coalition building or for mobilizing public support in elections. Therefore, the most important focal points for Russian foreign policy are likely to be those defined by a conjunction of interests, institutions, ideas, and international influences.

Future research on Russia needs to focus on these four factors, and promising theories of Russian foreign policy will be those that develop arguments about the causal linkages among them. The research by the authors in this volume suggests a model in which the most important causal ties link weak or uneven domestic political and economic institutions to instability and uncertainty in political competition and policymaking and in which ideas and international influences serve as important focal points for policy. This situation is unlikely to persist. As the institutional context stabilizes, interests and the policies that serve them will become clearer. It will become easier for political actors to identify common interests and to pool resources for joint efforts. We need theories that will tell us about the content of those interests and about the effects of Russia's developing institutions on those political processes. If a framework based on measuring differences in the sources of Russian and Soviet conduct can contribute to such a research program, those trained as Sovietologists may yet have a lot to offer the study of international relations.

Notes

Jeff Anderson and Carol Saivetz offered very helpful comments on this chapter, for which I am grateful.

1. See Robert A. Dahl, *Polyarchy: Participation and Opposition* (New Haven: Yale University Press, 1971), chap. 1; Samuel P. Huntington, *The Third Wave: Democratization in the Late Twentieth Century* (Norman: University of Oklahoma Press, 1991), chap. 1.

2. I am indebted for this concept of instability and cycling in Russian politics to Jo Andrews. See Josephine Andrews, "Legislative Instability: The Dynamics of Agenda Control in the Russian Parliament" (Ph.D. diss., Harvard University, 1995).

3. On definitions of institutions, see Douglass C. North, *Institutions, Institutional Change and Economic Performance* (Cambridge: Cambridge University Press, 1990), p. 3; Peter Hall, *Governing the Economy* (Cambridge: Cambridge University Press, 1986), chap. 1; Kathleen Thelen and Sven Steinmo, "Historical Institutionalism in Comparative Politics," chap. 1 in *Structuring Politics: Historical Institutionalism in Comparative Analysis,* ed. Sven Steinmo, Kathleen Thelen, and Frank Longstreth (Cambridge: Cambridge University Press, 1992). On "path dependence" see Matthew Evangelista's contribution to this volume.

4. Robert O. Keohane, *International Institutions and State Power: Essays in International Relations Theory* (Boulder: Westview Press, 1989), chap. 1.

5. Kenneth A. Shepsle and Barry R. Weingast, "Positive Theories of Congressional Institutions," *Occasional Paper* 92-18 (Center for American Political Studies, Harvard University, December 1992), pp. 13–18. For a study that assesses the link between institutions, technical knowledge, and policy, see Matthew Evangelista, "The Paradox of State Strength: Transnational Relations, Domestic Structures, and Security Policy in Russia and the Soviet Union," *International Organization* 49 (Winter 1995): 1–38.

6. For some evidence along these lines, see Jan S. Adams, "Who Will Make Russia's Foreign Policy in 1994?" *RFE/RL Research Report* 3 (11 February 1994): 36–40; Dominic Gualtieri, "Russia's New 'War of Laws,'" *RFE/RL Research Report* 2 (3 September 1993): 10–15; Vera Tolz, "Problems in Building Democratic Institutions in Russia," *RFE/RL Research Report* 3 (4 March 1994): 1–7.

7. On the composition and role of the Security Council, see, for example, Robert Orttung, "A Painful Price," *Transition* 1 (15 March 1995): 3–7, at p. 5; Victor Yasmann, "Security Services Reorganized: All Power to the Russian President?" *RFE/RL Research Report* 3 (11 February 1994): 7–14.

8. On the relative coherence and effectiveness of Russia's military policy toward the near abroad, see Fiona Hill and Pamela Jewett, "Back in the USSR: Russia's Intervention in the Internal Affairs of the Former Soviet Republics and the Implications for United States Policy Toward Russia," report of the Ethnic Conflict Project of the Strengthening Democratic Institutions Project, John F. Kennedy School of Government (Cambridge: Harvard University, January 1994).

9. Judith Goldstein and Robert O. Keohane, "Ideas and Foreign Policy: An Analytical Framework," in *Ideas and Foreign Policy: Beliefs, Institutions, and Political Change,* ed. Judith Goldstein and Robert O. Keohane (Ithaca: Cornell University Press, 1993), pp. 8–11.

10. Goldstein and Keohane, "Ideas and Foreign Policy," pp. 11–13.

11. Geoffrey Garrett and Barry R. Weingast, "Ideas, Interests, and Institutions: Constructing the European Community's Internal Market," in *Ideas and Foreign Policy,* ed. Goldstein and Keohane.

12. Thomas Risse-Kappen, "Ideas Do Not Float Freely: Transnational Coalitions, Domestic Structures, and the End of the Cold War," *International Organization* 48 (Spring 1994): 185–214.

13. Robert Putnam, "Diplomacy and Domestic Politics: The Logic of Two-Level Games," *International Organization* 42 (Summer 1988): 427–460, at pp. 454–456. For an elaboration of Putnam's framework and initial empirical studies of its implications, see Peter B. Evans, Harold K. Jacobsen, and Robert D. Putnam, eds., *Double-Edged Diplomacy: International Bargaining and Domestic Politics* (Berkeley: University of California Press, 1993). For a study of Soviet foreign policy under Gorbachev that developed many of these ideas independently, see Jack Snyder, "International Leverage on Soviet Domestic Change," *World Politics* 42 (October 1989): 1–30.

14. Peter Gourevitch, "The Second Image Reversed: The International Sources of Domestic Politics," *International Organization* 32 (Autumn 1978): 881–912.

About the Book

In this timely and pathbreaking volume, scholars in comparative politics and international relations build upon earlier theoretical work on the interaction of domestic and international systems, applying it innovatively to the study of post-Soviet Russian policy and conduct. Individual chapters focus on regime type, leadership politics, interest group politics, nationalism as ideology, international conflict and threat, and international economic opportunities and constraints. The complex interplay between domestic and international factors is highlighted.

Exploring both the origins and the outcomes of Russian policy and behavior, this book provides a telling measure of the direction and significance of political change since 1991.

About the Editor and Contributors

Matthew Evangelista is the author of *Innovation and the Arms Race: How the United States and the Soviet Union Develop New Military Technologies* (1988) and numerous articles in journals such as *International Security, World Politics,* and *International Organization.* He spent 1993–1995 as a visiting scholar at Harvard's Center for Science and International Affairs and plans to join the faculty of Cornell University's Department of Government in autumn 1996.

Ted Hopf is an assistant professor of political science at the University of Michigan and a faculty associate of the Center for Russian and East European Studies there. He is the author of *Peripheral Visions: Deterrence Theory and American Foreign Policy in the Third World, 1965–1990* (1994).

Bruce D. Porter is associate professor of political science at Brigham Young University. Prior to joining the BYU faculty in 1990, he was the Bradley Senior Research Associate of the Olin Institute for Strategic Studies at Harvard University. Dr. Porter also served previously as an analyst of Soviet foreign policy at Radio Free Europe in Munich, Germany; was a professional staff member of the Senate Armed Services Committee; and was executive director of the Board for International Broadcasting, the federal agency that oversees Radio Free Europe and Radio Liberty. He is author of the recently published *War and the Rise of the State: The Military Foundations of Modern Politics* (1994).

James Richter is associate professor of political science at Bates College in Lewiston, Maine. He is the author of *Khrushchev's Double Bind: International Pressures and Domestic Coalition Politics* (1994) and is now examining the links between international politics, national identity, and regional politics of Russia.

Jack Snyder is professor of political science and director of the Institute of War and Peace Studies at Columbia University. He is the author of *Myths of Empire: Domestic Politics and International Ambition* (1991).

Astrid S. Tuminez is a program officer for the Program on Preventing Deadly Conflict at the Carnegie Corporation of New York. She is also a Ph.D. candidate in political science at MIT and is writing a dissertation on "Russian Nationalism: Content, Empowerment, and Impact on Foreign Policy, 1856–1994." She holds a master's degree in Soviet Studies from Harvard University and was formerly assistant director of the Harvard Project on Strengthening Democratic Institutions.

Celeste A. Wallander is associate professor of government and faculty associate at the Center for International Affairs and the Russian Research Center at Harvard University. She is author of "International Institutions and Modern Security Strategies," *Problems of Communism* (1992), and "Opportunity, Incrementalism, and Learning in the Extension and Retraction of Soviet Global Commitments," *Security Studies* (1992). She is currently writing a book on the role of security institutions in German-Russian relations after the Cold War.

Kimberly Marten Zisk is assistant professor of political science and faculty associate of the Mershon Center at the Ohio State University. Her book, *Engaging the Enemy: Organization Theory and Soviet Military Innovation, 1955–1991* (1993), received the 1994 Marshall Shulman Prize from the American Association for the Advancement of Slavic Studies. Most recently she is the author of "Arzamas-16: Economics and Security in a Closed Nuclear City," *Post-Soviet Affairs* (1995). She was a visiting scholar at the Olin Institute for Strategic Studies at Harvard University during the 1993–1994 academic year, when her chapter in this volume was completed.

Index